W9-DDH-947

Measuring the Subjective Well-Being of Nations

A National Bureau
of Economic Research
Conference Report

Measuring the Subjective Well-Being of Nations

National Accounts of Time Use and Well-Being

Edited by **Alan B. Krueger**

The University of Chicago Press

Chicago and London

At the time of publication, ALAN B. KRUEGER was on leave from
Princeton University and the National Bureau of Economic Research,
serving as assistant secretary for economic policy and chief economist
for the U.S. Department of Treasury.

The University of Chicago Press, Chicago 60637
The University of Chicago Press, Ltd., London
© 2009 by the National Bureau of Economic Research
All rights reserved. Published 2009
Printed in the United States of America

18 17 16 15 14 13 12 11 10 09   1 2 3 4 5
ISBN-13: 978-0-226-45456-6 (cloth)
ISBN-10: 0-226-45456-8 (cloth)

Library of Congress Cataloging-in-Publication Data

Measuring the subjective well-being of nations : national accounts of
    time use and well-being / edited by Alan B. Krueger.
        p. cm.—(A National Bureau of Economic Research Conference
    Report)
        Papers originally presented at a conference at the National Bureau
    of Economic Research in Cambridge, Mass., Dec. 7–8, 2008.
        Includes index.
        ISBN-13: 978-0-226-45456-6 (cloth : alk. paper)
        ISBN-10: 0-226-45456-8 (cloth : alk. paper) 1. Happiness—
    Congresses. 2. Well-being—Congresses. 3. Life—Congresses.
    4. National characteristics—Congresses. I. Krueger, Alan B.
    II. National Bureau of Economic Research.
        BF575.H27M424 2009
        152.4′2072—dc22

                                                            2009005897

⊗ The paper used in this publication meets the minimum requirements
of the American National Standard for Information Sciences—
Permanence of Paper for Printed Library Materials, ANSI Z39.48-1992.

Relation of the Directors to the
Work and Publications of the
National Bureau of Economic Research

1. The object of the NBER is to ascertain and present to the economics profession, and to the public more generally, important economic facts and their interpretation in a scientific manner without policy recommendations. The Board of Directors is charged with the responsibility of ensuring that the work of the NBER is carried on in strict conformity with this object.

2. The President shall establish an internal review process to ensure that book manuscripts proposed for publication DO NOT contain policy recommendations. This shall apply both to the proceedings of conferences and to manuscripts by a single author or by one or more co-authors but shall not apply to authors of comments at NBER conferences who are not NBER affiliates.

3. No book manuscript reporting research shall be published by the NBER until the President has sent to each member of the Board a notice that a manuscript is recommended for publication and that in the President's opinion it is suitable for publication in accordance with the above principles of the NBER. Such notification will include a table of contents and an abstract or summary of the manuscript's content, a list of contributors if applicable, and a response form for use by Directors who desire a copy of the manuscript for review. Each manuscript shall contain a summary drawing attention to the nature and treatment of the problem studied and the main conclusions reached.

4. No volume shall be published until forty-five days have elapsed from the above notification of intention to publish it. During this period a copy shall be sent to any Director requesting it, and if any Director objects to publication on the grounds that the manuscript contains policy recommendations, the objection will be presented to the author(s) or editor(s). In case of dispute, all members of the Board shall be notified, and the President shall appoint an ad hoc committee of the Board to decide the matter; thirty days additional shall be granted for this purpose.

5. The President shall present annually to the Board a report describing the internal manuscript review process, any objections made by Directors before publication or by anyone after publication, any disputes about such matters, and how they were handled.

6. Publications of the NBER issued for informational purposes concerning the work of the Bureau, or issued to inform the public of the activities at the Bureau, including but not limited to the NBER Digest and Reporter, shall be consistent with the object stated in paragraph 1. They shall contain a specific disclaimer noting that they have not passed through the review procedures required in this resolution. The Executive Committee of the Board is charged with the review of all such publications from time to time.

7. NBER working papers and manuscripts distributed on the Bureau's web site are not deemed to be publications for the purpose of this resolution, but they shall be consistent with the object stated in paragraph 1. Working papers shall contain a specific disclaimer noting that they have not passed through the review procedures required in this resolution. The NBER's web site shall contain a similar disclaimer. The President shall establish an internal review process to ensure that the working papers and the web site do not contain policy recommendations, and shall report annually to the Board on this process and any concerns raised in connection with it.

8. Unless otherwise determined by the Board or exempted by the terms of paragraphs 6 and 7, a copy of this resolution shall be printed in each NBER publication as described in paragraph 2 above.

Contents

Introduction and Overview

Alan B. Krueger

Subjective well-being involves people's evaluations of their lives, encompassing how happy or satisfied they say they are overall, and their reported emotional experiences at specific times. Economists are often skeptical of self-reported data on subjective outcomes, but in recent years economists have increasingly analyzed data on subjective well-being. From 2000 to 2007, for example, there were 263 papers on subjective well-being according to a search of *Econ Lit,* up from just twenty-five in the 1990s.[1] If it can be measured, even approximately, there is no question that subjective well-being should be of interest to economists and other social scientists.

Perhaps related to the outpouring of research into subjective well-being, policymakers and statistical agencies around the world have shown increased interest in measuring subjective well-being as part of their national statistics. In addition to Bhutan, whose king called for a measure of Gross National Happiness in the early 1970s without having much idea of how to measure or define it, the governments of Canada, the United Kingdom, France, and Australia have initiated programs to consider developing indicators of subjective well-being. Are these efforts silly? Has research progressed to the point that happiness could be measured along with GDP or investment? Or even unemployment?

This volume considers a more limited goal than measuring Gross National Happiness, but a goal that dramatically departs from the standard economic measurements that guide policy. The goal is to develop a system of National Time Accounting (NTA). National Time Accounting is a frame-

At the time of publication, Alan B. Krueger was on leave from Princeton University and the National Bureau of Economic Research, serving as assistant secretary for economic policy and chief economist for the U.S. Department of Treasury.

1. These figures are based on a search on the terms "life satisfaction," "subjective well-being," or "self-reported happiness."

work for measuring, comparing, and analyzing the way people spend their time across countries, over historical time, or between groups of people within a country at a given time. Although time-use data have long been collected and studied, most past efforts to evaluate time use rely on researchers' external judgments regarding which activities constitute enjoyable leisure and which constitute arduous work and home production. The method for NTA described in the first chapter of this volume, "National Time Accounting: The Currency of Life," instead relies on individuals' own evaluations of their emotional experiences during their various uses of time. This approach is called "evaluated time use." One feature of our use of evaluated time use is that we explicitly allow for emotions to be multidimensional during specific time periods. Someone can feel happy, tired, and stressed all at the same time, for example.

The intended contribution of National Time Accounts is nicely summarized in figure I.1, which is borrowed from George Loewenstein's chapter. A society's well-being or "true welfare" is represented by the rectangle. Widely used measures from the National Income Accounts (NIA), such as gross domestic product (GDP) per capita and consumption per capita, only represent a component of total welfare because well-being depends on more than economic output and material consumption. In addition, aspects of life that contribute to economic output may detract from well-being. For example, an increase in pollution could be associated with decreased welfare but increased production and national income. Thus, the circle representing NIA partly falls outside the box representing total welfare. National Time Accounting partly overlaps with NIA, but also reflects other features of well-being that are not captured by NIA. For example, time spent socializing with friends is not measured in national income but is important for well-being. Key questions are: how big is the circle representing NTA? How much overlap is there between NTA and NIA? And how big is the area in the well-being box that is not measured by either NTA or NIA?

The readers of other National Bureau of Economic Research volumes should be warned that this volume deviates somewhat from the usual model. The volume is focused on measuring subjective well-being, and authors were invited to specifically use the NTA approach as a leaping-off point, to offer criticisms of the method or provide alternative ways of measuring subjective well-being. The first chapter, by Alan Krueger, Daniel Kahneman, David Schkade, Norbert Schwarz, and Arthur Stone, sets the scene. The chapter is the culmination of an eight-year effort by four psychologists and one economist (Krueger) to measure people's evaluated time use. The authors lay out their method of NTA and provide some illustrative findings based on a nationwide telephone survey of nearly 4,000 people that they conducted with the Gallup Organization in the spring and summer of 2006. Results from other paper-and-pencil diary-based surveys and real-time data collection efforts are also presented and compared.

Krueger et al.'s (implicit) perspective:

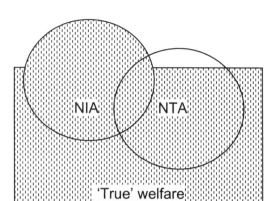

Fig. I.1   National Time Accounting in perspective

Put briefly, their method is based on collecting time-diary information from individuals. For various episodes of the day, they also collect information on individuals' reported emotional experiences, such as the intensity of pain, happiness, stress, and so forth. Their chapter provides some background information on the development of their survey instrument, and on the validity of their data. Interesting differences between various methods of collecting the enjoyment associated with various activities are explored. Based on their time diary data, Krueger et al. propose a summary measure of subjective well-being called the U-index, or percentage of time that an individual or group of individuals spends in an unpleasant emotional state. An unpleasant emotional state is defined as an interval in which the strongest emotion is a negative one. The U-index has several advantages over more conventional measures of subjective well-being. Most importantly, because it involves an ordinal ranking of individuals' reported positive and negative emotions, individuals can interpret and use the scales differently and the U-index is still meaningful as long as they assign the highest value to their most intense feeling. In addition, the U-index reflects more than one dimension of emotions.

Five main criticisms of this approach emerge from the other chapters in the volume. The first is that evaluated time use misses important features of experiences and life in general that are important for well-being. In terms of Loewenstein's Venn diagram, this argument is that NTA only represents a small fraction of the total well-being box. Indeed, Loewenstein argues in chapter 2, "I believe that much if not most of what makes life worthwhile is *not* captured by moment to moment happiness, but corresponds more closely, if not perfectly, to what Krueger et al. acknowledge to be absent from

NTA, namely 'people's general sense of satisfaction or fulfillment with their lives as a whole, apart from moment to moment feelings.'" He illustrates this point in a number of ways, perhaps most vividly by pointing to his father's experience in a French prisoner of war camp during World War II. Despite enduring hunger to the point that "he dug up worms for food and chewed on shoe leather," Loewenstein reports that his father considered his time in the POW camp the peak experience of his life. More generally, Loewenstein argues that NTA misses much of what gives people meaning in their lives.

In chapter 3, David Cutler evaluates NTA along similar lines. He notes, "The major issue is the distinction between the *process* of consumption and the *existential value* of consumption." According to Cutler, the U-index and evaluated time use more generally, are "very good at measuring the utility of the process that goes into consumption. They are less good at measuring the value of what comes out." Cutler also makes reference to Bentham's classic felicity calculus, which involved an enumeration of pleasures and pains. He argues that, "Pleasures of wealth, skill, amity, a good name, piety, and benevolence are generally missing" from the U-index. Finally, Cutler notes that some activities that are not particularly pleasurable at the time, such as work, are nonetheless engaged in for the benefits that they yield later on, such as the pleasure of using income to consume. Since the time-use data cover a representative snapshot of time, activities that involve investments in future well-being should be captured in the aggregate, although they are hard to attribute to specific activities.

Some of the components of well-being that are currently missing from evaluated time use can be incorporated in the measure. For example, respondents could be asked if they are hungry or uncomfortable. Moreover, respondents could be asked whether each moment of time was meaningful or a waste of time. But we suspect that even the latter will not capture the meaningfulness component of well-being to the extent that Loewenstein has in mind.

Still, it is useful to bear in mind that NTA reflects a dimension of well-being that is not captured in conventional economic statistics. Consumption statistics, for example, do not capture the sense of meaning or fulfillment in consumers' lives. Steven Landefeld, the director of the Bureau of Economic Analysis, evaluates NTA in comparison to the criteria often applied to the National Income Accounts in chapter 4. Although NTA does not have the advantage of double-entry bookkeeping—which is a central feature of the National Income Accounts—from his vantage point, "The National Time Accounts (NTAs) are a major step forward in the measurement of well-being." To some extent, the development of NTAs could relieve pressure to use the National Income Accounts to make welfare conclusions for which they are not well suited.

The second criticism of NTA, raised most prominently by William Nordhaus in chapter 5, is more fundamental. Nordhaus argues that emotions, and subjective experience more generally, are not interpersonally comparable. Nordhaus notes that to be interpersonally comparable a variable "must have a uniquely defined zero and a well-defined unit of increment." He further argues that the zero point (and presumably the increment) must be stable across time, people, and countries. He claims there simply is no interpersonally cardinal scale for reporting subjective data such as happiness and pain. If this is correct, happiness or pain cannot be compared across people. He goes further and implies that the strength of various emotions at a point in time cannot be compared by a given person. In this worldview, it is folly for a doctor to ask patients to rate their pain on a scale of zero to ten, as is commonly done, or to ask a given patient if her broken leg hurts more than her dislocated shoulder.

Now the U-index does not require that everyone use the same zero point and same increment. All that is required is that, at a moment in time, whatever zero point and increment people have in mind are applied to their rating of positive and negative emotions. Nordhaus recognizes this, but argues, "The U-index of KKSSS would appear to avoid the difficulties of some happiness indexes by its creation of an ordinal index. But, their procedure simply pushes the difficulty into the background." We shall have more to say about this criticism in the rejoinder, but for now we note that Nordhaus's critique is more a philosophical than empirical argument. It does not rest on any evidence, and is made in such a way that it is not empirically testable. Also note that even if one accepts the view that subjective data are not interpersonally comparable, it is nonetheless the case that subjective reports have predictive power. For example, across-subject differences in self-reported life satisfaction correlate with life expectancy, physiological measures, and job turnover.

The third line of criticism is the polar opposite of Nordhaus's interpersonal comparability critique: in chapter 6 Richard Layard laments that the measure of well-being that Krueger et al. emphasize is not a cardinal metric. This was a conscious decision. Krueger et al. chose the U-index precisely because it minimizes assumptions necessary for interpersonal comparisons of utility. The fraction of time spent in an unpleasant state can be compared across individuals even if the underlying cardinal utilities are not interpersonally comparable. But Layard points out that a cardinal measure is necessary to draw inferences about parameters that are essential for important policy questions, such as the diminishing marginal utility of income. Layard presents evidence on the curvature of the "utility function" with respect to income based on self-reported overall happiness data. The similarity of the parameters may indicate that the data provide interpretable cardinal measures, or it may be a coincidence of the way that individuals utilize response scales. We return to this point in the rejoinder. We note that Layard is not doctrinaire. He is not committed to the development of one well-being measure. Indeed, he begins his chapter by observing that the development of evaluated time-use data described in chapter 1 "represents an excellent use of time by its five authors."

A fourth criticism of NTA is contained in David G. "Danny" Blanchflower's chapter (chapter 7). Blanchflower compares the results of evaluated time use to those of more conventional well-being measures, including life satisfaction and happiness. Blanchflower notes that many of the findings from evaluated time-use data are replicated in more conventional data on subjective well-being. For example, both the U-index and conventional measures of life satisfaction and happiness show higher levels of well-being among wealthier, higher educated, and older individuals. Blanchflower points out an advantage of the NTA data, however. Namely, the evaluated time-use data can be used to understand why some groups are happier than others. That is, some differences in well-being between groups can be traced to differences in time use. Blanchflower highlights that this advantage comes at some cost. First, NTA data are costly and more difficult to collect than conventional subjective well-being data. Secondly, and more importantly, when it comes to data, sunk costs are not necessarily sunk. In particular, comparable historical and cross-country data on life satisfaction and happiness are valuable even if they are less informative than NTA. Blanchflower devotes considerable attention to exploring national differences in subjective well-being with overall life satisfaction and happiness data. He also notes that the contrast between the difference in subjective well-being between France and the United States using the U-index and life satisfaction is suggestive that NTA can help overcome biases in conventional happiness measures that are sometimes introduced when "nations have different languages and cultures" that lead to different reporting practices.

Finally, Erik Hurst (chapter 8) raises a fifth objection to our approach to NTA: some people seek out and want to experience negative emotions. For example, people sometimes pay money to watch movies that make them sad. This is a valid point. There are also some activities that people engage in that cause pain but raise happiness even more; for example, exercise. Over all episodes of the day, however, positive emotions and negative ones tend to be inversely correlated. The U-index presumes that an experience is unpleasant if a negative emotion is felt more strongly than a positive one, but, as Hurst argues, this may not be the case for all people all the time. Hurst raises another important point: people self-select the activities they engage in. Thus, it is not straightforward to infer that an activity that is rated as highly enjoyable by its average participant will be enjoyable to someone who does not partake in that activity. This type of selection problem is common in economic data, and can be addressed with econometric methods (e.g., instrumental variables) or by implementing a random assignment experiment. Despite noting these limitations of NTA, Hurst concludes, "Overall, I think this research design has merit."

Research on National Time Accounting is at an early stage. It took decades for the National Income and Product Accounts to be developed, and some thorny issues were never fully resolved. The chapters of this book closely examine one promising approach to developing National Time Accounts. The authors bring different expertise and different methods to evaluate NTAs, yet most are optimistic that progress can be made. But the early stage of the research program should be borne in mind. One important purpose of this volume is to stimulate further research and interest in developing National Time Accounts. Many of the criticisms of NTA that are identified by the scholars in this volume can be researched—some can be overcome by tweaking the current survey method or by using evaluated time use as the outcome of randomized control trials; some may be solvable with future advances in subjective measurement; and some must be borne in mind as limitations that will also leave users of NTAs with some uncertainty.

The chapters contained in this book were originally presented at a conference at the National Bureau of Economic Research in Cambridge, MA on December 7 and 8, 2008. The authors engaged in lively discussions about research opportunities involving NTAs and the potential for national statistical agencies to produce NTAs. The conference was supported in part by the National Institute of Aging, and Richard Suzman's participation and encouragement is gratefully acknowledged.

1

National Time Accounting
The Currency of Life

Alan B. Krueger, Daniel Kahneman, David Schkade,
Norbert Schwarz, and Arthur A. Stone

> Time is the coin of your life. It is the only coin you have, and
> only you can determine how it will be spent. Be careful lest you
> let other people spend it for you.
> —Carl Sandburg

1.1 Introduction

The development of the National Income and Product Accounts (NIPA) was arguably the foremost contribution of economics in the last century, and the National Bureau of Economic Research's role in developing the accounts remains an unparalleled achievement. Nearly every country tracks its national income today, and limiting fluctuations in national income is a goal of public policy around the world. The National Accounts have been used to estimate bottlenecks in the economy, to forecast business growth, and to inform government budgeting.[1] As then-Treasury Secretary Robert Rubin said, "the development of the GDP measure by the Department of

Alan B. Krueger is the Bendheim Professor of Economics and Public Policy at Princeton University. Daniel Kahneman is a senior scholar and professor of psychology and public affairs emeritus at the Woodrow Wilson School of Public and International Affairs, and the Eugene Higgins Professor of Psychology Emeritus, Princeton University. David Schkade holds the Jerome S. Katzin Endowed Chair and is associate dean and a professor of management at the Rady School of Management, University of California, San Diego. Norbert Schwarz is the Charles Horton Cooley Collegiate Professor of Psychology, a professor of business at the Stephen M. Ross School of Business, and research professor at the Institute for Social Research, University of Michigan. Arthur A. Stone is department vice-chair and Distinguished Professor of Psychiatry and of Psychology at Stony Brook University.

We thank the National Institute of Aging, the Hewlett Foundation, and Princeton University for generous financial support. We thank Leandro Carvalho, Marie Connolly, David Kamin, Amy Krilla, Molly McIntosh, and Doug Mills for excellent research assistance, and Ed Freeland, Jack Ludwig, John McNee, and Rajesh Srinivasan for survey assistance. We are grateful to colleagues too numerous to thank individually for their constructive comments and criticisms, but we acknowledge that they have improved our collective U-index.

1. In one important early application, Fogel (2001, 213) describes how Simon Kuznets and Robert Nathan "used national income accounting together with a crude form of linear programming to measure the potential for increased [military] production and the sources from

Commerce is a powerful reminder of the important things that government can and does do to make the private economy stronger and our individual lives better."[2]

Yet gross domestic product (GDP), national income, consumption, and other components of the National Accounts have long been viewed as partial measures of society's well-being—by economists and noneconomists alike. For one thing, the National Accounts miss "near-market" activities, such as home production (e.g., unpaid cleaning, cooking, and child care), which produce services that could be purchased on the market. Perhaps more significantly, the National Accounts do not value social activities, such as interactions between friends or husbands and wives, which have an important effect on subjective well-being. Because economic activity is measured by prices, which are marginal valuations in perfectly competitive markets, the National Accounts miss consumer surplus from market transactions. Diamonds are counted as more valuable than water, for example, yet one could question whether diamonds contribute more to society's well-being. Other limitations of the National Accounts that have long been recognized are: externalities improperly accounted for; prices distorted in imperfectly competitive markets; and the particular distribution of income in a country influences prices and marginal valuations. While attempts have been made to adjust the National Accounts for some of these limitations—such as by valuing some forms of nonmarket activity—these efforts are unlikely to go very far in overcoming these problems.

Many of these sentiments were alluded to by Robert Kennedy in his speech "On Gross National Product" at the University of Kansas on March 18, 1968:

> Too much and for too long, we seemed to have surrendered personal excellence and community values in the mere accumulation of material things. Our Gross National Product . . . if we judge the United States of America by that . . . counts air pollution and cigarette advertising, and ambulances to clear our highways of carnage. It counts special locks for our doors and the jails for the people who break them. It counts the destruction of the redwood and the loss of our natural wonder in chaotic sprawl. . . . And the television programs which glorify violence in order to sell toys to our children. Yet the Gross National Product does not allow for the health of our children, the quality of their education or the joy of their play. It does not include the beauty of our poetry or the strength of our marriages, the intelligence of our public debate or the integrity of our public officials. It measures neither our wit nor our courage, neither our wisdom nor our learning, neither our compassion nor our devotion

---

which it would come and to identify the materials that were binding constraints on expansion" prior to the U.S. entry in World War II.

2. Quoted from "GDP: One of the Great Inventions of the 20th Century," *Survey of Current Business,* January 2000.

to our country, it measures everything in short, except that which makes life worthwhile.[3]

The problem is not so much with the National Accounts themselves as with the fact that policymakers and the public often lose sight of their limitations, or misinterpret national income as the sole object of policy and primary measure of well-being.[4]

In this volume, we propose an alternative way of measuring society's well-being, based on time use and affective (emotional) experience. We call our approach National Time Accounting (NTA). National Time Accounting is a set of methods for measuring, categorizing, comparing, and analyzing the way people spend their time, across countries, over historical time, or between groups of people within a country at a given time.

Currently, time use is tracked according to the amount of time spent in various activities—such as traveling, watching television, and working for pay—but the evaluation and grouping of those activities is decided by external researchers and coders. Determining whether people are spending their time in more or less enjoyable ways than they were a generation ago is either impossible or subject to researchers' judgments of what constitutes enjoyable leisure activities and arduous work. In addition to the obvious problem that researchers may not view time use in the same way as the general public, other problems with this approach are that: (a) many people derive some pleasure from nonleisure activities; (b) not all leisure activities are equally enjoyable to the average person; (c) the nature of some activities changes over time; (d) people have heterogeneous emotional experiences during the same activities; and (e) emotional responses during activities are not unidimensional. The methods we propose provide a means for evaluating different uses of time based on the population's own evaluations of their emotional experiences, what we call *evaluated time use,* which can be used to develop a system of national time accounts.

We view NTA as a complement to the National Income Accounts (NIA), not a substitute. Like the National Income Accounts, NTA is also incomplete, providing a partial measure of society's well-being. National time accounting misses people's general sense of satisfaction or fulfillment with their lives as a whole, apart from moment to moment feelings.[5] Still, we will argue that evaluated time use provides a valuable indicator of society's well-being, and the fact that our measure is connected to time allocation has

---

3. Transcription available from: www.jfklibrary.org/Historical + Resources/Archives/Reference + Desk/Speeches/RFK/RFKSpeech68Mar18UKansas.htm.
4. Kennedy's point has resonance with at least one politician. In an interview, Barack Obama told David Leonhardt (2008) the following: "One of my favorite quotes is—you know that famous Robert F. Kennedy quote about the measure of our G.D.P.? . . . it's one of the most beautiful of his speeches."
5. For surveys of economics research using the more conventional measures of life satisfaction, see Frey and Stutzer (2002) and Layard (2005).

analytical and policy advantages that are not available from other measures of subjective well-being, such as overall life satisfaction.

There have been some attempts at NTA in the past, primarily by time-use researchers. Our approach builds on Juster's (1985) seminal observation that "an important ingredient in the production and distribution of well-being is the set of satisfactions generated by activities themselves" (333). To assess the satisfactions generated by activities, Juster asked respondents to rate on a scale from zero to ten how much they generally enjoy a given type of activity, such as their job or taking care of their children. Later research found that such general enjoyment ratings can deviate in important and theoretically meaningful ways from episodic ratings that pertain to specific instances of the activity (Schwarz, Kahneman, and Xu 2009). To overcome this problem, we utilize a time diary method more closely connected to the recalled emotional experiences of a day's actual events and circumstances. Gershuny and Halpin (1996) and Robinson and Godbey (1997), who analyzed a single well-being measure (extent of enjoyment) and time use collected together in a time diary, are closer forerunners to our approach.

Our project is distinguished from past efforts in that we approach NTA from more of a psychological well-being and Experience Sampling Method (ESM) perspective. For example, our measure of emotional experience is *multidimensional,* reflecting different core affective dimensions. And like ESM, we try to measure the feelings that were experienced during different uses of time as closely as possible. We also developed an easily interpretable and defensible metric of subjective well-being, which combines the data on affective experience and time use to measure the proportion of time spent in an unpleasant state.[6] And we use cluster analysis to determine which groups of activities are associated with similar emotional experiences to facilitate the tracking of time use with historical and cross-country data. Past research has not addressed how time-use has shifted among activities associated with different emotional experiences over time, or the extent to which cross-country differences in time allocation can account for international differences in experienced well-being. Lastly, our survey methods attempt to have respondents reinstantiate their day before answering affect questions, to make their actual emotional experiences at the time more vivid and readily accessible for recall.

Past calls for National Time Accounting have largely foundered. It is instructive to ask why these efforts were not more influential in academic circles and why government statistical agencies have not implemented them.

---

6. Because the earlier work focused on whether activities were enjoyable, it would not have been possible to construct our measure of time spent in an unpleasant state with their data. Our approach also differs fundamentally from Glorieux (1993), who asked survey respondents to classify their time use into different "meanings of time," such as social time, time for personal gratification, and meaningless time. Instead, we focus on the emotional experiences that occur over time.

One possible explanation is that it is difficult to collect time diary information along with affective experience in a representative population sample. To this end, we developed a telephone survey, called the Princeton Affect and Time Survey (PATS), patterned on the Bureau of Labor Statistics' (BLS's) American Time Use Survey (ATUS), that is practical and easily adaptable for use in ongoing official time-use surveys. Another possible explanation is that evidence on the validity of subjective well-being measures has progressed greatly in the last decade. While subjective data cannot be independently verified, a range of findings presented in section 1.3 suggests that self-reports of subjective experience indeed have signal. The earlier efforts may have been ahead of their time and taken less seriously than they should have because such evidence was not yet available. Finally, it is difficult to track down documentation on the precise methods used in past diary cum well-being surveys. To facilitate replication and extensions, we have posted our main data sets, questionnaires, and background documents on the web at www.krueger.princeton.edu/Subjective.htm.

The remainder of this chapter is organized as follows. Section 1.2 provides a conceptual framework for using evaluated time use in National Time Accounting and discusses perspectives on well-being in economics and psychology. Section 1.3 provides evidence on the link between self-reports of subjective well-being and objective outcomes, such as health and neurological activity. Section 1.4 introduces the evaluated time-use measures that we have developed and provides some evidence on their reliability and validity. Section 1.5 uses the PATS data to describe time use and affective experience across groups of individuals and activities. Section 1.6 provides a method for grouping activities into categories based on the emotional experiences that they are associated with. To illustrate the utility of our techniques, section 1.7 describes long-term historical trends in the desirability of time use and section 1.8 provides a cross-country comparison. Section 1.9 concludes by considering some knotty unresolved issues and by pointing to some opportunities for NTA in the future.

1.2   Conceptual Issues

1.2.1   Economics of Time Use, Goods, and Utility

In a standard economic model, households receive utility from their consumption of leisure and goods. People choose to work because of the income and hence, consumption of goods that work makes possible. Available time and the wage rate are the constraints that people face. The national income and product accounts only value market output (or, equivalently, paid inputs and profits). Some attempts have been made to value nonmarket time using the wage rate as the shadow price of leisure. Becker (1965) argued that households combine resources (e.g., food) and time to produce output (e.g., meals), just like firms. Thus, in Becker's model cooking only affects utility through the subsequent enjoyment of eating. Pollak and Wachter (1975) expand this framework to allow home production activities to affect utility through their direct effect on utility during the activities themselves and through the consumption of the output produced during the activities.

Dow and Juster (1985) and Juster, Courant, and Dow (1985) emphasize the notion of "process benefits," or the flow of utility that accrues during particular activities, such as work and consumption.[7] Juster, Courant, and Dow illustrate this idea in a Robinson Crusoe economy. Robinson can divide his time among three distinct activities: working in the market, cooking, and eating. He is constrained by the amount of food or clothing he can obtain through work, the amount of meals he can cook in a given period of time, and twenty-four hours in a day.[8] With the assumption that process benefits from activities are separable, utility can be written as:

$$(1) \qquad U = V_m(t_w,x_c) + V_c(t_c,x_c,x_f) + V_e(t_e,x_c,x_m),$$

where V_w, V_c, and V_e are the process benefits derived during work, cooking, and eating, respectively; x_c is the quantity of clothing; x_f is the quantity of food; x_m is the amount of meals cooked; and t is the amount of time devoted to each activity. Juster, Courant, and Dow make the critical but sensible assumption "that the process benefit obtained from each activity is independent of the time and goods devoted to other activities" (128). They defend this assumption by noting that "any stocks produced by activity i are permitted to affect the process benefits from other activities."[9]

The data that we collect are divided into episodes of varying length, not activities, so it is more natural to model the time devoted to episodes and the average process benefit during those episodes. Consider someone who spends her first t_1 hours of the day working, her next t_2 hours preparing meals, her next t_3 hours eating the meals prepared earlier, and her final t_4 hours working again. (Of course, this could easily be extended to allow for more episodes and other activities.) Under the assumption of separability, the utility function can be written as:

$$(2) \quad U_i = \int_0^1 v_1(t,X_c)dt + \int_0^2 v_2(t,X_c,X_f)dt + \int_0^3 v_3(t,X_c,X_m)dt + \int_0^4 v_4(t,X_c)dt.$$

Taking means of the flow utilities over the relevant intervals gives:

---

7. They define process benefits as the "direct subjective consequences from engaging in some activities to the exclusion of others. . . . For instance, how much an individual likes or dislikes the activity 'painting one's house,' in conjunction with the amount of time one spends in painting the house, is an important determinant of well-being independent of how satisfied one feels about having a freshly painted house." The idea of process benefits is closely related to Kahneman's notion of "experienced utility."

8. We ignore sleep to simplify the exposition.

9. An exception might be exercise. A period of exercising may raise someone's mood during the rest of the day. We return to this following.

(3) $U_i = t_1 \bar{v}_1(t_1, X_c) + t_2 \bar{v}_2(t_2, X_c, X_f) + t_3 \bar{v}_3(t_3, X_c, X_m) + t_4 \bar{v}_4(t_4, X_c).$

It follows that a person's total utility can be obtained from the duration weighted sum of average process benefits during the time the individual is engaged in each episode. There is no need to collect additional information on resources, constraints, or prices to summarize the person's well-being. Notice also that equation (3) does not require utility maximization. Even if the individual allocates his or her time suboptimally, if the mean process benefit can be estimated it is possible to estimate his or her well-being.

In this framework, which loosely guides our empirical work, the average well-being among N members of society, W, is $W = \Sigma U_i / N$. If one wants to put a dollar value on W, in principle it is possible to estimate the monetary price that people are willing to pay on the margin to increase their process benefit in some activity by one unit, and use the inverse of this figure as a numeraire. For example, the way workers trade off pay for a more or less pleasant job can give an estimate of the marginal willingness to pay to improve time spent in a pleasant state. Alternatively, the amount that people are willing to spend on various types of vacations can be related to the flow of utility they receive during those vacations to place a monetary value on additional utility. Although it is possible, under the assumption of rational decision making, to place a dollar value on W in this framework, we shy away from this step and focus instead on providing credible estimates of W.

Of course, measuring the flow of utility or emotions during various activities is no easy task, and some scholars doubt its feasibility entirely. Juster (1985) attempts to measure process benefits by using responses to the following question: "Now I'm going to read a list of certain activities that you may participate in. Think about a scale, from 10 to zero. If you enjoy doing an activity a great deal, rank it as a '10'; if you dislike doing it a great deal, rank it as a '0'; if you don't care about it one way or the other, rank it in the middle as '5'. . . . Keep in mind that we're interested in whether you *like* doing something, not whether you think it is important to do." The activities included: cleaning the house, cooking, doing repairs, taking care of your child(ren), your job, grocery shopping, and so forth. For activity j, the enjoyment score is assumed to equal the process benefit, Vj.

There are several important limitations to Juster's type of enjoyment data, which we describe as a "general activity judgment" measure, because it focuses on a general response to a domain of life, not specific events that actually occurred. First, respondents are likely to develop a theory of how much they should enjoy an activity in order to construct an answer to the question. Second, respondents may be sensitive to the interviewers' reactions to their answers. For example, someone may be concerned that they will be viewed as a bad parent or worker if they respond that they do not like taking care of their children or their job. Third, people are unlikely to correctly aggregate their experiences over the many times that they engaged in a particular activity in providing a general activity judgment. Other research (e.g., Kahneman, Wakker, and Sarin 1997) has found that individuals ignore the duration of events and instead place excessive weight on the end and peak of the experience when answering general evaluative recall questions. Fourth, and related, individuals are likely to exercise selection bias in choosing from the best or worst moments of past incidents of the specified activities. Results presented below cast some doubt on the validity of general activity judgments. Fifth, it is unclear if individuals utilize the enjoyment scales in an interpersonally comparable way.

Nonetheless, as a description of time use and well-being, the process benefit approach has many advantages. Most importantly, the output of home production does not have to be observed or evaluated. A major goal of our work, therefore, has been to develop more informative measures of the flow of emotional experience during specific moments of the day.

1.2.2   The Psychology of Well-Being

Contemporary psychology recognizes a variety of informative subjective well-being (SWB) measures. Our view of the structure of subjective well-being concentrates on two qualitatively distinct constituents that both contribute to SWB. The first component pertains to how people experience their lives moment to moment as reflected in the positive and negative feelings that accompany their daily activities. We refer to this component as "experienced happiness," or the average of a dimension of subjective experience reported in real time over an extended period. The second component pertains to how people evaluate their lives. It is typically assessed with measures of life-satisfaction, like "Taking all things together, how satisfied would you say you are with your life as a whole these days?" There are many ways in which these components of SWB can be measured, but we view them as reflecting overlapping but distinct aspects of people's lives.

Much of the variance of both experienced happiness and life satisfaction is explained by variation in personal disposition that probably has a significant genetic component (Diener and Lucas 1999; Lykken 1999). We focus here on two other determinants: the general circumstances of people's lives (marital status, age, income) and the specifics of how they spend their time.

Evaluating one's life as a whole poses a difficult judgment task (see Schwarz and Strack 1999). Like other hard judgments, the evaluation of one's life is accomplished by consulting heuristics—the answers to related questions that come more readily to mind (Kahneman 2003). Experimental demonstrations of priming and context effects provide evidence for the role of such heuristics in reports of life satisfaction (Schwarz and Strack 1999). Two heuristic questions that are used are: "How fortunate am I?" and "How good do I feel?" The first involves a comparison of the individual's circumstances to conventional or personal standards, while the second calls attention to recent affective experience. Research indicates, for example, that reported life satisfaction is higher on sunny than on rainy days, consistent with the influence of the weather on their temporary moods. If individuals are first asked explicitly about the weather, however, they become aware that their current feelings may only reflect a temporary influence, which eliminates the effect of weather on reported life satisfaction (Schwarz and Clore 1983).

In addition to personal effects, affective experience is determined by the immediate context and varies accordingly during the day; most people are happier sharing lunch with friends than driving alone in heavy traffic. Russell (1980) provides a theory of core affect, in which emotions are described along two dimensions. One dimension ranges from pleasure to displeasure, and the other from highly activated to deactivated. Happiness, for example, is an activated, pleasurable state. We define an individual's experienced happiness on a given day by the average value of this dimension of affective experience for that day. Experienced happiness, so defined, is influenced by the individual's allocation of time: a longer lunch and a shorter commute make for a better day. A person's use of time, in turn, reflects his or her circumstances and choices. Favorable life circumstances are more strongly correlated with activation than with experienced happiness.

A classic puzzle in SWB research involves the limited long-term hedonic effects of outcomes that are greatly desired or feared in anticipation and evoke intense emotions when they occur (Brickman, Coates, and Janoff-Bulman 1978). In a recent study using longitudinal data, Oswald and Powdthavee (2005) find that average life satisfaction drops after the onset of a moderate disability but fully recovers to the predisability level after two years.[10] This process is known as adaptation or habituation. Oswald and Powdthavee find that adaptation takes place but is incomplete for severe disabilities. Life events such as marriage and bereavement have substantial short-run effects on happiness and life satisfaction, but these effects are mainly temporary (e.g., Clark et al. 2003). Findings like these invite the idea of a potent process of hedonic adaptation that eventually returns people to a set point determined by their personality (see Diener, Lucas, and Scollon [2006]; Headey and Wearing [1989]).

Kahneman and Krueger (2006) conclude that adaptation to both income and to marital status is at least as complete for measures of experienced happiness as for life satisfaction. This conclusion is also consistent with Riis et al. (2005), who used experience sampling methods to assess the feelings of end-stage renal dialysis patients and a matched comparison group. They found no significant differences in average mood throughout the day between the dialysis patients and the controls.

10. Smith et al. (2005) find that the onset of a new disability causes a greater drop in life satisfaction for those in the bottom half of the wealth distribution than for those in the top half, suggesting an important buffering effect of wealth, although low-wealth individuals still recovered some of their predisability well-being.

A focus on time use and activities suggests two factors in addition to hedonic adaptation for understanding the stability of SWB. First, although personality surely matters, the claim that an individual's experienced happiness must return to a set-point that is independent of local circumstances is probably false. For someone who enjoys socializing much more than commuting, a permanent reallocation of time from one of these activities to the other can be expected to have a permanent effect on happiness (Lyubomirsky, Sheldon, and Schkade 2005). Second, one must recognize that there are substantial substitution possibilities when it comes to activities. People who suffer injuries, for example, can substitute games like chess or checkers for competitive sports in their leisure time. These substitution possibilities are probably not anticipated. Thus, the largely unanticipated opportunity to substitute activities could attenuate the actual loss or gain in SWB associated with major changes in life circumstances, relative to anticipations.

A final observation is that the withdrawal of attention is another mechanism of adaptation to life changes. Attention is normally associated with novelty. Thus, the newly disabled, lottery winner, or newlywed are almost continuously aware of their state. But as the new state loses its novelty it ceases to be the exclusive focus of attention, and other aspects of life again evoke their varying hedonic responses. Research indicates that paraplegics are in a fairly good mood more than half the time as soon as one month after their crippling accident. Intuitive affective forecasts will miss this process of attentional adaptation, unless they are corrected by specific personal knowledge (Ubel et al. 2005).

1.2.3   The U-Index: A Misery Index of Sorts

Two challenges for developing a measure of the process benefit of an activity are that the scale of measurement is unclear, and different people are likely to interpret the same scale differently. Indeed, modern utility theory in economics dispenses with the concept of cardinal utility in favor of preference orderings.

Survey researchers try to anchor response categories to words that have a common and clear meaning across respondents, but there is no guarantee that respondents use the scales comparably. Despite the apparent signal in subjective well-being data (documented in the next section), one could legitimately question whether one should give a cardinal interpretation to the numeric values attached to individuals' responses about their life satisfaction or emotional states because of the potential for personal use of scales. This risk is probably exacerbated when it comes to comparisons across countries and cultures.

We propose an index, called the U-index (for "unpleasant" or "undesirable"), designed to address both challenges.[11] The U-index measures the

---

11. The remainder of this section borrows heavily and unabashedly from Kahneman and Krueger (2006).

proportion of time an individual spends in an unpleasant state. The average U-index for a group of individuals can also be computed. This statistic has the virtue of being immediately understandable, and has other desirable properties as well. Most importantly, the U-index is an ordinal measure *at the level of feelings*.

The first step in computing the U-index is to determine whether an episode is unpleasant or pleasant. There are many possible ways to classify an episode as unpleasant or pleasant. The data collected with Experience Sampling Methods (ESM) or the Day Reconstruction Method (DRM) include descriptions of an individual's emotional state during each episode in terms of intensity ratings on several dimensions of feelings, some of which are positive (e.g., "Happy," "Enjoy myself," "Friendly") and some of which are negative (e.g., "Depressed," "Angry," "Frustrated"). We classify an episode as unpleasant if the most intense feeling reported for that episode is a negative one—that is, if the maximum rating on any of the negative affect dimensions is strictly greater than the maximum of rating of the positive affect dimensions.[12] Notice that this definition relies purely on an *ordinal ranking* of the feelings within each episode. Respondents can interpret the scales differently. It does not matter if respondent A uses the two to four portion of the zero to six intensity scale and Respondent B uses the full range. As long as they employ the same personal interpretation of the scale to report the intensity of their positive and negative emotions, the determination of which emotion was strongest is unaffected.[13] It is reassuring to note that in cognitive testing conducted by the Bureau of Labor Statistics, ten subjects were asked whether the affective dimension that they gave the highest rating to was the most intense feeling they had during the episode, and all of the respondents said yes for each sampled episode.[14]

To define the U-index mathematically, let I_{ij} be an indicator that equals 1 if a time interval denoted j of duration h_{ij} for person i is considered unpleasant and 0 otherwise. As mentioned previously, I_{ij} equals 1 if the emotion that was rated as most intensive for that time interval is a negative one. For an individual, the U-index over a given period of time is $\Sigma_j I_{ij} h_{ij} / \Sigma_j h_{ij}$. For a group of N individuals, the U-index is defined as:

$$U = \Sigma_i \left(\frac{\Sigma_j I_{ij} h_{ij}}{\Sigma_j h_{ij}} \right) / N.$$

12. Our approach bears some resemblance to a procedure proposed by Diener, Sandvik, and Pavot (1991), which categorized moments as unpleasant if the average rating of positive emotions was less than the average rating of negative emotions. Unlike the U-index, however, averaging ratings of feelings requires a cardinal metric. Notice also that because the correlations between negative emotions tend to be low, their procedure will categorize fewer moments as unpleasant than the U-index.

13. Formally, let $f(\ )$ be any monotonically increasing function. If P is the maximum intensity of the positive emotions and N is the maximum intensity of the negative emotions, than $f(P) > f(N)$ regardless of the monotonic transformation.

14. Memo from Kathy Downey, research psychologist, Office of Survey Methods Research, BLS, July 21, 2008.

Notice that the U-index for a group is the equally weighted U-index for the individuals in the group. The group U-index can be interpreted as the average proportion of time that members of the group spend in an unpleasant state.

From a psychological perspective, the U-index has some desirable attributes. First, the predominant emotional state for the majority of people during most of the time is positive, so any episode when a negative feeling is the most intense emotion is a significant occurrence. It is not necessary to have more than one salient negative emotion for an episode to be unpleasant. Second, the selection of a negative feeling as more intense than all positive ones is likely to be a mindful and deliberate choice: the maximal rating is salient, especially when it is negative, because negative feelings are relatively rare. Third, because at a given moment of time, the correlation of the intensity among various positive emotions across episodes is higher than the correlation among negative emotions, one dominant negative emotion probably colors an entire episode and it is potentially misleading to average negative emotions.

Of course, the dichotomous categorization of moments or episodes as unpleasant or pleasant obscures some information about the intensity of positive and negative emotions, just as a dichotomous definition of poverty misses the depths of material deprivation for those who are below the poverty line. However, we see the ordinal definition of unpleasant episodes as a significant advantage. In addition to reducing interpersonal differences in the use of scales, the question of how to numerically scale subjective responses is no longer an issue with our dichotomous measure. The categorization of moments into unpleasant and pleasant moments emphasizes what can be most confidently measured from subjective data.

The U-index can be used to compare individuals (what proportion of the time is this person in an unpleasant emotional state?), demographic groups (do men or women spend a higher proportion of time in an emotional state considered unpleasant?), and situations. The U-index can also be aggregated to the country level (what proportion of time do people in France spend in an emotional state classified as unpleasant) and can be used to compare countries. Notice that because the U-index is aggregated based on time, it takes on useful cardinal properties. Like the poverty rate, for example, one could compute that the U-index is X percent lower for one group than another, or has fallen by Y percent from one year to another.

1.3   Is There Useful Signal in What People Report About Their Subjective Experiences?

Economists often treat self-reported data with a high degree of suspicion, especially when those data pertain to subjective internal states, such as well-being or health. Is there any useful signal in what people tell us about their subjective experiences? To answer this question, we first discuss how social scientists assess the validity of self-reports of behavior and subsequently develop a strategy for assessing the validity of self-reports of subjective experiences before we turn to relevant empirical findings. Following the review of the evidence, we identify some limiting conditions and highlight that self-reports of affect are most meaningful when they pertain to recent specific episodes in a person's life, a fact that we exploit later in the design of the Day Reconstruction Method and the Princeton Affect and Time-use Survey.

1.3.1 Rationale

Many surveys ask respondents to report on their behavior. The validity of such reports can be assessed by comparing them with external records at the individual or aggregate level. For example, banking records can be used to evaluate the validity of self-reported expenditures at the individual level (e.g., Blair and Burton 1987), and national sales figures can be used to assess the validity of purchase reports in representative sample surveys at the aggregate level (e.g., Sudman and Wansink 2002). Neither of these strategies is feasible for assessing the validity of self-reported feelings, like moods, emotions, worries, or pain. Feelings are subjective experiences and the final arbiter is the person who experiences them. The same holds for other subjective evaluations, like reports of life-satisfaction, which pertain to individuals' subjective assessments of the quality of their lives. The subjective nature of feelings and evaluations precludes direct validation against objective records. It is also expected that comparisons of subjective and objective reports will not be identical, because people interpret the objective world in idiosyncratic ways.

Nevertheless, one can gauge the validity of these reports in other, less direct ways. To begin with, one can assess interpersonal agreement: do "close others" perceive the person in ways that are compatible with the person's self-reports? While interpersonal agreement is comforting, it is less than compelling and subject to numerous biasing factors. As a more informative alternative, one can relate self-reports of subjective experience to objective outcomes with the expectation that there should be at least a modest correspondence. If reports of positive affect are associated with increased longevity, for example, they obviously capture *something* real—yet it remains unclear whether that something is indeed positive affect or some other variable correlated with its expression (the so-called "third variable" explanation). Perhaps people who present themselves in a positive light when answering questions also follow other strategies of social interaction that reduce daily friction and benefit health. Such ambiguities are attenuated when studies that do not rely on self-reports for the assessment of affect show similar results. Finally, interpretative ambiguities are further attenuated when experimental results, based on random assignment, support the naturalistic observation; for example, when induced positive affect also has beneficial health consequences. Such supporting results will typically be more limited in scope due to ethical constraints on the experimental induction of affect (especially negative affective states such as stress or anger) and the more limited time frame of experimental studies.

We next review illustrative findings from longitudinal studies that show self-reported affect predicts some important objective outcomes in life. Paralleling these naturalistic observations, a growing number of experimental studies documents compatible effects of induced affect, based on random assignment of participants to positive or negative "affect induction" conditions. For example, positive affect can be induced by giving subjects a cookie or placing a dime in a spot where they can find it. Other approaches to inducing affect include placing subjects in a situation where they overhear a compliment or insult, showing subjects a funny versus sad movie, asking subjects to recall a happy versus sad event, and giving subjects a task that is easy or impossible to perform; see Schwarz and Strack (1999).

1.3.2   Affect and Objective Outcomes: Social Life

In a comprehensive review of cross-sectional and longitudinal studies, Lyubomirsky, King, and Diener (2005) observed that a preponderance of positive over negative affect predicts numerous beneficial outcomes, from the quality of one's social life and work life to longevity and the quality of one's health. Here, we focus on studies that are particularly informative with regard to the validity of affective self-reports, namely studies in which (a) the person's affect was assessed through self-reports several months or years prior to the observed outcome; (b) the outcome itself is objective (e.g., longevity or health status rather than subjective satisfaction with one's health); and (c) studies in which the affect assessment is *not* based on self-reports show compatible effects.

Finding a Spouse

Most people would prefer to be married to a partner who is happy and satisfied rather than depressed and dissatisfied. Consistent with this preference, several longitudinal studies show that people who report in sample surveys that they are happy (Marks and Fleming 1999) or satisfied with their lives (Lucas et al. 2003; Spanier and Fuerstenberg 1982) are indeed more likely to marry in the following years. For example, Marks and Fleming (1999) observed in a fifteen-year longitudinal study with a representative sample of young Australians that those who were 1 standard deviation above the mean of happiness reports were 1.5 times more likely to marry in the ensuing years; those 2 standard deviations above the mean were twice as likely to marry.

This relationship can also be observed with measures of affect that do *not* rely on self-report. For example, Harker and Keltner (2001) coded the affect expressed in women's college yearbook photographs, following the well-established procedures of Ekman's facial action coding system (Ekman and Rosenberg 1997). They observed that women who expressed genuine positive affect (in the form of a Duchenne smile) at age twenty-one were more likely to be married by age twenty-seven and less likely to remain single through middle adulthood. Of course, people may report being happy because they anticipate being married in the next year, but the long lag in the Ekman and Rosenberg study is harder to reconcile with reverse causality.

Helping Others

Several studies show that self-reported daily mood is associated with the likelihood of helping others. For example, Lucas (2001) observed that students who reported a preponderance of positive mood in their daily diaries also reported spending more time helping others than did those with less positive moods. Similarly, Csikszentmihalyi, Patton, and Lucas (1997) found that self-reported helping behavior increased with the percentage of time spent in a good mood among school-age youths.

Numerous experimental studies, with random assignment to different affect induction conditions, support the link between positive mood and prosocial behavior. People in induced positive moods are more likely to help others by donating money (Cunningham, Steinberg, and Grev 1980), blood (O'Malley and Andrews 1983), and time (Berkowitz 1987) to worthy causes. Receiving a cookie or finding a dime is sufficient to elicit increased prosocial behavior (Isen and Levin 1972).

Income

Several studies show a positive relationship between self-reported positive affect at a given time and later income. Diener et al. (2002) observed that self-reported cheerfulness at college entry predicted income sixteen years later, controlling for numerous other variables, including parents' income. For example, the most cheerful offspring of well-off parents earned $25,000 more per year than the least cheerful offspring. Similarly, Marks and Fleming (1999) observed in their Australian panel study of young adults that respondents' self-reported happiness in one wave predicted the size of the pay raises they had received by the time of the next interview, two years later. Finally, Russian respondents who reported high happiness in 1995 enjoyed higher incomes in 2000 and were less likely to have experienced unemployment in the meantime (Graham, Eggers, and Sukhtankar 2006).

1.3.3   Affect and Objective Outcomes: Health

Numerous longitudinal studies show that happy people have a better chance to live a long and healthy life (for reviews see Lyubomirsky, King, and Diener [2005]; Howell, Kern, and Lyubomirsky [2007]). This observation holds for mortality in general as well as for specific health outcomes;

moreover, it is supported by studies that relied on affect measures other than self-report.

Mortality

Based on data of the Berlin Aging Study, Maier and Smith (1999) reported that a preponderance of self-reported positive over negative affect (assessed with the Positive and negative affect schedule [PANAS]) predicted mortality in a sample of 513 older adults three to six years later. Studies with clinical samples reinforce this observation. For example, Devins et al. (1990) observed that end-stage renal patients who reported overall happiness were more likely to survive over a four year period than were their less happy peers. Similarly, Levy et al. (1988) found that women who reported more joy in life were more likely to survive a recurrence of breast cancer over a seven year period. Studies based on personality tests that assess enduring affective predisposition replicate this conclusion (see Lyubomirsky, King, and Diener [2005] for a review).

Complementary support for the observed relationship between positive affect and mortality comes from studies that asked the interviewer to rate the respondent's affective state. In one study (Zuckerman, Kasl, and Ostfeld 1984), healthy as well as unhealthy respondents who were rated as happier enjoyed lower mortality than their peers over a two-year period; Palmore (1969) replicated this observation over a more impressive period of fifteen years. Finally, in a study that attracted broad attention, Snowdon and his colleagues (Danner, Snowdon, and Friesen 2001; Snowdon 2001) analyzed autobiographical essays that young catholic nuns of the American School Sisters of Notre Dame had written in 1930, when most were in their early twenties. Coding the essays for emotional content, they discovered that positive affect expressed in these early essays was highly predictive of mortality by the time the writers were eighty to ninety years old. On average, nuns whose essays placed them in the top quartile of positive affect in the sample lived ten years longer than nuns whose essays placed them in the bottom quartile. Given that all nuns lived under highly comparable conditions in terms of daily routines, diet, and health care, this finding provides particularly compelling evidence for the repeatedly observed relationship between positive affect and longevity.

Physiological Associations

Several conceptual models in the fields of health psychology and behavioral medicine posit a central role for positive and negative affect in the translation of the psychosocial environment into physiological states and, subsequently, health outcomes, such as those mentioned previously. Empirical demonstrations of affect-physiology associations are a compelling source of validation for affect. We present representative findings in two physiological systems—the immune system and the endocrine system—because of their close linkage with health outcomes.

Immune Response

Alterations in immune system functioning—either above or below normative levels—can result in greater susceptibility to invading organisms and neoplastic diseases, and to autoimmune conditions. Therefore, many studies have examined how psychosocial factors and affect are related to various compartments of the immune system.

Several longitudinal studies observed that the frequency of self-reported hassles and uplifts and their accompanying affect is predictive of immune response. In one daily study, Evans et al. (1993) related participants' daily reports of life-events and mood over a two-week period to markers of immune function in daily saliva samples. They observed a higher secretion of immunoglobulin A on days that were characterized by many positive and few negative events. Stone and colleagues showed through their daily studies of events, mood, and symptoms that the impact of daily events on the secretory immune system was mediated through changes in negative and positive affect associated with daily events (Stone et al. 1987; Stone et al. 1996). A similar line of work by Vitaliano et al. (1998) monitored natural killer (NK) cell activity in cancer survivors. They found that participants who reported more uplifts than hassles (and presumably decreased levels of negative affect based on prior work [Stone 1987]) in daily life showed higher NK cell activity eighteen months later, an indicator of enhanced immune function.

Moving to more major events, a classic extensive line of work by Kiecolt-Glaser and colleagues demonstrated that naturalistic situations such as students taking exams or maritally distressed individuals discussing their marital situation results in declines in immune functioning (e.g., Kiecolt-Glaser et al. 1988). Changes in the immune system have been shown by the same investigators to have health consequences, such as in the resolution of experimentally induced wounds.

A particularly interesting series of studies by Cohen and colleagues demonstrated that people's level of affect is associated with their susceptibility to an experimentally induced viral infection and this is strongly supportive of the role of affect in physiology. In particular, recent evidence has indicated that proinflammatory cytokines are associated with positive affect (Doyle, Gentile, and Cohen 2006) when measured on a daily basis.

Beneficial immune function effects of positive affect were also observed in experimental studies, based on random assignment to different affect induction conditions. For example, watching a humorous video clip has been found to increase NK cell activity and several other immune function markers (Berk et al. 2001), including salivary immunoglobulin A (Dillon,

Minchoff, and Baker 1985) and salivary lysozyme (sLys) concentration (Perera et al. 1998). Induction of stressful situations has also produced changes in immune function. For example, Stone et al. (1993) exposed participants to challenging mental tasks and they subsequently had lower responsiveness of t-cells stimulated with standard antigens compared to participants who were not exposed. A recent review article by Marsland, Pressman, and Cohen (2007) concludes that positive affect is associated with up-regulation of the immune system.

Hormones

Many bodily functions are regulated by the actions of hormones, which are biological active substances secreted by various organ systems. One hormone that has been of particular interest to psychosocial researchers is cortisol, a product of the hypothamalic-pituatary-adrenal (HPA) system. Cortisol is often called the "stress hormone." It affects aspects of metabolism in general, but of special interest for this discussion is its impact of the immune system and its anti-inflammatory role.

Observational and experimental studies have confirmed that cortisol levels are responsive to changes in affect and to experiences that are closely linked with affect changes. In an impressive line of research, Kirschbaum and colleagues (Kirschbaum, Pirke, and Hellhammer 1993) showed that a laboratory manipulation involving stressful student presentations quickly increased levels of cortisol; such changes could at least temporarily suppress the immune system. Supporting the experimental work, there is evidence from naturalistic studies that sampled respondents' affect and cortisol repeatedly throughout the day. Those studies showed that momentary negative affect is associated with higher levels of cortisol and positive affect with lower levels of cortisol (relative to when affect levels were at the opposite level) (Smyth et al. 1998). Furthermore, both state (momentary) and trait measurement of affect is associated in the same manner with cortisol levels (Polk et al. 2005).

Neurological Activity

Findings from neuroscience research also lend some support for the view that subjective reports are related to individuals' emotional states. By way of background, note that there is strong clinical and experimental evidence that the left prefrontal cortex of the brain is associated with the processing of approach and pleasure, whereas the corresponding area in the right hemisphere is active in the processing of avoidance and aversive stimuli. In particular, the left prefrontal cortex is more active when individuals are exposed to pleasant images or asked to think happy thoughts, while the right prefrontal cortex is more active when individuals are shown unpleasant pictures and asked to think sad thoughts. A study using several measures of psychological well-being reported a statistically significant correlation of 0.30 between survey evidence on life satisfaction and the left-right difference in brain activation (Urry et al. 2004).

In a striking demonstration of the validity of subjective reports, Coghill and colleagues compared subjects' self-reported pain levels to functional magnetic resonance imaging (fMRI) while applying a *standardized* pain stimulus to seventeen subjects. The pain stimulus consisted of hot presses against the lower leg. They found that individuals reporting higher levels of pain to the thermal pain stimulus produced greater activation of various cortical regions of the brain, some of which corresponded with the stimulated limb, than individuals who reported lower pain ratings to the same stimulus (see figure 1.1; Coghill, McHaffie, and Yen [2003]). The strong implication of this work is that variation in self-reports to standard stimuli are not simply a function of interpersonal differences in scale usage, but reflect, at least in part, differential neural processes associated with the perception of pain. They concluded, "By identifying objective neural correlates of subjective differences, these findings validate the utility of introspection and subjective reporting as a means of communicating a first-person experience" (8358).

Other Systems

Levels of positive and negative affect have also been associated with and shown to affect other physiological systems and we mention some of them here. Positive affect has been shown to increase performance on cognitive tasks and this could be associated with brain dopamine levels (Ashby, Isen, and Turken 1999). Relatedly, measures of brain activity have been associated with affective levels (Wheeler, Davidson, and Tomarken 1993). Some aspects of cardiovascular function and affect have been studied. Shapiro and colleagues (Shapiro, Jamner, and Goldstein 1997) used daily monitoring of affect and blood pressure to show that specific mood states such as anger were associated with increased levels of blood pressure.

1.3.4   Assessing Subjective Experiences

As our review indicates, there is systematic signal in people's self-reports of their affective experiences. Nevertheless, self-reports of affect are subject to systematic methodological biases, which depend on the assessment method used. Next, we summarize what has been learned (for reviews see Robinson and Clore [2002]; Schwarz [2007]).

When people report on their *current* feelings, the feelings themselves are accessible to introspection, allowing for more accurate reports on the basis of experiential information. But affective experiences are fleeting and not available to introspection once the feeling dissipated. Accordingly, the opportunity to assess emotion reports based on experiential information is limited to methods of momentary data capture (Stone et al. 2007) like

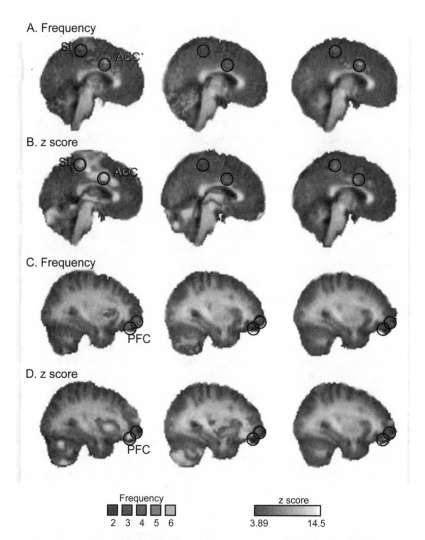

Fig. 1.1   Brain regions displaying different frequencies of activation between high- and low-(pain rating) sensitivity subgroups

Source: Reproduced from: Coghill, McHaffie, and Yen (2003). Please see original image for references to color in the following note.

Notes: Circles are centered on regions where the peak differences between groups were located. Colors in *A* and *C* correspond to the number of individuals displaying statistically significant activation at a given voxel (frequency), whereas colors in *B* and *D* correspond to the *z*-score of the subgroup analysis. Slice locations in *A* and *B* are –2 mm from the midline, whereas slice locations in *B* and *C* are 32 mm from the midline (in standard stereotaxic space). Structural MRI data (gray) are averaged across all individuals involved in corresponding functional analysis.

experience sampling (Stone, Shiffman, and DeVries 1999), which we address in more detail in section 1.4. Once the feeling dissipated, the affective experiences need to be reconstructed on the basis of other information. When the report pertains to a specific *recent episode,* people can draw on episodic memory, retrieving specific moments and details of the recent past. Such reports can often recover the actual experience with some accuracy, as indicated by their convergence with concurrent reports (e.g., Kahneman et al. 2004; Stone et al. 2006). The Day Reconstruction Method, presented in section 1.4, takes advantage of this observation.

In contrast, *global* reports of past feelings are based on semantic knowledge. When asked how they "usually" feel during a particular activity, people draw on their general beliefs about the activity and its attributes to arrive at a report. The actual experience does not figure prominently in these global reports because the experience itself is no longer accessible to introspection and episodic reconstruction is not used to answer a global question. Finally, the same semantic knowledge serves as a basis for *predicting* future feelings, for which episodic information is not available to begin with (Schwarz, Kahneman, and Xu 2009; Xu and Schwarz 2009). These hedonic predictions, in turn, often serve as a basis for behavioral *choice* (March 1978).

These processes result in a systematic pattern of convergences and divergences in affect reports. First, concurrent reports and retrospective reports pertaining to specific recent episodes usually show good convergence, provided that the episode is sufficiently recent to allow detailed reinstantiation in episodic memory. Second, retrospective global reports of past feelings and predictions of future feelings also show good convergence, given that both are based on the same semantic inputs. Hence, global memories are likely to "confirm" predictions. Third, choices are based on predicted hedonic consequences, and are therefore usually consistent with predictions and global memories. However, fourth, global retrospective reports as well as predictions and choices will often diverge from concurrent and episodic reports, given that the different types of reports are based on different inputs. As a result, a person's expectations and global memories go hand in hand, but often fail to reflect what the person actually experienced moment to moment (for a review see Schwarz, Kahneman, and Xu 2009).

These observations have important implications for the assessment of affective experience in time-use studies. They highlight that global reports of how much one usually enjoys a given activity are a fallible indicator of people's actual affective experience in situ. Such global reports were used in Juster and colleagues' pioneering studies (e.g., Juster and Stafford 1985). Our work builds on Juster's (1985) conceptual approach while heeding the lessons learned from recent psychological research by employing measures of affective experience that pertain to specific episodes of the preceding day. Next, we turn to the development of these measures.

1.4   Methods for Collecting Evaluated Time-Use Data: From EMA to DRM to PATS

The Experience Sampling Method (ESM) and Ecological Momentary Assessment (EMA) were developed to collect information on people's reported feelings in *real time* in natural settings during selected moments of the day (Csikszentmihalyi 1990; Stone and Shiffman 1994). Participants in real-time studies carry a handheld computer that prompts them several times during the course of the day (or days) to answer a set of questions immediately.[15] Participants are typically shown several menus, on which they indicate their physical location, the activities in which they were engaged just before they were prompted, and the people with whom they were interacting. They also report their current subjective experience by indicating the extent to which they feel the presence or absence of various feelings, such as angry, happy, tired, and impatient. Momentary real-time surveys are often viewed as the gold standard for collecting data on affective experience because it minimizes effects of judgment and of memory. As a convention, we will refer to studies that collect data on emotions in real time as ESM studies throughout the remainder of the chapter (because we are focusing on experience rather than environmental features).

So far, however, real-time data collection has proved prohibitively expensive and burdensome to administer to large, representative samples. An alternative to ESM that relies on a short recall period is the Day Reconstruction Method (DRM), which is described in Kahneman et al. (2004). The DRM combines elements of experience sampling and time diaries, and is designed specifically to facilitate accurate emotional recall.[16] Respondents—who participated in the survey in a central location—were provided with four packets containing separate questionnaires, and were asked to answer them in sequence. The first packet had standard questions on life, health, and work satisfaction and demographics. Satisfaction questions were asked first so that answers were not contaminated by the other questions and diary that followed. Second, respondents filled out a time diary summarizing episodes that occurred in the preceding day. The third packet asked respondents to describe each episode of the day by indicating the following: when the episode began and ended, what they were doing (by selecting activities from a provided list), where they were, and with whom they were interacting. To ascertain how they felt during each episode in regards to selected affective dimensions, respondents were also asked to report the intensity of their feelings along twelve categories on a scale from zero ("Not at all") to six ("Very Much"). The affective categories were specified by descriptors,

15. Other survey technologies can also be used for EMA, such as paper diaries and cell phones.
16. Robinson and Godbey (1997), Gershuny and Halpin (1996), and Michelson (2005) have used data collected from related survey techniques.

Survey Techniques for Collecting Data on Evaluated Time Use

Experience Sample Method (ESM) and Ecological Momentary Assessment (EMA). ESM and EMA are techniques for collecting data on time use and emotional experiences in real time. Respondents typically carry a computer device (a Personal Digital Assistant, called a PDA, for example) and indicate features of their activity and the feelings prior to being signaled by the device. EMA studies typically collect environmental information as well and may include physiological measurements (e.g., blood pressure, cortisol).

Day Reconstruction Method (DRM). DRM is a paper-and-pencil questionnaire that first collects time diary information from individuals for the preceding day. The diaries can list personal details, as they are not collected. Then, for each indicated episode, individuals indicate the nature of the activity, who was present, and the extent to which various emotions were present or absent.

Princeton Affect and Time Survey (PATS). PATS is a telephone survey patterned after the American Time Use Survey. After individuals report the activities of the preceding day (who with, what doing, where, when started and ended), three fifteen-minute intervals are randomly sampled and respondents are asked the extent to which various emotions were present or absent during that time.

mostly adjectives, such as happy, worried/anxious, and angry/hostile. The anchor, "Not at all," is intended to be a natural zero point that has a common meaning across respondents for these descriptors. The final packet contained personality and work questions. Subjects were paid $75 for filling out the DRM questionnaire, which usually took forty-five to seventy-five minutes to complete.

The emotions that respondents were asked to rate for each episode in the DRM were selected in part to represent points along the Russell (1980) affect circumplex. This distinguishes the DRM from the small number of past diary studies that included a question on how much individuals enjoyed (or liked/disliked) the activity they were doing. Russell models emotions as consisting of two core dimensions, *pleasantness* (pleasant versus unpleasant) and *activation* (aroused versus unexcited), with emotions positioned on a circle in this space. We interpret the duration-weighted average of the reported affect intensities as the average flow of "process benefits" or experienced well-being during the interval.

An early version of the Day Reconstruction Method was applied to a sample of 909 working women in Dallas and Austin, which we refer to as the Texas DRM (Kahneman et al. 2004).[17] Another DRM survey was conducted of 810 women in Columbus, Ohio and 820 women in Rennes, France in the spring of 2005.[18] A major goal of the Texas DRM study was to determine whether, despite its reliance on memory, the DRM reproduces results found in ESM. We looked in particular for features of experience captured by ESM and DRM that deviate from people's lay intuitions. If DRM reproduces these patterns we can conclude that it captures respondents' actual experiences during the preceding day rather than their general intuitions about what their experiences "must have been like." One comparison along these lines is shown in figure 1.2, which shows hourly mean ratings of "tired" in the DRM and from an independent study that used experience sampling. Whereas people's intuitions might hold that tiredness rises monotonically throughout the day, ESM studies show that tiredness reaches a minimum around noon. The DRM data replicate this V-shaped pattern, and the results obtained with ESM and DRM methods are remarkably similar. Moreover, this V-shaped pattern of tiredness was found in four subsequent DRM studies.

Other results of the Texas DRM conformed reasonably well to basic results frequently observed in Experience Sampling, despite differences in the sample demographics.[19] For example, the incidence of negative emotions is relatively rare in DRM—"angry/hostile" was rated above zero only 23 percent of the time, while feeling "happy" was rated above zero 95 percent of the time. The same pattern is found in ESM studies. The correlations among the emotions, particularly the positive ones, were quite high across episodes—around 0.7 for positive emotions and 0.4 for negative emotions. This pattern also replicates ESM findings. For example, the correlation of happy and "enjoying myself" across episodes is 0.73 in the DRM and 0.80 for a specialized sample of arthritis patients who participated in an ESM study.[20] Unfortunately, we are not aware of a real-time data capture study that collected sufficiently comparable data to compare activity ratings in the two methods.

Though not definitive, these findings suggest that DRM provides a reasonable approximation to the results of the more demanding ESM.

We also compared the DRM to a set of general activity judgment questions that closely replicated Juster (1985). Specifically, we asked the following questions shown in table 1.1 to 252 women in Texas in 2002 who were recruited in the same fashion as the Texas DRM sample.

17. The sample consisted of 535 respondents who were recruited through random selection from the driver's license list plus a screen for employment and age eighteen to sixty, and another 374 workers in three occupations: nurses, telemarketers, and teachers. Because most results were similar for both subsamples, we present results for the full sample.

18. Sampled individuals were identified by random-digit dialing.

19. See Kahneman et al. (2004) for further examples of nonintuitive patterns obtained with both methods.

20. This correlation was computed using a sample of eighty-four arthritis patients who were prompted to report their feelings on a zero to 100 visual analog scale three to twelve times a day, over an entire week.

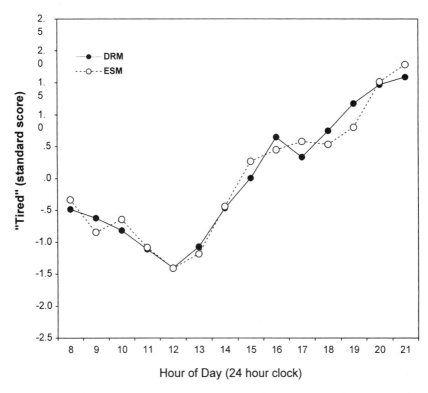

**Fig. 1.2   Comparison of pattern of tiredness over the day based on DRM and
ESM samples**
Source: Kahneman et al. (2004).
Note: Points are standard scores computed across hourly averages within each sample.

We then used just the adjective "enjoy" on a zero to six scale from the Texas
DRM to compute the average reported enjoyment while women engaged in
these thirteen activities according to the diary study. Table 1.2 compares the
ranking of activities from the two approaches. The correlation between the
ranks is 0.69. With small samples and some possible differential selection as
to who participated in the activities on the diary day, the results should be
read cautiously. Still, the results of the global ratings are quite similar to
Juster (1985). The original Juster survey found that work and child care
ranked particularly highly in terms of enjoyment, while our replication survey finds a similar result, especially for child care. More important, however, the DRM affect reports paint a different picture. For example, child
care is reported as more enjoyable when asked about as an activity than in
the diary-based study.[21] Work is ranked eighth in the Juster-like survey,

21. Robinson and Godbey (1997) found a similar result comparing his diary-based study
to Juster's ranking.

Table 1.1   Juster-like question in our replication survey

We would like to learn how likable or dislikable various activities are. Below we list a number of different things that you may often likely to do in your life. For each one, please circle the response that indicates how much you *like or dislike* it: (if one does not apply to you, you may skip it)

	Dislike a great deal									Like a great deal	
Commuting to work	−5	−4	−3	−2	−1	0	1	2	3	4	5
Working in your main job	−5	−4	−3	−2	−1	0	1	2	3	4	5
Having lunch on a workday	−5	−4	−3	−2	−1	0	1	2	3	4	5
Socializing at work	−5	−4	−3	−2	−1	0	1	2	3	4	5
Commuting to home from work	−5	−4	−3	−2	−1	0	1	2	3	4	5
Socializing with friends	−5	−4	−3	−2	−1	0	1	2	3	4	5
Talking on the phone at home	−5	−4	−3	−2	−1	0	1	2	3	4	5
Taking care of your children	−5	−4	−3	−2	−1	0	1	2	3	4	5
Doing housework	−5	−4	−3	−2	−1	0	1	2	3	4	5
Cooking/preparing food	−5	−4	−3	−2	−1	0	1	2	3	4	5
Having dinner on a workday	−5	−4	−3	−2	−1	0	1	2	3	4	5
Relaxing at home	−5	−4	−3	−2	−1	0	1	2	3	4	5
Watching TV	−5	−4	−3	−2	−1	0	1	2	3	4	5

perhaps not as highly as in the original because of our focus on women, but still higher than in the DRM. Interestingly, socializing after work is ranked much more highly in the DRM than in the general activity question. The contrast between these results, together with the contrast between the DRM and the original Juster rankings of activities, highlights the importance of collecting event-based data. Asking people to respond about how they feel about activities in general tends to provide a different ranking than when their actual experiences are used to guide their reported feelings during those activities (for a more detailed discussion see Schwarz Kahneman, and Xu 2009).[22]

1.4.1   PATS: A Phone Survey Version of DRM

The DRM is also burdensome and difficult to implement in a national sample. We designed the Princeton Affect and Time Survey to collect data

22. Gershuny and Halpin (1996) also cast doubt on the utility of general activity judgments. They analyzed data from a survey of British married couples in 1986 that asked a set of general questions about enjoyment with various activities. Respondents also maintained a diary for five days in which they reported their main activity during thirty-minute intervals and, for each interval, how much they enjoyed their main activity, on a scale of 1 (very much) to 5 (not at all). Looking across subjects for a given activity, the proportion of the variation in the diary-derived enjoyment scale explained by the corresponding general activity enjoyment response was low, only 11 percent for supervising kids and 10 percent for cooking. Thus, people did a poor job predicting their own reported emotional experiences with a general activity enjoyment question.

Table 1.2   **Rank of activities in terms of average enjoyment from DRM and general activity enjoyment question similar to Juster (1985)**

Activity	DRM (enjoy)	Juster enjoy/dislike
Child care	9	2
Commuting from work	12	11
Commuting to work	13	13
Cooking	8	9
Dinner	3	3
Housework	10	12
Lunch	4	4
Phone at home	7	10
Relaxing	2	1
Socializing after work	1	7
Socializing at work	6	5
Watching TV	5	6
Working	11	8

from respondents over the phone more expeditiously. A related goal was to develop a module that could be added to the U.S.' main time-use survey, the ATUS. The PATS survey works as follows. We started with the BLS ATUS questionnaire and eliminated a small number of questions that were not relevant. Respondents were first asked to describe each episode (defined as an interval of time in which the respondent was engaged in a specified activity; the average respondent reported 17.8 episodes) of the preceding day, using the ATUS protocols. Information about the activity individuals engaged in—what they were doing, where they were, and who was with them—was collected for each episode.

After the entire day was described in this manner, three episodes were randomly selected in proportion to duration and without replacement.[23] For these episodes, respondents were asked a five-minute module of questions, covering the extent to which they experienced six different feelings (pain, happy, tired, stressed, sad, and interested) during each episode on a scale from zero to six. They were instructed that a zero meant they did not experience the feeling at all at the time and a six meant the feeling was very strong. Specifically, respondents were asked to report their feelings during a randomly selected fifteen-minute interval of the sampled episodes. They were also reminded of what activity they said they were doing at that time in the diary part of the questionnaire. The order in which the feelings were presented was randomly assigned across respondents from six different permutations. The sampled episodes were ordered chronologically in the

23. More specifically, the BLAISE computer program divided the day into fifteen-minute intervals and randomly selected three fifteen-minute intervals. If any of those intervals was in the same episode, additional fifteen-minute intervals were selected that were in other episodes so an episode was only included at most once.

module. We also collected information on whether the individual was interacting with someone during sampled episodes.

The adjectives used in the PATS only partially overlap with those used in our DRM studies for a few reasons. First, we asked a smaller number of adjectives to save respondent time. Second, we avoided using compound adjectives, which we thought could be confusing to respondents over the phone. Third, the Gallup Organization conducted a set of twenty-five cognitive interviews with respondents to check their understanding of the affect questions and to make sure the questions made sense during most nonsleeping activities. These interviews helped us narrow down the set of emotions asked about.

The survey was administered by the Gallup Organization on our behalf in a random digit dial telephone survey of U.S. residents from May to August of 2006. Interviews were conducted in English and Spanish. A total of 3,982 people completed the survey, for a response rate of 37 percent. Weights were developed by Gallup to make the sample representative of the general population in terms of geographic region, gender, age, and race. The weights were based on counts from the Current Population Survey (CPS). Sixty-one percent of the unweighted respondents were women, a majority were white (88 percent), 90 percent had a high school education or higher, and 40 percent had household income less than $40,000 per year. The average age was 51.4 years. Reweighting the sample to represent the population resulted in some significant distributional changes. Most notably, compared with the unweighted sample, the weighted sample had fewer women (53 percent), higher income (36 percent below $40,000), and a lower average age (45.2 years). Unless otherwise noted, we apply sample weights in all of the statistics we report based on PATS.

1.4.2   Evaluating PATS

We will use the PATS to illustrate NTA, so it is important to evaluate its properties in comparison to other time-use data sets and in comparison to results for affective experience captured in ESM and DRM.

Figure 1.3 shows that the allocation of time across activities (weighting individuals by sample weights) from the PATS closely matches that in the ATUS for the same months of 2004 and 2005. The correlation between time spent in these activities from the two surveys is an impressive 0.99. This high concordance suggests that the weighted sample is representative of the population, at least in terms of time use.

In figure 1.4 we show the distribution of responses to the questions about feeling happy and tired over episodes in the PATS and Texas DRM. These adjectives were selected because they display different patterns—strongly skewed to the left for happy and slightly skewed to the left for tired except for a prominent mode at zero. It is reassuring that the distributions are very similar in both methods. Moreover, the incidence of reports of negative emotions was rare in PATS as was found in DRM and ESM.

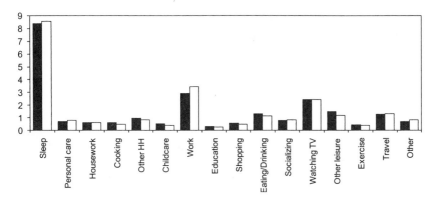

Fig. 1.3   Average hours per major activity in PATS and ATUS

Notes: PATS shown in black and ATUS in white. PATS was conducted in May–August 2006 and ATUS is for May–August 2004–05.

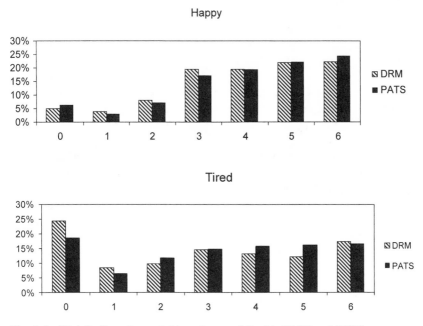

Fig. 1.4   Distribution of reported happiness and tired in PATS and DRM

We can also compare correlations between feelings across episodes in PATS to those in DRM and ESM. The correlation between feeling happy and feeling tired, for example, is –0.13 for women in the PATS, –0.21 in the Texas DRM survey of women, and –0.34 in a Columbus, Ohio DRM survey of women. The correlation between feeling happy and stressed is –0.29 across women's episodes in PATS, and –0.44 in the Columbus DRM.

The correlation between pain and happiness across episodes in the PATS is −0.10, while the corresponding correlation across moments in ESM data is −0.20 for the sample of arthritis patients mentioned previously. These results suggest that the correlation between pairs of reported emotions in the PATS is a little weaker than the corresponding correlations in ESM and DRM, but they point in the same direction and are qualitatively similar.

With only three sampled episodes per interview, it is probably more difficult for respondents to reproduce their precise pattern of tiredness over the day. Still, the correspondence between the diurnal pattern of tiredness in PATS and DRM and ESM is reasonable (see fig. 1.5). The pattern displayed by the PATS data is much less V-shaped than was the case in the other surveys, but the increasing pattern of tiredness in the afternoon and evening is clearly evident. The correlation between the average rating of tiredness each hour in PATS and DRM is 0.87, and between PATS and ESM is 0.86. Moreover, the PATS data show similar age interactions to what we found earlier; namely, a sharper decline in tiredness in the morning for younger respondents.

The correlation between reported life satisfaction and net affect across people was also similar in PATS and the Texas DRM. In the (random sample component of the) Texas DRM, the correlation between life satisfaction and net affect is 0.44 and in the PATS it is 0.35. Because net affect can be computed for only three episodes per person in the PATS, however, one would expect the 0.35 correlation to be biased downward. To make a fairer comparison, we randomly selected three episodes per person from the DRM. In this more comparable sample, the correlation fell to 0.39, quite close to the 0.35 computed with PATS. Krueger and Schkade (2008) provide estimates of the reliability of life satisfaction and net affect. Using their estimates to adjust for attenuation bias, the correlation between life satisfaction and net affect would rise from 0.44 to around 0.70. This figure suggests that interpersonal variations in average net affect over many days reflects about half of the variability in life satisfaction.

Table 1.3 considers how the average rating of happy compares across common activities in the PATS and the random sample of the Texas DRM, both on a zero to six scale.[24] The Pearson correlation between the two measures is 0.78, and the rank-order correlation is 0.74. Childcare is the largest outlier, with a one-half point lower rating in the DRM. Television is another outlier, with the DRM exceeding the PATS.[25] In these respects, the PATS ranking of activities are intermediate between the rankings in the Juster-like survey and the DRM. It is possible that in the PATS, respondents reflect more on the activity in general than the particular episode. Another possibility is that

---

24. Attempts were made to make the activities as comparable as possible.
25. See Kubey and Csikszentmihalyi (1990) for a real-time study of subjects' emotional experiences while watching television.

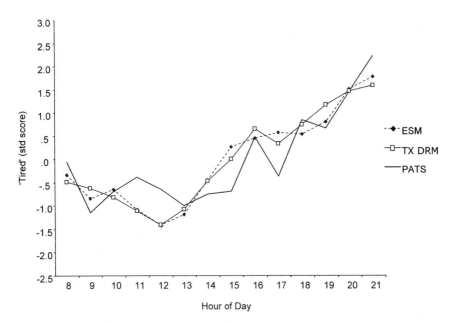

Fig. 1.5   Comparison of pattern of tiredness over the day based on PATS, DRM, and ESM samples

Notes: Points are standard scores computed across hourly averages within each sample.

Table 1.3   **Comparison of PATS and DRM average happiness rating (0–6) by activity**

Activity	PATS	DRM	Difference
Housework	3.77	4.10	−0.33
Commuting	3.80	3.84	−0.04
Working	3.82	3.74	0.08
Watching TV	3.91	4.32	−0.41
Computer	4.06	3.94	0.12
Shopping	4.11	4.00	0.11
Preparing food	4.25	4.27	−0.02
On the phone	4.47	4.00	0.47
Relaxing	4.49	4.55	−0.06
Eating	4.57	4.43	0.14
Child care	4.59	4.06	0.53
Socializing	4.74	4.48	0.26
Prayer/worship	4.97	4.56	0.41
Exercising	5.09	4.77	0.32
Unweighted average	4.37	4.23	0.15

Notes: PATS sample is men and women combined. DRM sample is random component of Texas survey.

Table 1.4   **Average response by order of affect questions in PATS sample**

	Average					
	Happy	Tired	Stressed	Sad	Interested	Pain
Question order						
First	4.35	2.31	1.37	0.71	4.34	0.89
Second	4.22	2.62	1.41	0.68	4.10	0.97
Third	4.19	2.67	1.62	0.69	3.90	0.98
Fourth	4.18	2.65	1.58	0.83	3.92	0.96
Fifth	3.88	2.67	1.49	0.70	4.10	1.03
Sixth	3.99	2.71	1.54	0.69	4.07	1.08
All	4.13	2.61	1.50	0.72	4.07	0.99

Notes: One of the following six different orderings was randomly selected for each respondent. Order 1: Happy, Tired, Stressed, Sad, Interested, Pain; Order 2: Tired, Stressed, Sad, Interested, Pain, and Happy, Order 3: Stressed, Sad, Interested, Pain, Happy, and Tired; Order 4: Sad, Interested, Pain, Happy, Tired, and Stressed; Order 5: Interested, Pain, Happy, Tired, Stressed, and Sad; Order 6: Pain, Happy, Tired, Stressed, Sad, and Interested. Results are unweighted.

differences in the sample populations between PATS and the DRM account for the discrepancies.

Table 1.4 summarizes results on how the order of emotions affected reported intensity of feelings in PATS. As mentioned, we randomly assigned respondents to one of six different orderings for the affect questions. Once an order was selected, the same order was used for each of the three sampled fifteen-minute intervals. The order effect for each of the emotions is statistically significant at the 0.025 level, and usually much lower. As a general rule, when positive emotions were asked about early on, their ratings tended to be higher, and when negative emotions were asked about early on, their ratings tended to be lower. If happy was asked first, for example, its mean response was 4.35, compared with 3.99 when it was asked last; when pain was asked first its mean response was 0.89, compared with 1.08 when it was asked last. Interestingly, the adjective "interested" behaved like a positive emotion in this regard. Table 1.2 combines results for the first, second, and third episode that was inquired about. Surprisingly, when we disaggregated the order effects were not notably stronger for the first of the three episodes. We expected to find stronger order effects for the first episode, as the order was known to respondents by the second and third episode. One interpretation of these results is that the first emotion provides an anchor for the subsequent ones. Respondents are typically in a positive mood before the affect questions are asked (judging from the high frequency of positive affect), and the response to the first emotion question is anchored relative to this positive feeling. Because the order in which emotions were presented was randomly assigned to respondents in PATS, our results should not be biased by order effects in any event.

It is also worth noting that the particular ordering used did not have a significant effect on the level of the U-index (p-value = 0.37 for joint F-test of constant U-index). Thus, a salutary feature of the U-index is that it is apparently robust to order effects, because the anchoring that produces the order effects does not substantially alter the ordinal ranking of emotional ratings.

We can examine how the weather relates to the PATS affect and satisfaction data. Table 1.5 summarizes results from Connolly (2007), who merged daily weather data from the National Climate Data Center to the PATS survey. Specifically, she merged data on the mean temperature and amount of rainfall on the interview day and diary day (which is the day prior to the interview day), as well as the normal temperature and rainfall for the season and geographic area. Because temperature is highly correlated on adjacent days, it was not possible to estimate separate effects of the temperature on the interview and diary day. Rainfall, however, varies considerably from day to day. Women's reports of their life satisfaction and affect were more sensitive to the weather than men's, so we focus on results for women here. As in Schwarz and Clore's (1983) survey, Connolly found that life satisfaction was lower in the PATS if women were interviewed on rainy days. Life satisfaction was also lower in areas with higher normal precipitation levels and temperature. Temperature on the interview day was unrelated to life satisfaction, but a higher temperature on the diary day was associated with lower net affect. Since PATS was conducted in the late spring and summer, one might expect hotter days to be associated with lower net affect. Rain on the interview day was insignificantly related to net affect, while a small amount of rain on the diary day was associated with lower net affect. These

Table 1.5   **Summary of effects of weather on reported well-being in the PATS survey**

Variable	Life satisfaction	Net affect
Normal rainfall	—	0
Rain on interview day	—	0
Rain on diary day	0	–/0
Normal temperature	+	0
Temperature on interview day	0	n.a.
Temperature on diary day	n.a.	—

Notes: Connolly entered dummy variables for ranges of the rain and temperature variables in her regression analysis. A negative sign here indicates a negative and statistically significant effect of the climate measure, a positive sign indicates a positive and statistically significant effect of the climate measure, and n.a. indicates that the measure was not included in the particular analysis because of multicolinearity. Sample consists of women from PATS. The satisfaction regression also controlled for demographic variables (education, age, marital status, race, and ethnicity). The net affect regression also controlled for activity dummies, month, day, state, and demographic variables. See tables 3.4, 3.12, and 3.16 of Connolly (2007) for the underlying estimates.

results suggest that the weather influences reported net affect in the PATS data in a plausible way that is consistent with the true effect of the weather on people's moods, while the weather on the interview day is unrelated to net affect reported for the preceding day, as one would hope.

Finally, Alan Krueger and Arthur Stone have conducted a small scale study of 168 workers in Syracuse, NY and Stony Brook, NY who participated in a specially designed ESM study on three consecutive days in the spring and summer of 2008 (on a Thursday, Friday, and Saturday). A day later, participants also completed the PATS questionnaire referring to the same days covered by the ESM survey. In the ESM component of the survey, respondents were asked about their feelings on six occasions on each day, after being prompted by a PDA. The PATS component asked about emotions during three randomly selected fifteen-minute intervals. Because it proved impossible to conduct the study on a representative sample, subjects were recruited through advertising and were offered $120 for their participation. But because we compare reported emotions from the two survey modes for the *same* individuals, any systematic differences are likely to be due to the survey methods. To avoid confusion, we call the PATS component of this survey *PATS-2*. The PATS-2 interviewing was also conducted by Gallup. The emotions inquired about in the PATS-2 and ESM questionnaires included those in the original PATS (happy, sad, stressed, pain, etc.). We use these data to compare the real-time responses of respondents to their recalled experiences in the PATS-2 instrument.

Figure 1.6 reports the average rating of the emotions from the two surveys. The negative emotions received a slightly higher rating in the ESM than in the PATS-2 survey, which may partly reflect their order on the ESM questionnaire (in the PATS-2 the order was randomly assigned). The differences

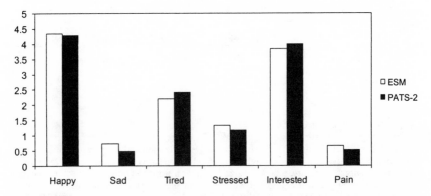

Fig. 1.6   Average of subjects' ratings in ESM and PATS-2 for same sample members
Notes: Order of emotions was randomized in PATS-2. Sample is 165 individuals who responded in both surveys. Except for happy, all differences are significant at 0.005 level in paired *t*-test.

are qualitatively small, however, even though they are usually statistically significant. Clearly, the pattern of intensity across emotions is the same regardless of whether the emotions were recalled or collected in real time.

For the 105 moments in time that were sampled in both the ESM and PATS-2 surveys (those that by chance happen to have overlapped), we can calculate the correlation between the emotions from the two surveys. The correlations ranged from 0.41 for happiness to 0.54 for pain. The correlation of the U-index measured in overlapping moments was 0.54. These correlations are lower than one might hope, but still nontrivial. Moreover, they could be biased slightly downward because the PATS refers to a fifteen-minute slice while the ESM data are for a moment in time.

A larger sample can be used to compare the ratings of activities because it is not necessary to restrict the sample to overlapping moments. Table 1.6 reports the U-index during various activities for the two survey modes. We restrict the sample to activities with at least forty-five sampled episodes in PATS-2 to reduce sampling error. In both survey modes the U-index is low for social activities and eating, and high for work and travel time. The correlation of the measures across the activities is 0.83, and the rank correlation is 0.86. Given the sampling variability inherent in the activity-level U-indices, it is also noteworthy that if we weight the activities by the PATS-2 sample size (which ranges from forty-five to 423), the correlation rises to 0.90. Finally, we note that we used the ESM-PATS-2 data to compute the correlation of person-level averages. That is, for each individual we computed the average of the (up to eighteen) ESM ratings and of the (up to nine) PATS-2 ratings of each emotion, and computed the correlation between them. The correlation ranged from 0.75 for happiness to 0.86 for pain. These correlations are attenuated by sampling variability, however, as we only sampled a small number of random moments from each person's day. If the correlation is adjusted for sampling variability, it rises to 0.92 for happiness and 0.94 for pain.

Table 1.6	Average U-Index during popular activities, as measured by ESM and PATS-2 for the same sample	
Activity	ESM	PATS-2
Work	0.157	0.156
Housework	0.093	0.117
Socializing	0.088	0.076
Travel	0.143	0.144
Grooming	0.156	0.133
Eating/drinking	0.080	0.043
Recreation	0.114	0.068
All activities	0.126	0.112

Notes: U-index equals one if rating of stress, sad, or pain exceeds happiness. Activities are based on PATS-2 questionnaire.

We conclude that the PATS instrument and real-time reporting do a reasonably similar job characterizing individuals or activities. They are less consistent in describing feelings at specific moments, although the measures are still positively correlated and the mean reported emotion over all moments is remarkably similar regardless of whether it is reported in real-time or recalled a day later.

1.5   Well-Being across Groups and Activities

1.5.1   Differences in Well-Being between Groups

We use the PATS to compare affective experience across groups of individuals and frequent uses of time. Table 1.7 reports the average U-index for several demographic groups, and some of those results are highlighted here. (Table 1A.1 presents results of the effect of demographic and other variables on the U-index in a multiple regression framework.) The U-index is 2 points lower for men than women (p-value < 0.10). The U-index is higher for blacks and hispanics than for whites. The U-index falls with household income and education. Those in households with income below $30,000 per year spend almost 50 percent more time in an unpleasant state than do people with income above $100,000 per year (22.5 percent versus 15.7 percent). The data indicate a mild inverse U-shape pattern in unpleasant moments with age for women. These patterns are often found in life satisfaction data and in our earlier DRM studies.

Married men and women have the same U-index, 17.4 percent. The U-index for never married men and cohabiting men is also around 17 percent. The U-index is notably higher for unmarried women and divorced men. The former result is a contrast to our previous DRM studies, which found that married and unmarried women exhibited a similar U-index. Interestingly, the U-index is around 23 percent for all groups of unmarried women, divorced, widowed, cohabiting, and never married. In a regression, the married-unmarried gap is not accounted for by controlling for demographic variables or activities. Controlling for differences in household income, however, accounts for more than half of the marriage gap in the U-index for women.

1.5.2   Activities

Table 1.8 reports the U-index and mean of five reported emotions during various primary activities. The order of activities is ranked by the U-index. The U-index is relatively low during discretionary activities, including religion/prayer, sports and exercise, relaxing and leisure, and socializing. Watching television is rated in the middle of the activities shown, as are food preparation and volunteering. The highest U-index activities include housework, working for pay, household management, receiving medical care, edu-

Table 1.7   **U-Index for various demographic groups, PATS data**

Demographic	(%)	
Sex		
Men	17.6	
Women	19.6	
Race/ethnicity		
White	17.5	
Black	23.8	
Hispanic	21.9	
Household income		
< $30,000	22.5	
$30,000–$50,000	18.6	
$50,000–$100,000	18.6	
> $100,000	15.7	
Education		
< High school	20.5	
High school	21.3	
Some college	19.6	
College	15.6	
Master's	16.6	
Doctorate	11.3	
	Men (%)	Women (%)
Age		
15–24	18.8	18.9
25–44	17.1	20.5
45–64	18.7	20.9
65+	15.6	16.1
Marital Status		
Married	17.4	17.4
Divorced/separated	24.3	24.5
Widowed	20.2	22.3
Never married	16.9	23.2
Cohabiting	17.3	23.3

Notes: U-index is proportion of time that rating of sad, stressed, or pain exceeds happy.

cation, and caring for adults. This pattern is quite plausible, although it deviates in some important respects from the Juster-like general activity results.

Some of the ratings of the specific emotions are also worth discussing. The intensity of both pain and happiness are high during episodes of sports and exercise, especially for men. This pattern, which is not surprising, may result from elevated endorphins during exercise. The low rating of "interested" during education-related activities might be related to the high dropout rate of college-age students in the United States. Telephone calls seem to evoke a high level of diverse emotions, with above-average ratings of happy, stressed, sad, and interest. Medical care is rated as an especially painful

Table 1.8   U-Index and average of selected emotions by activity

ATUS activity category	U-index (%)	Happy	Stressed	Sad	Interested	Pain	No. of episodes
Religious	6.4	4.97	0.90	0.66	5.09	0.61	151
Sports and exercise	7.4	5.08	0.84	0.25	4.92	1.20	321
Eating and drinking	9.7	4.57	1.11	0.52	4.03	0.80	1,206
Relaxing and Leisure	13.4	4.34	1.08	0.70	4.55	0.91	1,173
Socializing	13.5	4.74	1.21	0.66	4.65	0.88	528
Lawn and garden	14.2	4.23	0.98	0.47	3.92	1.37	318
Child care	15.6	4.63	1.76	0.39	4.41	0.56	376
Shopping	16.9	4.11	1.42	0.45	4.04	0.85	342
Volunteer	17.7	4.22	1.40	0.61	4.86	0.57	53
Watching TV	18.1	3.91	1.17	0.82	3.97	0.94	1,946
Food prep and clean-up	19.0	4.02	1.58	0.62	3.62	1.07	595
Travel	20.7	4.05	1.69	0.59	3.46	0.81	1,150
Telephone calls	23.5	4.47	2.02	1.14	4.99	0.86	128
Personal care	23.6	4.02	1.83	0.91	3.32	1.30	172
Housework	24.0	3.55	1.46	0.61	3.16	1.02	538
Working	26.9	3.80	2.37	0.69	3.99	0.71	1,671
Household management	27.9	3.50	1.85	0.82	3.94	0.76	235
Medical care	29.0	3.64	2.50	0.75	4.06	1.66	77
Education	32.3	3.62	2.66	0.87	3.87	0.82	143
Adult care	33.8	3.54	1.89	1.46	3.63	1.34	67
All	18.6	4.13	1.53	0.66	4.03	0.88	11,781

Source: Authors' calculations based on PATS.

Notes: U-index indicates the proportion of fifteen-minute intervals in which stressed, sad, or pain exceeded happy.

activity, particularly by women. The emotional experience of watching television appears quite close to the overall average emotional experience during the day, except for stress, which is below average.

A salutary feature of the PATS is that the same individual reports on multiple episodes of the day. As a result, individual fixed-effects (means) can be removed when studying differences in activities. Table 1.9 reports the U-index and affective ratings during the various activities after removing individual fixed effects. In essence, this analysis compares the emotional ratings of the same individual as he or she moves from one activity to another. In general, the activities are ranked similarly with or without fixed effects removed. The correlation between the U-index across activities in Table 1.8 and 1.9 is 0.93. The biggest movement occurs for medical care and personal care, both of which become less unpleasant when person-effects are removed, indicating that the people who tend to engage in these activities have a higher-than-average U-index during other episodes of the day. Because people tend to seek medical care when they are in pain or ill, this finding is quite plausible.

Table 1.9   **U-index and average of selected emotions by activity after removing individual fixed effects**

ATUS activity category	U-index (%)	Happy	Stressed	Sad	Interested	Pain	No. of episodes
Religious	8.3	4.81	0.94	0.83	5.14	0.88	151
Eating and drinking	10.7	4.49	1.14	0.55	3.99	0.78	1,206
Sports and exercise	11.9	4.89	1.22	0.48	4.87	1.48	321
Socializing	13.0	4.68	1.21	0.59	4.65	0.84	528
Child care	13.6	4.59	1.44	0.49	4.49	0.65	376
Relaxing and leisure	15.1	4.35	1.24	0.68	4.49	0.88	1,173
Watching TV	15.7	4.00	1.16	0.71	4.01	0.77	1,946
Lawn and garden	16.7	4.21	1.21	0.55	3.92	1.25	318
Personal care	17.4	4.07	1.47	0.60	3.20	0.96	172
Food prep and clean-up	17.6	4.02	1.42	0.51	3.39	0.92	595
Shopping	18.0	4.15	1.68	0.63	4.01	0.92	342
Travel	19.8	4.06	1.62	0.63	3.64	0.89	1,150
Telephone calls	20.4	4.50	1.73	0.94	5.14	0.84	128
Volunteering	20.7	4.28	1.72	0.81	4.71	0.96	53
Medical care	22.6	3.76	2.20	0.83	4.52	1.22	77
Housework	25.6	3.56	1.57	0.68	3.11	1.08	538
Household management	27.4	3.70	1.68	0.78	4.00	0.76	235
Education	28.7	3.55	2.39	0.90	4.09	0.80	143
Working	28.8	3.83	2.34	0.78	4.09	0.89	1,671
Adult care	32.0	3.50	1.79	1.15	3.37	1.23	67
All	18.6	4.13	1.53	0.66	4.03	0.89	11,781

Source: Authors' calculations based on PATS.

Notes: U-index indicates the proportion of fifteen-minute intervals in which stressed, sad, or pain exceeded happy.

Another feature of the PATS is that affect can be modeled before, during, and after participating in a specific activity. Figure 1.7 illustrates this point by showing the average rating of the emotion "happy" in relation to the occurrence of an episode involving sports or exercise. Specifically, we regressed the happiness rating on the number of minutes before or after an episode involving exercise with an interaction to allow for a different slope before and after exercise, for the subset of people who exercised on the interview day. The model was estimated both with and without person fixed effects. Time zero corresponds to the period of exercise. Especially in the model that removes person fixed effects, an inverse-V pattern is evident: Happiness rises as a period of exercise approaches and then decays afterwards. With more observations, a less constraining model could be estimated.

Krueger and Mueller (2008) use the PATS data to compare the well-being of employed and unemployed individuals. Many previous studies have found that the unemployed are much less satisfied with their lives (e.g., Clark and Oswald 1994). The PATS data likewise show significantly lower average

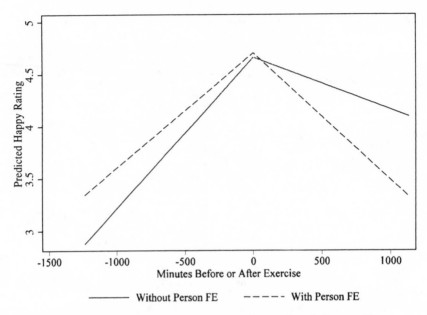

Fig. 1.7   Happiness rating before and after exercise, results of a linear spline

life satisfaction and a significantly higher U-index for the unemployed than employed. The PATS data enable one to further ask: during which activities are the unemployed particularly unhappy or sad? The results indicate that the unemployed are particularly sad during time periods involving job searching and television viewing.

1.5.3   Interaction Partners

The presence of others during an episode affects the pleasantness of the experience. Table 1.10 presents the U-index for men and women, disaggregated by who else was present during the episode. The tabulations do not control for other features of the episode, but the pattern is generally similar when we control for the activity engaged in during the episode as well as person fixed effects. For simplicity, we present the unadjusted results here.

When people are alone, the U-index is higher than when they interact with others. The identity of the "others" matters, however. For men, the U-index is lower when friends and relatives are present. Spending time with coworkers is associated with a higher U-index for both men and women, primarily because work has a high incidence of negative emotions, particularly stress. Spending time with the boss makes the experience of work notably more unpleasant. The pattern for men and women is similar, except for the striking elevation in the U-index for women when it comes to spending time

Table 1.10   **U-Index by whom with based on PATS data**

	Men (%)	Women (%)	p-value for difference between men and women
Alone	18.3	21.9	0.033
Spouse	15.8	15.3	0.808
Children	10.2	17.7	0.034
Parents	7.2	27.1	0.025
Friends	11.8	12.8	0.792
Coworkers	25.9	27.5	0.615
Boss/supervisor	46.9	30.5	0.522

with one's parents or children.[26] These differences are partly explained by the different mix of activities that men and women engage in when they are with their parents and children. For example, men spend relatively more of their time with children watching television and traveling than do women, while women spend relatively more of their time with children engaged in child care and doing chores. Even holding activities constant, however, there are sizable differences in the U-index between men and women when they are in the company of their parents or children.

1.5.4   Day of Week

Table 1.11 reports the U-index by day of the week (i.e., the diary day). A test of a constant U-index across days is rejected at the 0.01 level. Not surprisingly, weekend days are associated with less unpleasant feelings than weekdays, although the U-index is slightly lower on Fridays than on Saturdays. (For many people, apparently the weekend starts on Friday.) The U-index is lowest on Sundays and slightly higher on Mondays than on Tuesdays through Thursdays. Almost half of the weekend-weekday difference in the U-index can be accounted for by the different mix of activities that take place on the weekend. The empirical support for the song "rainy days and Mondays always get me down" thus far is limited, as a statistical test does not find the U-index on Monday to be significantly higher than on other weekdays ($t = 1.41$), and the evidence on rain on the diary day cited in table 1.5 was mixed as well.[27]

1.5.5   Goods and Time Use

In the standard economic model, people consume goods to increase their utility. Time-use data are notably lacking in information on goods

26. The ranking in Table 1.9 for women is exactly the same as was found for interaction partners in the Texas DRM, except parents were not separately identified in the DRM.
27. Stone et al. (1985) provide related evidence.

Table 1.11   U-Index by day of week based on PATS data

		(%)
	Monday	21.7
	Tuesday	19.0
	Wednesday	20.9
	Thursday	20.1
	Friday	16.8
	Saturday	17.7
	Sunday	13.7

consumption. Instead, it can be hoped that the activity description reflects the goods consumed during an episode or that no goods are involved. In many situations, however, this is likely to be inadequate. For example, food must be involved during episodes of eating, but we lack information on the quantity or quality of food. Dinners at McDonalds' or the French Laundry are obviously not equivalent experiences, yet these events are lumped together in the time-use data. When computed at the episode level, the U-index potentially reflects features of the episode, such as consumption of goods, that are not captured elsewhere in the data. Unobserved features of activities, including goods consumption, surely account for some of the variability in emotional responses across respondents engaged in a given activity.

The largest expenditure item for most people is their housing. Wong (2007) merged data on housing values and other housing characteristics to the Columbus DRM to explore the effect of housing consumption on subjective well-being. She finds that respondents who live in larger or more expensive homes do not report higher net affect while they are at home (either absolutely or in comparison to time spent away from home). This conclusion holds for both women with and without children living at home. She also finds that reported joy from one's house and home is unrelated to the market value of the home but is positively related to the market value of the homes in the neighborhood.

To illustrate the effect of the consumption of goods on the affective experience of time use, in the PATS we collected information on the size of the television set being viewed during episodes of watching television. Because television absorbs such a large proportion of people's time, this seemed a particularly worthwhile activity to focus on. Specifically, we asked respondents whether the television screen they were watching was greater than or smaller than twenty-five inches. (If we were to redo the survey today, we might ask about flat screen versus not-flat screen.) We regressed each of the reported emotions during television watching on an indicator for the size of the television set, education, household income, and the mean affect rating during other episodes of the day. The results indicated some emotional benefit from watching a larger television: stress was lower ($t = -2.7$) and net affect was higher ($t = 2.0$) if a larger television was being watched. Although we would not make too much out of this result, it does suggest the utility of collecting information on the nature of the goods involved during participation in certain activities.

Clearly more could be done in connecting goods to the quality of experiences. For example, the nature of kitchen equipment could be related to affect during episodes involving cooking, and the make and model of cars could be related to affect during episodes of travel. Note, however, that goods only affect people's hedonic experience when they attend to them. For example, Schwarz, Kahneman, and Xu (2009) explored how the quality of the car driven (as indexed by the car's Bluebook value) affects the driver's emotional experience. They found that drivers feel better driving luxury cars than economy cars—but only during episodes that are car-focused; that is, in the 2 percent of episodes that the drivers categorized as "driving for fun." In the other 98 percent of driving episodes, like commuting to work or shopping, the type of car driven was unrelated to drivers' emotional experiences. In short, the car only made a difference when the car was on the driver's mind. However, drivers are not aware of this contingency and drivers of luxury cars reported that they "generally" feel much better while driving than drivers of economy cars. Such discrepancies between global and episodic reports of enjoyment highlight that global reports of one's "usual" experience are based on general beliefs about the type of activity, which are often at odds with actual experience as captured by episodic assessments.

1.5.6   Decomposing Group Differences: The Case of Age and Income

Age

Past research finds that older individuals report fewer negative emotional experiences and greater emotional control than younger individuals (e.g., Gross et al. 1997). Consistent with this result, we find that the U-index is lower for those age sixty-five and older than for the younger population. The younger group works more and spends more time taking care of children, activities associated with stress (see fig. 1.8). How much of the difference in the U-index between young and old is accounted for by differences in their activities? Here we provide an example of how the difference in well-being between groups can be attributed to differences in time allocated across activities and differences in affect derived from a given set of situations and a residual.

To simplify the analysis, we focus on the gap in the U-index between people age twenty-five to sixty-four and those sixty-five and over. We also confine our attention to weekdays, when differences in activities are more pronounced. Table 1.12 summarizes our results. The U-index is 20.4 percent

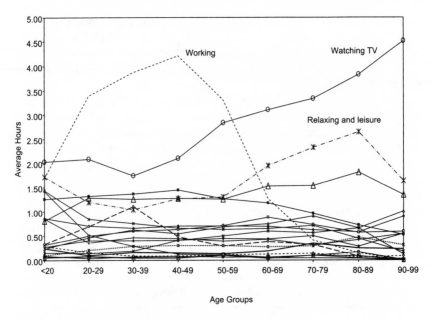

Fig. 1.8   Time spent in various activities by age, 2005 ATUS

Table 1.12   Decomposition of U-index for 25 to 64-year-olds and those 65 and over

Group	Actual (%)	Predicted (%)	Unexplained by activities (%)
25–64-year-olds	20.4	20.0	0.4
65+	16.1	17.5	−1.4
Difference	4.3	2.5	1.8

Notes: Table gives actual episode-level U-index and the predicted U-index using the overall sample's average U-index at the activity-level. Seventy-two harmonized activities are used.

for the younger group and 16.1 percent for the older group, a gap of 4.3 points ($p = 0.007$). If we compute the U-index using each group's actual time allocation and the average activity ratings for the combined sample (so the entire difference is due to differences in time allocated across activities), the gap is predicted to be 2.5 points.[28] Thus, 58 percent (= $100 \times 2.5/4.3$) of the difference in the U-index between young and working-age is solely a result of differences in their activities. The remaining 1.8 point gap is a result of differences in emotional responses to the same set of activities or an interaction between differences in ratings and differences in time allocation.

28. This is mostly a result of the difference in working hours. During weekdays the younger group spent 24 percent of its awake time at work compared with just 2.6 percent for the older group. The U-index is 9 points higher during work-related episodes. So 9 percent × (.24–.026) = 1.9 points of the 2.5 points is due to the difference in time spent at work.

Table 1.13   **Decomposition of U-index by income group**

Group	Actual (%)	Predicted (%)	Unexplained by activities (%)
< 40,000	23.2	20.4	2.8
≥ $75,000	19.0	21.4	−2.4
Difference	4.2	−1.0	5.2

Notes: Table gives actual episode-level U-index and the predicted U-index using the overall sample's average U-index at the activity-level. Seventy-two harmonized activities are used.

A further indication that choice of activity plays a role here comes from comparing the weekend and weekdays. On the weekend, the U-index falls to 16.8 percent for the younger group, not very different from the U-index for the older group during the week.[29]

Income

Unlike the gap in U-index between older and younger groups, differences in time use across activities do not help explain the difference in U-index between income groups. To illustrate, we divided the sample of people age twenty-five to sixty-four into two groups, those in families with annual income less than $40,000 and those in families with annual income of $75,000 or more. Table 1.13 summarizes our results.

The U-index is 23.2 percent for the lower income group and 19.0 percent for the higher income group, a gap of 4.2 points. If we recompute the U-index using each group's actual time allocation and the average activity ratings for the combined sample (so the entire difference is due to differences in time allocated across activities), the gap is predicted to be −1 point. That is, the lower income group spends slightly more time in activities that are rated lower on the U-index. So the higher income group has a comparatively lower U-index because it rates the same activities as more enjoyable than does the lower income group. Episodes of TV watching, for example, have a lower U-index for the higher income group.

One reason why differences in activities might explain a large share of the age gap in the U-index but not of the income-gap involves reverse causality. High-income earners may earn high incomes, in part, because they have cheerful personalities that enable them to prosper in the job market. Those who tend to be depressed and unhappy, on the other hand, are likely to suffer an income loss as a result. Causality runs, at least in part, from personality trait to income. Differences in personalities between income groups are likely to permeate their feelings throughout the day, regardless of the

---

29. The U-index also falls for the older group, but by a smaller amount, to 13.4 percent. Perhaps the elderly are more cheerful on the weekend because they interact with more cheerful younger people on those days.

activities individuals engage in. In contrast to income groups, personality differences between age groups are likely to be less important because age is exogenously determined.

1.6   Identifying Affectively Similar Activities

Summarizing time-use data at the activity level can be unwieldy.[30] The ATUS, for example, has hundreds of detailed activity codes. To make the analysis tractable, it is necessary to group activities into common categories. But classifying activities requires judgments of what activities are similar. Should gardening and lawn care be classified with leisure activities or with home production activities, for example? Researchers may have a different view of the enjoyment derived from such activities than the general public would. (See Aguiar and Hurst [2007] and Ramey and Francis [2006] for alternative results in which researchers classified time use into broad categories, such as leisure, home production, and market work. For results of an alternative approach that classifies leisure based on individuals' interactions with others, see Nadal and Sanz [2007]).

Rather than externally assign activities to groups, we propose an alternative approach: use the average of the emotional ratings that respondents reported during each activity to assign activities with similar emotional experiences to the same group. Specifically, we use K-means cluster analysis to identify K groups of activities associated with similar emotional experiences. Cluster analysis is a family of techniques for assigning observations to groups (clusters) in a way that minimizes the discrepancies within groups and maximizes discrepancies between groups. For a single outcome measure (e.g., happy), the K-means cluster technique minimizes the within-cluster variance, which also has the feature of maximizing the between-cluster variance in means. The interpretation is more complicated with more than one outcome measure, but the intuition is the same. The algorithm for the Stata cluster procedure used here minimizes the sum of squared Euclidean distances of the emotions associated with the activities from their cluster means (which is equivalent to maximizing between group differences as well due to a multivariate extension of the Pythagorean identity from analysis of variance [ANOVA]).

We illustrate this approach using ratings of pain, happy, tired, stressed, sad, and interested to cluster activities. Activities form the unit of observation. For each activity, we computed the weighted average of each of those six emotional responses. Activities in the PATS were originally coded with the same system that the Census Bureau uses for ATUS. Because we will use the groups to make historical comparisons in section 1.7, we converted the ATUS activity codes to seventy-two "harmonized" codes used in the

---

30. This section and the next one borrow heavily from Krueger (2007).

American Heritage Time Use Studies (AHTUS).[31] These harmonized codes are activity codes that can be compared over time in a consistent way. We set K to equal 6, mainly because 6 is a tractable number of categories and because it is not very different from the number of categories that researchers have used in the past. It would be possible to explore the sensitivity of the results to other values of K, or to select K on the basis of a goodness of fit test.

Two additional features of the analysis are worth noting. First, the activities were weighted by their relative frequencies.[32] Thus, the resulting clusters can be thought of as minimizing the weighted sum of within-group variances. Second, because cluster analysis is an iterative procedure that can be sensitive to the starting point, we executed the cluster command thirty-five times using random starting points and selected the estimates with the highest Calinski and Harabasz pseudo-F statistic, defined as:

$$F = \frac{\text{trace}(B)/(g - 1)}{\text{trace}(W)/(n - g)},$$

where B is the between-cluster sum of squares and cross-products matrix, W is the within-cluster sum of squares and cross-products matrix, g is the number of groups, and n is the sample size.

Table 1.14 reports the optimal cluster assignments for the most common activities and the average ratings for each of the six emotions. In addition, the table reports net affect, the positive emotion (happy) less the average of the negative ones (sad, pain, stressed). Many of the cluster assignments make intuitive sense. Paid work performed at home and away from home, for example, are both in cluster 6, as is helping someone with homework. Home production activities, including cleaning and putting away dishes, are mostly assigned together in cluster 5. There are some unexpected results, however. For example, time on a second job is classified in cluster 2 while other paid work is in cluster 6. Unfortunately, we did not collect occupation or industry for secondary jobs. Compared with surveyed episodes during the main job, people on a second job were much less likely to work with coworkers and were more likely to work alone or with their spouse.

In addition to tracking and organizing time use, another application of the classification of activities that result from this exercise would be for non-market NIPAs. In particular, a question often arises in valuing nonmarket

31. The concordance was from the Center for Time Use Research (www.timeuse.org/athus/documentation). The concordance contains ninety-two activities, fourteen of which could not be coded in the ATUS. We combined child care regardless of the child's age. We omitted sleeping and napping and a small number of infrequent activities that were not covered by PATS, resulting in seventy-two harmonized activities.

32. Because Stata does not have a weight option with cluster, we created a new data set in which each activity could be represented multiple times, in proportion to its relative frequency.

Table 1.14   Clusters assigned based on six emotions, 2006 PATS

Activity	Cluster	Net effect	Happy	Tired	Stress	Sad	Interested	Pain	No. of episodes
Personal medical care	1	0.21	2.34	3.69	2.21	1.06	2.70	3.10	24
Financial/government services	1	0.32	2.87	3.19	3.40	1.86	3.34	1.92	20
Homework	1	0.80	2.71	3.08	3.32	0.94	3.08	1.47	43
Purchase medical services	1	2.08	3.67	2.77	2.51	0.74	4.08	1.63	80
Writing by hand	2	2.79	3.46	1.97	0.96	0.52	3.69	0.53	34
Purchase routine goods	2	3.08	4.03	2.29	1.46	0.52	3.96	0.88	218
Other child care	2	3.08	3.93	2.43	1.32	0.48	3.79	0.73	30
Use computer	2	3.24	3.99	2.17	1.16	0.55	4.52	0.55	240
Second job, other paid work	2	3.40	4.39	2.49	1.42	0.66	4.48	0.90	67
Other meals and snacks	2	3.61	4.47	2.42	1.15	0.58	3.91	0.83	971
Walking	2	3.95	4.66	1.56	0.64	0.27	4.21	1.22	56
General voluntary acts	3	3.36	4.22	2.41	1.40	0.61	4.86	0.57	53
Conversation, phone, texting	3	3.42	4.55	2.44	1.50	0.93	4.61	0.98	377
Read books	3	3.49	4.36	2.35	0.94	0.83	4.81	0.87	474
Receive or visit friends	3	3.79	4.71	2.71	1.25	0.59	4.77	0.90	187
Read to/with, talk with children	3	3.92	4.73	2.61	1.45	0.39	4.72	0.58	35
Travel related to consumption	3	4.04	5.02	2.87	1.86	0.51	4.23	0.55	18
Other in-home social, games	3	4.08	4.77	2.23	1.04	0.25	4.92	0.78	121
Pet care, walk dogs	3	4.14	4.91	2.89	1.06	0.49	4.51	0.75	104
Worship and religious acts	3	4.24	4.97	1.70	0.90	0.66	5.09	0.61	151
Sports and exercise	3	4.26	5.09	2.87	0.89	0.25	4.97	1.34	208
Café, bar	3	4.39	5.00	2.24	0.88	0.29	4.59	0.66	255

Activity								
General out-of-home leisure	3	4.39	4.91	1.91	0.46	4.49	0.69	29
Purchase personal services	3	4.43	5.06	2.08	0.69	4.33	1.05	22
Parties or receptions	3	4.72	5.24	2.04	0.88	5.00	0.38	90
Hunting, fishing, boating, hiking	3	4.73	5.32	1.91	0.74	5.26	0.68	30
Attend sporting event	3	4.74	5.24	1.73	0.78	4.97	0.69	21
Play with children	3	4.81	5.41	2.49	0.74	4.69	0.86	40
Listen to music (cd, etc.)	3	4.81	5.33	1.56	0.38	5.06	0.84	22
Watch television, video	4	2.94	3.91	2.94	1.17	3.97	0.94	1,946
Food preparation, cooking	4	3.14	4.25	2.65	1.63	3.91	1.11	452
Relax, think, do nothing	4	3.25	4.40	2.77	1.31	3.96	1.34	313
Gardening	4	3.34	4.26	2.79	0.92	3.88	1.41	306
Set table, wash/put away dishes	5	2.28	3.32	2.81	1.45	2.76	0.93	145
Laundry, ironing, clothing repair	5	2.46	3.33	2.28	1.11	2.73	0.94	187
Adult care	5	2.56	3.90	2.56	1.72	3.82	1.10	87
Cleaning	5	2.63	3.72	2.85	1.61	3.54	1.05	327
Other domestic work	5	2.63	3.76	2.59	1.85	3.87	0.90	368
Travel related to leisure/other	5	3.00	4.02	2.73	1.66	3.43	0.79	1,120
Wash, dress, personal care	5	3.11	4.31	3.16	1.78	3.39	1.02	140
Home repairs, maintain vehicle	6	2.22	3.50	2.76	1.97	3.95	1.03	89
Paid work at home	6	2.35	3.47	2.66	2.01	4.00	0.71	207
Regular schooling, education	6	2.42	3.77	3.73	2.69	4.01	0.48	70
Main paid work (not at home)	6	2.55	3.83	2.72	2.44	3.98	0.71	1,425
General care of older children	6	3.55	4.54	3.41	1.98	4.36	0.54	235

activities whether an activity should be valued at the wage rate, at the market wage for hiring someone to perform a task, or at some other price. Another issue concerns whether particular activities such as schooling are primarily consumption activities or investment activities. One answer to this question is that activities that are as stressful and uninteresting as someone's main job should be valued at the same wage as the main job. Likewise, activities that are as enjoyable as socializing should be treated as leisure. The cluster analysis provides a means for identifying activities that are associated with similar emotional experiences. For example, time spent in school does not appear to be a consumption activity in our data, and time spent taking care of teenagers appears as taxing as one's main job.

Table 1.15 reports the mean of the emotions and net affect for each cluster of activities. The lowest rated cluster in terms of net affect is cluster 1, which includes receiving medical care, purchasing medical services, seeking government services, and doing homework. Cluster 2 involves tasks like writing and using a computer. The most enjoyable and interesting activities are in cluster 3, including religious activities, exercise, attending parties, listening to music, playing with children, and recreation. Cluster 4 is a mixture of activities, such as watching television, relaxing, cooking, and gardening, that are close to average in terms of affect ratings. Cluster 5, which includes domestic activities such as doing laundry, ironing, caring for adults, and cleaning, is slightly above cluster 6 (work) in terms of net affect but well below it in terms of interest.

If we were to assign value-laden terms to describe the clusters, we could think of cluster 1 as unpleasant personal maintenance, cluster 2 as moderately enjoyable tasks, cluster 3 as engaging leisure and spiritual activities, cluster 4 as neutral downtime and cooking, cluster 5 as mundane chores, and cluster 6 as work-like activities.

One caveat to bear in mind is that average affect ratings are conditional on engaging in the activity for a given length of time. People probably sort into the activities that they engage in based, in part, on how much utility

Table 1.15   Average of emotions by cluster

Cluster	Happy	Tired	Stressed	Sad	Interested	Pain	Net effect
1	3.09	2.97	2.92	1.18	3.57	1.80	1.12
2	4.29	2.31	1.18	0.55	4.06	0.78	3.45
3	4.79	2.37	1.05	0.56	4.79	0.84	3.97
4	4.05	2.87	1.23	0.76	3.95	1.06	3.04
5	3.86	2.72	1.64	0.63	3.44	0.89	2.80
6	3.88	2.83	2.35	0.69	4.04	0.69	2.63

Notes: Averages are weighted by episode frequency and sample weights. All emotions are reported on a 0 to 6 scale. Sample is PATS data. Based on July 5, 2007, cluster6_freqwgt_ctus_best.log.

they derive from them. If the cluster analysis is redone using residuals of the six emotions after removing person effects, however, 83 percent of activities (weighted by frequency) remain in the same cluster as in the original assignment that did not remove person effects. Thus, the cluster analysis seems to provide a reasonably robust and plausible set of groups of activities that can be used to compare time use over time or between countries.

1.7   Comparing Time Use over Time in Groups of Activities and Generally

We propose three techniques for tracking time use over time: (a) following groups of activities defined in section 1.6, (b) computing an overall U-index based on the U-index associated with various activities at a point in time; and (c) computing the U-index at the episode level. To illustrate the first two techniques, we used data from a project originally of the Yale University Program on Nonmarket Accounts, known as the American Heritage Time Use Studies (AHTUS). The AHTUS consists of five time-use surveys conducted from 1965 and 1966 through 2003. The disparate activity codes were harmonized to a common set of seventy-two main activities (plus missing/unclassified). In addition, we merged the harmonized activity codes to the 2005 ATUS and include it as well. The underlying sources of the harmonized data are described in the following box. Unfortunately, it is not possible to compute the episode-level U-index over time as PATS-like data are not available in earlier years, so we just illustrate the technique. We hope that data will be available in the future for episode-level analyses.

Historical Time-Use Surveys

- 1965–1966: Original source is Multinational Comparative Time-Budget Research Project conducted by the University of Michigan's Survey Research Center. $N = 1,968$.
- 1975–1976: Original source is American's Use of Time: Time Use in Economic and Social Accounts, conducted by the University of Michigan's Survey Research Center. $N = 5,869$.
- 1985: Original source is American's Use of Time, conducted by the University of Maryland's Survey Research Center. $N = 2,308$.
- 1992–1994: Original source is National Human Activity Pattern Survey, conducted by the University of Maryland's Survey Research Center. $N = 5,964$.
- 2003: Original source is ATUS, conducted by Census Bureau for Bureau of Labor Statistics. $N = 15,999$.
- 2005: Original source is ATUS, conducted by Census Bureau for Bureau of Labor Statistics. $N = 10,112$.

Sample weights were used for all estimates using the AHTUS data sets. Because we lack affect ratings during sleep, we focus on the waking day.[33] One issue that we can only partially address is that the data sets use different methods and sampling frames. For example, the 1965 to 1966 survey sampled people from households in which someone was employed in a nonagricultural industry, and only covered certain months of the year. The samples were restricted to those from age nineteen to sixty-four to have a consistent age range. The average age was fairly similar in the data sets, ranging from 38.4 in 1985 to 40.6 in 2003.

1.7.1   Tracking Groups of Activities

Table 1.16, panels A and B, present the average proportion of women's and men's awake time spent in the harmonized activities, respectively. A motivation of the cluster analysis was to classify these activities into affectively similar categories so that changes in time use could be tracked in a more manageable set of categories.

Specifically, for each person we first computed the average percentage of the awake day spent in each of the six clusters previously described. We next averaged over every individual in the sample.[34] Table 1.17, panel A, summarizes the results for men and women combined. The picture that emerges is one of stability for clusters 1 (unpleasant personal maintenance), 2 (moderately enjoyable tasks), and 6 (work-like activities). Time spent on cluster 4 (neutral downtime) is up while cluster 3 (engaging leisure) and cluster 5 (mundane chores) are down. Overall, these figures suggest that affectively neutral downtime activities like watching television have gained at the expense of mundane chores and engaging leisure activities over the last forty years.

Panels B and C of table 1.17 report separate results for men and women, respectively. For men, the share of the day devoted to cluster 6 (work-like activities) has declined by 6 percentage points since 1965 and 1966, while the share devoted to cluster 4 (neutral downtime) has increased by 8.5 points. Women, not surprisingly, have increased time in cluster 6 activities by 5 percentage points because of higher labor force participation, while time spent on mundane chores fell even more, by almost 7 points. The amount of time women spend in cluster 3 (engaging leisure) fell by roughly the same amount (3 points) as their time devoted to cluster 4 (neutral downtime) increased. These shifts, on balance, do not suggest significant improvements in affective experience for women over this entire forty-year time span.

---

33. Sleep rose from 7.95 hours in 1965 and 1966 to 8.5 hours in 2005, or by 2.3 percentage points on a twenty-four hour day.

34. Because a small number of activities (accounting for less than 3 percent of awake time each year) were not assigned to clusters in the PATS, they are omitted here. The percentages were renormalized to sum to 100 percent accordingly.

Table 1.16　　　**Percentage of days spent in each activity, 1965–1966 to 2005**

Main Activity	1965–1966 (%)	1975–1976 (%)	1985 (%)	1992–1994 (%)	2003 (%)	2005 (%)
	A. Women					
1　General or other personal care	1.52	0.20	0.79	0.32	0.25	0.09
2　Wash, dress, personal care	5.80	4.90	6.67	5.84	5.22	4.96
3　Personal medical care	0.06	0.11	0.04	0.06	0.44	0.64
4　Meals at work	0.74	0.69	0.72	0.00	0.05	0.03
5　Other meals and snacks	7.09	7.83	7.32	6.88	5.27	5.51
6　Main paid work (not at home)	14.32	14.07	15.83	21.10	19.51	19.13
7　Paid work at home	0.62	0.56	1.36	0.81	1.36	1.28
8　Second job, other paid work	0.14	0.17	0.26	0.01	0.64	0.62
9　Work breaks	0.51	0.34	0.18	0.06	0.02	0.02
10　Other time at workplace	0.23	0.19	0.16	0.00	0.00	0.00
11　Time looking for work	0.00	0.08	0.08	0.06	0.18	0.14
12　Regular schooling, education	0.19	0.30	0.33	1.01	0.61	0.43
13　Homework	0.30	0.42	0.48	0.77	0.79	0.70
14　Short course or training	0.21	0.20	0.28	0.04	0.06	0.21
15　Other education or training	0.72	0.03	0.16	0.09	0.02	0.02
16　Food preparation, cooking	7.46	7.08	5.77	4.09	3.74	3.77
17　Set table, wash/put away dishes	3.71	2.26	1.87	0.68	1.23	1.22
18　Cleaning	5.94	5.76	4.52	4.79	3.97	4.58
19　Laundry, ironing, clothing repair	4.43	2.45	1.99	1.58	2.21	2.37
20　Home repairs, maintain vehicle	0.30	0.60	0.40	0.39	0.32	0.28
21　Other domestic work	1.58	0.59	1.49	1.40	1.26	1.24
22　Purchase routine goods	1.90	2.94	3.10	0.93	3.35	3.31
23　Purchase consumer durables	0.14	0.12	0.08	2.60	0.01	0.02
24　Purchase personal services	0.27	0.26	0.16	0.18	0.26	0.19
25　Purchase medical services	0.13	0.25	0.30	0.37	0.43	0.33
26　Purchase repair, laundry services	0.33	0.16	0.10	0.09	0.12	0.11
27　Financial/government services	0.06	0.14	0.20	0.12	0.09	0.10
28　Purchase other services	1.52	0.10	0.19	0.10	0.06	0.06
29　General care of older children	3.47	2.36	2.23	1.44	2.60	2.37
30　Medical care of children	0.09	0.12	0.07	0.02	0.16	0.17
31　Play with children	0.32	0.30	0.41	0.33	0.87	0.81
32　Supervise/help with homework	0.25	0.13	0.16	0.18	0.52	0.45
33　Read to/with, talk with children	0.24	0.36	0.18	0.06	0.38	0.43
34　Other child care	0.30	0.57	0.23	0.43	0.54	0.53
35　Adult care	0.67	1.10	0.51	0.51	1.65	1.35
36　General voluntary acts	0.45	0.29	0.43	0.05	0.91	0.78
37　Political and civic activity	0.09	0.04	0.01	0.00	0.02	0.00
38　Worship and religious acts	0.95	1.09	0.84	1.02	0.98	0.89
39　General out-of-home leisure	0.16	0.18	0.16	0.00	0.19	0.21
40　Attend sporting event	0.11	0.26	0.28	0.31	0.22	0.16
41　Theater, concert, opera	0.02	0.09	0.06	0.14	0.11	0.08
42　Museums, exhibitions	0.01	0.04	0.01	0.06	0.06	0.05
43　Café, bar	0.11	0.27	0.49	0.30	1.63	1.44
44　Parties or receptions	1.54	0.55	0.55	0.69	0.68	0.61
45　Sports and exercise	0.34	0.60	0.98	1.50	0.90	0.84

(continued)

Table 1.16 (continued)

Main Activity	1965–1966 (%)	1975–1976 (%)	1985 (%)	1992–1994 (%)	2003 (%)	2005 (%)
46 Walking	0.10	0.13	0.25	0.00	0.31	0.26
47 Cycling	0.00	0.03	0.02	0.00	0.03	0.02
48 Physical activity/sports with child	0.05	0.13	0.15	0.10	0.02	0.04
49 Hunting, fishing, boating, hiking	0.08	0.21	0.25	0.00	0.08	0.10
50 Gardening	0.27	0.55	0.36	0.26	0.82	0.80
51 Pet care, walk dogs	0.13	0.37	0.57	0.44	0.60	0.65
52 Receive or visit friends	4.97	4.78	2.94	4.01	4.62	1.81
53 Other in-home social, games	0.46	0.69	0.71	0.56	0.58	0.80
54 Artistic activity	0.07	0.15	0.11	0.09	0.02	0.02
55 Crafts	1.24	1.44	0.76	0.55	0.11	0.17
56 Hobbies	0.04	0.04	0.02	0.03	0.02	0.03
57 Relax, think, do nothing	0.59	1.16	0.74	1.81	1.77	1.69
58 Read books	3.02	2.97	2.68	2.44	1.96	2.15
59 Listen to music (cd, etc.)	0.08	0.20	0.08	0.04	0.10	0.07
60 Listen to radio	0.28	0.19	0.23	0.11	0.07	0.11
61 Watch television, video	8.47	12.74	13.02	14.87	13.60	14.68
62 Writing by hand	0.74	0.23	0.39	0.72	0.19	0.15
63 Conversation, phone, texting	1.60	2.20	3.37	1.42	0.92	3.45
64 Use computer	0.00	0.00	0.08	0.26	0.89	1.00
65 Imputed travel	0.00	0.05	0.00	0.00	0.33	0.03
66 Travel related to personal care	0.71	0.96	0.86	1.76	1.56	0.97
67 Travel related to work	1.35	1.37	1.97	2.26	1.68	1.66
68 Travel related to education	0.11	0.13	0.22	0.23	0.13	0.11
69 Travel related to consumption	2.13	2.06	2.33	2.22	2.50	1.26
70 Travel related to child care	0.55	0.53	0.53	0.36	0.77	0.72
71 Travel related to volunteering/worship	0.39	0.91	0.67	0.37	0.27	0.26
72 Travel related to leisure	1.89	1.87	2.04	2.00	1.71	1.56
73 Missing/unclassified	1.34	2.79	2.18	1.66	0.47	2.92
B. Men						
1 General or other personal care	0.93	0.19	0.74	0.34	0.25	0.17
2 Wash, dress, personal care	4.60	4.04	4.93	4.10	3.67	3.51
3 Personal medical care	0.06	0.04	0.02	0.04	0.31	0.60
4 Meals at work	1.55	1.18	0.90	0.00	0.05	0.06
5 Other meals and snacks	7.49	8.42	7.63	7.13	5.55	5.93
6 Main paid work (not at home)	34.98	30.28	25.57	29.27	28.44	27.41
7 Paid work at home	0.97	1.76	2.62	1.23	1.54	1.89
8 Second job, other paid work	0.96	0.71	0.54	0.06	1.00	0.96
9 Work breaks	1.16	0.60	0.27	0.08	0.03	0.03
10 Other time at workplace	0.68	0.40	0.35	0.00	0.00	0.00
11 Time looking for work	0.00	0.16	0.12	0.10	0.30	0.15
12 Regular schooling, education	0.32	0.67	0.64	1.23	0.64	0.50
13 Homework	0.73	0.76	0.93	0.93	0.68	0.90
14 Short course or training	0.26	0.25	0.20	0.03	0.03	0.09
15 Other education or training	0.29	0.09	0.12	0.07	0.04	0.00
16 Food preparation, cooking	0.84	1.03	1.44	1.52	1.42	1.42
17 Set table, wash/put away dishes	0.35	0.22	0.38	0.14	0.33	0.30
18 Cleaning	0.94	1.79	2.13	2.54	1.88	1.89

Table 1.16   (continued)

Main Activity	1965–1966 (%)	1975–1976 (%)	1985 (%)	1992–1994 (%)	2003 (%)	2005 (%)
19 Laundry, ironing, clothing repair	0.11	0.10	0.26	0.30	0.42	0.45
20 Home repairs, maintain vehicle	0.99	1.75	1.80	1.64	1.49	1.47
21 Other domestic work	0.79	0.72	1.35	1.13	0.88	0.84
22 Purchase routine goods	1.05	1.31	1.69	0.44	2.17	1.95
23 Purchase consumer durables	0.18	0.15	0.10	1.24	0.03	0.01
24 Purchase personal services	0.09	0.05	0.06	0.04	0.06	0.06
25 Purchase medical services	0.17	0.14	0.19	0.21	0.24	0.28
26 Purchase repair, laundry services	0.25	0.13	0.15	0.18	0.13	0.11
27 Financial/government services	0.04	0.13	0.16	0.10	0.08	0.07
28 Purchase other services	1.02	0.11	0.23	0.10	0.05	0.04
29 General care of older children	0.40	0.48	0.38	0.25	0.83	0.84
30 Medical care of children	0.00	0.02	0.01	0.00	0.05	0.01
31 Play with children	0.46	0.17	0.23	0.20	0.60	0.54
32 Supervise/help with homework	0.08	0.05	0.04	0.05	0.23	0.17
33 Read to/with, talk with children	0.06	0.11	0.08	0.07	0.12	0.12
34 Other child care	0.11	0.13	0.06	0.15	0.25	0.25
35 Adult care	0.47	0.91	0.54	0.40	1.22	1.13
36 General voluntary acts	0.21	0.24	0.26	0.10	0.72	0.67
37 Political and civic activity	0.10	0.02	0.00	0.03	0.00	0.05
38 Worship and religious acts	0.59	0.76	0.54	0.65	0.74	0.57
39 General out-of-home leisure	0.03	0.08	0.19	0.00	0.22	0.17
40 Attend sporting event	0.14	0.30	0.28	0.40	0.26	0.29
41 Theater, concert, opera	0.05	0.08	0.09	0.06	0.09	0.16
42 Museums, exhibitions	0.02	0.05	0.03	0.03	0.06	0.01
43 Café, bar	0.66	0.48	0.83	0.78	1.67	1.65
44 Parties or receptions	1.40	0.59	0.61	0.61	0.62	0.52
45 Sports and exercise	0.72	1.24	1.75	2.21	1.39	1.36
46 Walking	0.16	0.19	0.26	0.00	0.23	0.22
47 Cycling	0.00	0.03	0.03	0.00	0.05	0.07
48 Physical activity/sports with child	0.04	0.07	0.10	0.04	0.04	0.07
49 Hunting, fishing, boating, hiking	0.52	0.63	0.99	0.00	0.53	0.50
50 Gardening	0.16	0.38	0.61	0.33	1.39	1.64
51 Pet care, walk dogs	0.06	0.34	0.52	0.40	0.45	0.47
52 Receive or visit friends	3.29	3.36	2.50	3.60	3.86	1.63
53 Other in-home social, games	0.54	0.52	0.51	0.51	1.00	1.06
54 Artistic activity	0.11	0.05	0.09	0.03	0.02	0.00
55 Crafts	0.01	0.22	0.03	0.04	0.18	0.13
56 Hobbies	0.28	0.32	0.30	0.04	0.04	0.06
57 Relax, think, do nothing	0.31	1.21	0.77	1.74	1.75	1.93
58 Read books	3.46	2.61	2.42	2.44	1.55	1.44
59 Listen to music (cd, etc.)	0.10	0.42	0.13	0.08	0.26	0.32
60 Listen to radio	0.44	0.28	0.33	0.24	0.12	0.13
61 Watch television, video	11.21	12.77	14.55	16.41	16.08	17.25
62 Writing by hand	0.27	0.12	0.23	0.60	0.12	0.11
63 Conversation, phone, texting	0.99	1.53	2.05	0.73	0.44	2.69
64 Use computer	0.00	0.00	0.17	0.58	1.24	1.25

(*continued*)

Table 1.16   (continued)

Main Activity	1965–1966 (%)	1975–1976 (%)	1985 (%)	1992–1994 (%)	2003 (%)	2005 (%)
65 Imputed travel	0.00	0.04	0.01	0.00	0.24	0.03
67 Travel related to work	3.68	3.19	3.45	3.35	2.86	2.69
68 Travel related to education	0.19	0.27	0.17	0.22	0.15	0.09
69 Travel related to consumption	1.63	1.41	1.86	1.59	2.12	0.95
70 Travel related to child care	0.28	0.21	0.23	0.11	0.32	0.26
71 Travel related to volunteering/worship	0.37	0.81	0.62	0.35	0.24	0.18
72 Travel related to other purposes	2.06	1.97	2.58	2.35	1.79	1.71
73 Missing/unclassified	1.60	2.67	2.00	2.23	0.47	2.47

Note: Based on PATS data.

Table 1.17   **Average percent of day by cluster, 1965–1966 to 2005**

Cluster	1965–1966 (%)	1974–1975 (%)	1985 (%)	1992–1994 (%)	2003 (%)	2005 (%)
Panel A: All						
1	4.2	3.6	3.9	5.8	4.4	3.8
2	10.7	12.1	11.8	9.5	11.1	11.5
3	19.8	19.6	19.0	16.5	18.3	17.1
4	16.3	20.3	20.1	21.2	20.6	22.3
5	17.6	15.2	16.3	14.6	14.0	14.1
6	31.4	29.2	28.9	32.4	31.6	31.2
Panel B: Men						
1	4.5	4.0	4.2	5.0	3.9	3.6
2	10.7	11.5	11.2	9.4	10.8	11.1
3	18.2	17.5	17.8	15.5	17.4	16.1
4	14.5	17.3	18.8	20.7	20.9	23.0
5	9.7	10.2	12.6	11.4	10.4	10.2
6	42.4	39.5	35.4	38.0	36.5	36.0
Panel C: Women						
1	4.0	3.2	3.6	6.5	4.9	3.9
2	10.7	12.5	12.3	9.6	11.3	11.9
3	21.2	21.5	20.2	17.3	19.2	18.1
4	17.9	23.0	21.3	21.6	20.2	21.7
5	24.7	19.6	19.6	17.2	17.5	17.9
6	21.5	20.1	23.0	27.8	26.9	26.5

1.7.2 Activity-Based U-Index

In addition to classifying and tracking time use in categories, it is useful to summarize time allocation in a single welfare measure. The U-index can be used for this purpose. As before, the U-index measures the percent of moments spent in an unpleasant state during each activity, where an unpleasant state is defined as one where a negative emotion (sad, stress, or pain) strictly dominates the positive emotions (happy in this case).

Specifically, we first computed the U-index for each harmonized activity using the 2006 PATS data for a pooled sample of men and women. For example, the U-index during paid work was 27 percent, during exercise it was 8 percent, and during television viewing it was 18 percent. We next computed the weighted average U-index where the weights were the percent of awake time the average person spent in each activity. Formally, the weighted average U-index, denoted $\overline{\overline{U}}_t$, each year is:

$$\overline{\overline{U}}_t = \frac{\Sigma_i w_{it}(\Sigma_j p_{ijt}\overline{U}_j)}{\Sigma_i w_{it}},$$

where w_{it} is the sample weight for individual i, p_{ijt} is the proportion of time individual i spent in activity j in year t, and $\overline{U}_j$ is the U-index for activity j from the PATS.

Panel A of table 1.18 reports the results. The activity-based U-Index shows very little trend over the last forty years for men and women combined or for women as a group. For men, however, there has been a shift away from activities associated with unpleasant feelings. To put the estimates in context, note that the difference between the activity-based U-index on weekends and weekdays is about 3 percentage points.[35] Thus, the 1 point drop in the U-index from 1965 and 1966 to 2005 is about one-third of the difference in unpleasant feelings associated with activities during the week and those on the weekend.

Although the U-index is highly correlated across activities for men and women, there are some notable differences in a small number of activities. Women, for example, find supervising/helping with homework and voluntary acts less unpleasant than do men. Thus, we computed the U-index separately for men and women. We then assigned the gender-specific U-index for each activity to each observation in the historical sample, and computed the activity-level U-index separately for men and women. Panel B of table 1.18 and figure 1.9 display the results, combining 2003 and 2005 for presentation. The results are generally consistent with those in panel A, though they are noisier. The gender-specific weighted U-index displays no trend for women and has trended downward for men over the last forty years, indicating an improvement in daily experience.

Table 1.19 presents regressions to control for possible changes in the age and education composition of the samples, as well as the survey day and month. The unit of observation for the regressions is an individual. The dependent variable is the duration-weighted U-index for each person's activities on the survey day, or $\Sigma_j p_{ijt}\overline{U}_j$, where $\overline{U}_j$ is the U-index for activity

---

35. With episode-level data, the weekend-weekday difference is about twice as large.

Table 1.18 U-index based on time in various activities each year

	1965–1966 (%)	1975–1976 (%)	1985 (%)	1992–1994 (%)	2003 (%)	2005 (%)
	A. U-index from men and women combined					
All	20.1	19.5	19.5	20.0	19.3	19.6
Men	20.9	20.4	20.1	20.2	19.6	19.9
Women	19.4	18.7	19.0	19.8	19.2	19.4
	B. Gender-specific U-indices and time allocation					
Men	20.2	20.1	19.2	18.8	18.7	19.0
Women	20.8	19.4	20.0	21.0	20.1	20.4

Note: A small number of missing and unclassified activities were assigned the mean U-index each year.

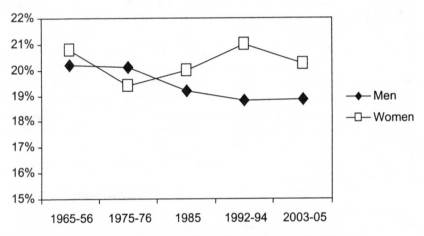

Fig. 1.9 Activity-level U-index over time, using gender-specific U-indexes

j for men and women combined. The regression-adjusted estimates reveal a similar pattern: very little shift toward or away from unpleasant activities, on net, for women, but about a 1 percentage point shift away from activities associated with unpleasant feelings for men since the mid-1960s.

Dispersion in Activity-Level U-Index

The activity-level U-index masks some important trends across people and groups. The standard deviation of the activity-level U-index was calculated across people each year (see fig. 1.10). This measure of dispersion has grown by about 15 percent over the forty-year period. Thus, the spread in time people spend in activities according to their frequency of unpleasant moments is increasing over time.

Table 1.19   **Regression models for activity-based U-index**

	All		Men		Women	
	Coefficient	Standard error	Coefficient	Standard error	Coefficient	Standard error
Intercept	20.905	0.224	21.108	0.356	19.862	0.279
Year = 1975–1976	−0.518	0.074	−0.338	0.118	−0.689	0.094
Year = 1985	−0.544	0.070	−0.731	0.111	−0.363	0.088
Year = 1992–1994	−0.031	0.071	−0.677	0.113	0.551	0.089
Year = 2003	−0.682	0.070	−1.255	0.110	−0.130	0.090
Year = 2005	−0.409	0.070	−0.950	0.109	0.110	0.089
Tuesday	−0.137	0.071	−0.122	0.113	−0.149	0.090
Wednesday	0.007	0.071	0.035	0.113	−0.023	0.090
Thursday	−0.194	0.071	−0.049	0.112	−0.325	0.090
Friday	−0.513	0.071	−0.553	0.112	−0.474	0.090
Saturday	−2.231	0.071	−2.599	0.113	−1.893	0.090
Sunday	−3.018	0.072	−3.431	0.113	−2.645	0.090
February	0.022	0.089	−0.128	0.140	0.158	0.113
March	0.203	0.092	−0.072	0.146	0.451	0.115
April	0.056	0.095	−0.179	0.149	0.243	0.121
May	−0.118	0.093	−0.272	0.146	0.004	0.117
June	−0.146	0.089	−0.302	0.142	−0.018	0.112
July	−0.406	0.111	−0.351	0.177	−0.470	0.139
August	−0.405	0.107	−0.473	0.171	−0.363	0.134
September	−0.018	0.096	−0.221	0.152	0.177	0.121
October	0.088	0.095	0.028	0.150	0.109	0.120
November	0.142	0.087	−0.031	0.140	0.313	0.109
December	0.102	0.089	0.082	0.140	0.092	0.113
Age	0.036	0.011	0.054	0.017	0.018	0.013
Age-Squared	−0.001	0.000	−0.001	0.000	0.000	0.000
Female	−0.921	0.038	—		—	
< HS	−0.048	0.059	−0.025	0.093	−0.113	0.074
Some college	0.438	0.052	0.511	0.084	0.329	0.066
College	0.152	0.056	0.103	0.087	0.142	0.072
> College	0.009	0.075	−0.006	0.112	−0.054	0.099
R^2	0.104		0.115		0.084	
Sample Size	40,388		17,921		22,467	

Notes: Dependent variable is the duration-weighted average U-index. Regressions are estimated by weighted least squares. Person weights have been normalized to sum to one in each sample. Weighted mean (and standard deviation) of the dependent variable is 19.7 percent (4.0) for all, 20.1 percent (4.3) for men and 19.3 percent (3.8) for women. All explanatory variables are dummy variables except age and age-squared. Base year is 1965–1966. Dashed cells indicate there is no coefficient, since the gender variable is a constant for women and men.

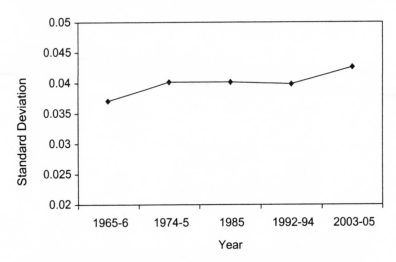

Fig. 1.10   Dispersion of activity-level U-index across people, 1965–1966 to 2003–2005

Additionally, the U-index has declined by more for men with a high school degree or less schooling than it has for men with a college degree or higher (see fig. 1.11). This result is consistent with Aguiar and Hurst's (2007) finding that leisure time increased more for the less educated than highly educated, partially offsetting the rise in income associated with additional schooling.

1.7.3   Episode-Level U-Index

Table 1.7 provides what we refer to as episode-level estimates of the U-index for various groups. These are tabulations of the proportion of time spent in an unpleasant state where the episode is the unit of observation. The calculations do not require information on activities. If the nature of activities changes over time, the episode-level U-index will reflect this change. The episode-level U-index will also reflect the presence of others during the episode and other features of the episode. Moreover, if the U-index is calculated at the episode level, it allows for the fact that some people may respond emotionally to the same activity in different ways. Because activity and other measured features of episodes account for a small proportion of variability in affect—for example, controlling for seventy-one activity dummies only accounts for 6 percent of the variability in reported happiness across episodes—tracking changes over time in the episode-level U-index can be more informative than tracking how changes in activities are likely to affect well-being.

Unfortunately, an episode-level U-index—either for a representative national sample or for selected groups—can only be calculated for 2006 because the PATS data set is cross-sectional. Nevertheless, the PATS data

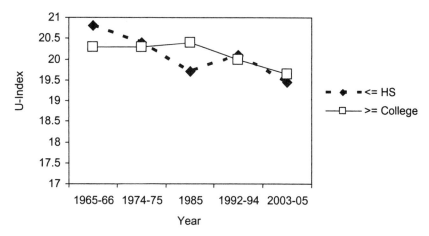

Fig. 1.11   U-index for men, by education, 1965–1966 to 2003–2005

provide proof of the applicability of the idea and a baseline against which future measurements can be compared. If the affect questions are added to subsequent time-use surveys, such as ATUS, then the episode-level U-index can be computed at regular intervals in the future.

1.8   International Comparison

In addition to comparing subjective well-being over time, social scientists and policymakers have long been interested in comparing SWB across countries.[36] This interest partly stems from a desire to rank countries based on SWB. Additionally, cross-country data have been used to study the effect of various public policies, economic conditions, and institutions (e.g., Blanchflower 2007; Alesina, Glaeser, and Sacerdote 2002; Frey and Stutzer 2002). The most common measures of SWB in these studies are reports of overall life satisfaction or happiness, which reflect global evaluations of one's life relative to some standard. In this section, we compare SWB in two "representative" cities, one in France and the other in the United States, and ask whether the standard measure of life satisfaction and the DRM yield the same conclusion concerning relative well-being. Specifically, we designed a survey to compare overall life satisfaction, time use, and recalled affective experience during episodes of the day for random samples of women in Rennes, France and Columbus, Ohio. These cities were selected because they represent "middle America" and "middle France." We also present results using time allocation derived from national samples in the United States

---

36. This section is based on work that we did together with Claude Fischler. For a more detailed report see Krueger et al. (2009).

and France to extend our analysis beyond these two cities. This comparison illustrates national time accounting in a cross-national context.

To preview the main results, based on the standard life satisfaction question, we find that Americans report higher levels of life satisfaction. Yet based on the DRM we find that the French spend their days in a more positive mood, on average. Moreover, the national time-use data indicate that the French spend relatively more of their time engaged in activities that tend to yield more pleasure than do Americans. Our results suggest that considerable caution is required in comparing standard life satisfaction data across populations with different cultures. In particular, the Americans seem to be more emphatic when reporting their well-being. The U-index apparently overcomes this inclination.

1.8.1   Study Design

The sample consists of 810 women in Columbus, Ohio and 820 women in Rennes, France. They were invited to participate based on random-digit dialing in the spring of 2005. Respondents were paid approximately $75 for their participation in both countries. The age range spanned eighteen to sixty-eight, and all participants spoke the country's dominant language at home. The Columbus sample was older (median age of forty-four versus thirty-nine), more likely to be employed (75 percent versus 67 percent) and better educated (average of 15.2 years of schooling years versus 14.0) than the Rennes sample. In addition, the Rennes sample was more likely to be currently enrolled in school (16 percent versus 10 percent). The differences in demographic characteristics partly reflect different circumstances in the countries (e.g., the employment rate is 8 percentage points higher in the United States than in France, and average education is 0.9 years higher in the United States), and partly reflect idiosyncrasies of our two cities and sample. Because we compare SWB measured with different methods for the *same* samples, our results should reflect differences in the methods, not demographic differences between the samples.

Essentially the same protocols as those used in the Texas DRM were followed. Groups of participants were invited for a weekday evening to a central location, where they completed a series of questionnaires contained in separate packets. The first packet included general satisfaction and demographic questions. The wording of the life satisfaction question closely followed the World Values Survey (although we use a different response set). The second packet asked respondents to construct a diary of the previous day as a series of episodes, noting the content and the beginning and ending time of each.[37] The average number of episodes described was 13.2 in Columbus and 14.5 in Rennes.

---

37. About 300 participants in each country were recruited for Mondays to describe a weekend day. Half of them were instructed to describe the preceding Saturday and half the preceding Sunday. Data were not collected pertaining to Fridays.

In the third packet, respondents completed a form for *each* of the episodes they had previously listed. The form included a list of twenty-two activities and eight interaction partners, with an instruction to mark all that apply. Respondents who had checked multiple activities were requested to indicate the one that "seemed the most important to you at the time" (we call it *focal*). Unless specifically noted, all analyses refer to focal activities. The form also requested ratings of ten emotions that were experienced at the time on a scale from zero (not at all) to six (very strongly). We focus on the following emotions: "happy," "tense/stressed," "depressed/blue," and "irritated/angry." The questionnaire was translated back and forth between French and English to ensure common meanings, and some questions were modified and deleted as a result of this procedure.

The data were reweighted by day of week to be representative of a random day. Weekdays received 5/7th of the weight and Saturday and Sunday received 1/7th of the weight in the weighted samples. Additional details of the procedures and all questionnaires are available online.[38]

1.8.2   Life Satisfaction

Table 1.20 contains tabulations of reported life satisfaction in the two cities. As in most populations, reports of being very unsatisfied are rare. The American women, however, are twice as likely to say they are very satisfied with their lives as are the French women (26 percent versus 13 percent). Furthermore, assigning a number from one to four indicating life satisfaction, a common practice, also indicates that the Americans are more satisfied, on average, and the difference is statistically significant at the .05 level.

On further inspection, however, table 1.20 provides less clear cut evidence that the Americans' responses exhibit higher life satisfaction. American respondents are overrepresented in both extremes, in both the very satisfied and the unsatisfied categories. If the top two categories on the satisfaction scale (very satisfied and satisfied) are combined, the French actually indicate higher life satisfaction: 83 percent versus 77 percent. Thus, it is unclear from these data whether the French are less satisfied or less prone to use the extreme ends of the scales. The propensity to express oneself in extremes can be influenced by cultural and social expectations. Cultural and social norms may discourage French women from reporting themselves as very satisfied compared with Americans.

1.8.3   Comparing SWB with the U-Index

The U-index is less susceptible to a tendency for the Americans to be more emphatic than the French as long as both apply their interpretation of the scales consistently to positive and negative emotions. To take an extreme example, suppose the French only use the zero to five portion of the zero to six scale, while the Americans utilize the full scale. Provided that the French

---

38. See http://management.ucsd.edu/faculty/directory/schkade/fa-study/.

Table 1.20   **Distribution of reported life satisfaction in Columbus, OH and Rennes, France**

	U.S. (%)	France (%)
Not at all satisfied	1.6	1.1
Not very satisfied	21.4	16.1
Satisfied	51.0	70.0
Very satisfied	26.1	12.9

Notes: Life satisfaction is based on the question, "Taking all things together, how satisfied are you with your life as a whole these days?" Sample size is 810 women for Columbus and 816 women for Rennes. Chi-square test of identical distributions rejects at $p < 0.001$.

use the zero to five range consistently for reporting positive and negative emotions—that is, an emotion reported as a five is always experienced more intensively than an emotion reported as a four—then, apart from integer concerns, the U-index is unaffected by this differential use of scales. As commonly applied, however, the standard life satisfaction measure is not robust to such reporting differences across people because the French would appear as less satisfied if they express themselves less emphatically.

The first row of table 1.21 reports the average episode-level U-index for the two samples. In this case, the U-index for an episode is defined as equal to one if the maximum rating of "tense/stressed," "depressed/blue," or "irritated/angry" strictly exceed the rating of "happy," and zero if not. The U-index was weighted by the proportion of each person's waking day spent in an episode to derive an overall estimate. In contrast to reported life satisfaction, the U-index is 2.8 percentage points lower in the French sample (16 percent) than in the American sample (18.8 percent). Thus, the French appear to spend less of their time engaged in unpleasant activities (i.e., activities in which the dominant feeling is a negative one) than do the Americans in our samples.

We explored whether the lower U-index for the French is a result of any single negative emotion, or combinations of them. The lower U-index for the French appears to be a fairly robust result. If we required that at least two negative feelings were rated more strongly than happy, for example, the U-index was still 2.8 points lower in France than in the United States (10.1 percent versus 7.4 percent) And if we dropped any one of the negative emotions and compared the remaining two to happy, the U-index was lower in France than in the United States in each case. These results suggest that the lower U-index in France is not due to the rating of any particular negative emotion in our study.

The other rows of table 1.21 provide comparisons of the episode-level U-index for various subpopulations. The general pattern is sensible. For example, the U-index in both countries is considerably lower on weekends

Table 1.21   **U-index for various groups in Columbus, OH and Rennes, France DRM surveys**

Group	U.S.	France	Difference
All	0.188	0.160	0.028**
Enrollment status			
Nonstudent	0.181	0.144	0.037**
Student	0.243	0.229	0.014
Employment status			
Employed	0.189	0.143	0.046***
Unemployed	0.219	0.190	0.029
Household income			
Bottom half	0.203	0.173	0.030*
Top half	0.169	0.143	0.026
Day of week			
Weekday	0.205	0.174	0.031*
Weekend	0.144	0.122	0.022

Notes: U-index is computed as proportion of time in which the rating of the maximum of tense, blue, and angry is strictly greater than the rating of happy. *P*-values are for test of country differences for each group.
***Significant at the 1 percent level.
**Significant at the 5 percent level.
*Significant at the 10 percent level.

than on weekdays. The French-American gap is largest for nonstudents, employed people, low-income people, and during the week. Interestingly, in both countries—but especially in the United States—the U-index of the unemployed is much higher during the week than it is during weekends. This pattern suggests that observing others go to work during the week worsens the mood of the unemployed during weekdays.

There is greater inequality in the U-index across people in the American sample than in the French sample. Figure 1.12 displays the average U-index by quintile of the individual-level U-index distribution in each country. The average woman in Columbus in the top quintile of the distribution spent 57.5 percent of her time in an unpleasant state, while her counterpart in Rennes spent 49.0 percent of her time in an unpleasant state. Regression analysis indicated that the gap in the upper tail is only partially accounted for by independent variables such as the log of household income, a quadratic in age, school enrollment, and day of week. Controlling for these variables reduced the U.S.-French gap in the upper quintile from 8.5 points to 5.3 points.

Another issue concerns vacations. In our sample, the French report taking twenty-one more vacation days than the Americans. We were not able to interview people if they were away from home, so we did not sample most vacation days. Accounting for vacations would almost certainly lower the U-index in France relative to the United States, as vacation days are likely to have a lower U-index than nonvacation days. The following back of the

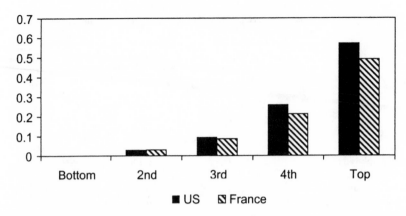

Fig. 1.12   Average U-index by quintile of the U-index distribution in U.S. and France based on DRM surveys

envelope calculation suggests, however, that this is not a large bias. The twenty-one day difference in vacations amounts to only 5.8 percent of the year. If the U-index is 10 points lower on vacation days than nonvacation days, which is almost double the difference on weekdays and weekends, then the French U-index would be an additional 0.58 percentage points lower than the American U-index.

1.8.4   Counterfactual Cross-Country Comparisons: Activity Level Analysis

Table 1.22 presents the U-index for twenty-one activities and the proportion of the day the average person devoted to each activity based on the DRM. (These activities are different from those in some of our other DRMs because of translation issues.) If more than one activity was engaged in at a time, we selected the activity that was indicated by respondents as being most important at the time. Activities such as working, commuting, and child care have a high U-index, and activities such as walking, making love, and exercising have a low U-index, similar to our earlier findings.

Both the pattern of time allocation and the U-index for each activity are similar in the two countries, with correlations of 0.93 and 0.85, respectively. The most notable exceptions to this pattern are that the Americans find child care substantially more unpleasant than do the French, and the French spend less time engaged in child care and more time eating. The latter is explained mainly by the fact that Americans are much less likely to indicate eating as their main activity when they engage in multiple activities that include eating. It is also worth noting that the French women in our sample are slightly less likely to have children living at home (56 percent versus 60 percent).

Table 1.22   **The U-index and allocation of time across activities based on DRM surveys**

Focal activity	U-index per activity		Percent of time (%)	
	U.S.	France	U.S.	France
Walking	0.04	0.09	0.63	1.69
Making love	0.05	0.03	0.77	0.98
Exercise	0.06	0.03	0.88	1.21
Playing	0.07	0.02	1.47	1.26
Reading, nonwork	0.09	0.07	2.97	4.36
Eating	0.10	0.09	5.22	11.11
Prayer	0.11	0.16	1.70	0.25
TV	0.12	0.14	7.07	7.32
Relaxing	0.13	0.13	2.88	2.85
Preparing food	0.14	0.13	2.92	3.29
Talking, nonwork	0.14	0.12	9.35	11.58
Grooming	0.15	0.14	5.19	4.76
Other	0.16	0.13	8.54	5.72
Housework	0.18	0.23	5.91	5.16
Sleep	0.18	0.15	2.70	2.32
Other travel	0.20	0.20	3.23	3.22
Shop	0.22	0.20	4.86	4.35
Computer, nonwork	0.23	0.22	2.52	2.28
Child care	0.24	0.11	6.85	4.50
Commute	0.27	0.26	2.22	1.68
Work	0.29	0.26	22.10	20.12

The data in table 1.22 can be used to perform counterfactual calculations. Specifically, we can use the time allocation across activities for one country to weight the U-index for the other country and thus create a "synthetic" U-index. To be more precise, define the synthetic U-index using country j's time allocation $(\overline{H}_i^j)$ and country k's U-index $(\overline{U}_i^k)$ for activities denoted i as $U_{j,k} = \Sigma_i \ \overline{H}_i^j \overline{U}_i^k$. The "synthetic" U-index indicates how the average French woman, say, would feel if she experienced her activities in the same way as the average American woman. Table 1.23 reports the synthetic U-indexes for each country.[39]

The results indicate that if the French and American women's allocation of time is weighted by either the average American woman's rating of activities or the average French woman's rating of activities, the average French woman is predicted to have a lower synthetic U-index than the average American woman. But only about one-third to 40 percent of the between-

39. Notice that when the same country's time allocation and activity-level U-indexes are used the synthetic U-index is slightly different from the episode-level U-indexes reported in the first row of table 1.8. This discrepancy arises because there is a weak correlation between time allocation and the U-index at the individual level.

Table 1.23   **Synthetic U-index based on country's aggregate time allocation and country's U-index by activity**

| | Country's time | | | |
Country's U-index	U.S.	France	Difference	t-ratio
U.S.	0.189	0.177	0.012	1.02
France	0.169	0.159	0.010	0.90

Notes: Standard errors for *t*-ratios are derived from a bootstrap procedure that takes into account sampling variability in the U-index and in the time allocation. Calculations based on data in table 1.3.

country difference in the U-index comes about because of differences in time allocation. Moreover, with small samples to compute time allocation, the difference in the synthetic U-index is not statistically significant regardless of which country's activity ratings are used.

We can calculate the synthetic U-indexes using larger samples of time allocation data from national time-use surveys, however. This provides a check on whether our results for Rennes and Columbus can be extended to the countries as a whole, and yields more precise estimates. Specifically, we analyzed national time-use data on American women from the 2003 to 2004 ATUS and on French women from the 1998 to 1999 *Enquête Emploi du Temps* survey by INSEE. We restrict both samples to women age eighteen to sixty. Although the French data are from an earlier time period, they are the most recent national data publicly available, and time allocation does not change very rapidly over time within countries. Because the activity categories in national time-use data are not harmonized, we collapsed the activities in these surveys into six broad categories: work, compulsory activities, active leisure, passive leisure, eating, and other. The U-index for these categories was computed from the DRM for Rennes and Columbus for the same activities.

Results are reported in table 1.24. The national time allocations are generally similar to what we found for Rennes and Columbus. In particular, using national data the French women spend less time working, less time participating in passive leisure (e.g., watching TV), and more time participating in active leisure (e.g., exercise and reading) and eating than do the American women. As was found before, the French allocation of time produces a slightly lower synthetic U-index regardless of whether the American or the French U-index is used to rate each activity. Using either U-index to rate the activities, the French allocation of time produces about a 1 percentage point lower synthetic U-index. With the larger national time-use samples, the differences are statistically significant at the 0.10 level, although they are similar in magnitude to the differences reported in table 1.23.

Table 1.24   **National time-use data for U.S. and France and synthetic U-indices**

	Work/commute (%)	Compulsory (%)	Passive leisure (%)	Active leisure (%)	Eating (%)	Other (%)
	Fraction of awake time spent in each activity					
U.S.	24.6	35.2	24.8	7.5	6.6	1.3
France	21.8	34.8	18.1	10.6	14.3	0.5
	Average U-index per activity					
U.S.	0.29	0.19	0.15	0.10	0.10	0.15
France	0.26	0.17	0.14	0.09	0.09	0.13

Notes: Synthetic U-index based on country's aggregate time allocation from national time-use data and country's U-index by activity from DRM.

	Country's time			
Country's U-index	U.S.	France	Difference	*t*-ratio
U.S.	0.193	0.184	0.010	1.67
France	0.173	0.164	0.009	1.74

Standard errors for *t*-ratios are derived from a bootstrap procedure that takes into account sampling variability in the U-index and in the time allocation. The work activity combines working and commuting; the compulsory activity combines shopping, housework, preparing food, and grooming; passive leisure combines watching TV, nonwork computer use, relaxing, and napping; activity leisure combines exercise, walking, making love, playing, and talking.

1.9   Conclusion

National Time Accounting provides a method for tracking time allocation and assessing whether people are experiencing their daily lives in more or less enjoyable ways. This chapter demonstrates how NTA can be used to compare groups of individuals, countries and eras. Many economists argue that a decline in the amount of time spent working has been a major source of improvement in Americans' daily lives over the last century (Fogel 1999). Shifts in time use among nonwork activities also affect the experience of daily life. If nonwork time increases in the next century as much as it did in the last century, it will be even more important to understand the experience of nonwork time. Tracking the U-index over time, either at the episode level or at the activity level, provides a means for measuring whether daily life is becoming more or less pleasant, and of understanding why. To facilitate NTA in the future, we think that adding a module on affective experience to ongoing time-use surveys, such as ATUS, should be a priority.

The PATS data on evaluated time use that we developed for NTA and summarize here reinforce some findings from the previous literature on overall happiness and life satisfaction and provide new results and puzzles. At the individual level within a country, the demographic correlates of experienced well-being and life (or happiness) satisfaction mostly have the same sign. Life satisfaction and the U-index, however, yield a different ranking of France and the United States, most likely because of cultural differences in reporting that lead the French to appear less satisfied. In addition, experienced well-being measures provide a means for decomposing differences between groups that is not possible with conventional life satisfaction data. For example, we show how differences in subjective well-being between age groups can be attributed to a component due to differences in time allocation and a component due to differences in feelings for a given set of activities. This analysis revealed that differences in time use account for a majority of the difference in experienced well-being between younger and older individuals. Unlike previous attempts to measure experienced well-being in the time-use literature, we emphasize that subjective-well being is multidimensional, and propose the U-index as a simple means to reflect the nonlinear relationship among emotions in a National Time Accounting framework.

Like the NIPAs, NTA is a descriptive, not prescriptive, technique. The method of NTA does not lead to immediate policy recommendations. For example, the fact that spending time socializing may be more enjoyable than working for pay for the average person does not necessarily lead to the recommendation that people should socialize more and work less. Paid work is obviously required to afford a certain lifestyle. A similar limitation applies to the NIPAs: although national income would be increased if all workers trained for higher paying professions, there are psychic and monetary costs that must be taken into account before making such a policy recommendation. To draw policy conclusions, we would recommend using the PATS or related instruments to measure outcomes of policy relevant experiments, such as the Moving to Opportunities public housing experiment.

Existing time-use data sets provide several opportunities for additional applications of NTA. One possibility is to use the harmonized international time-use data sets to compare how people in different countries devote time to various activities and to evaluate the activities by their average emotional experience according to the PATS. The clusters of activities identified in section 1.6 would seem particularly appropriate for comparing time use across countries. Another possibility is to use existing time-use data for the United States to study the effect of aging on the allocation of time across activities by following cohorts as they age. Again, the clusters of similar activities identified in section 1.6 could facilitate the analysis.

Several extensions, unresolved issues, and research issues concerning NTA should also be noted. First, although we based the emotions that we surveyed partly on the Russell circumplex and partly on practicality, the precise set of emotions could be tailored for the particular application at hand. For example, studies related to health and aging might focus on feelings of aches, pain, weariness, fatigue, and disorientation. In addition, PATS might be adapted to measure people's sense of purpose about their daily routines. People could be asked whether they considered their use of time during sampled episodes to be meaningful or a waste of time. If additional emotions are included, the robustness of the U-index to the set of surveyed emotions can be further explored, although some features of experience (e.g., meaningfulness) would seem to represent separate subjective components of well-being.

Another issue concerns the context of time use. That is, the precise situations that people are engaged in during their daily activities. Available time-use surveys collect only coarse information on the nature of activities. The fact that activity dummies account for such a small share of the variability in affective experience suggests that important features of activities are not measured by time-use surveys. Thus, tracking the change in activities over time weighted by the activity-level U-index (or some other activity-level measure of emotional experience) is susceptible to missing important changes in people's affective experiences because a great deal of what generates emotional experience occurs within a given set of measured activities.

A related issue is that the nature of some activities changes over time. For example, the experience of television viewing is likely to be quite different today than forty years ago, when there were few channels, television sets were black and white, and Tivo was not available to skip over commercials. While changes in the nature of activities present a problem for all studies that track time use over historical time, the problems are particularly apparent for NTA. In some respects, the problem is akin to changes in product quality in the consumer price index. The prospect of tracking affective experience at the episode-level in the future, however, provides a way to avoid problems caused by changes in the nature of activities because it would not depend on the a priori assignment of activities. In addition, a time-series of episode-level data on affective experience would enable research into the changing hedonic nature of activities.

Data on emotional experience might also be used to explain people's choices. What types of preferences are consistent with observed time allocation patterns if people seek to maximize some function of their flow of emotional experiences? What other considerations besides maximization of emotional experience is needed to rationalize observed choices about time allocation in a maximizing framework? Or, if maximization is considered too strong an assumption, can people's time allocation be explained by a small set of heuristics? Of course, modeling behavior with data on subjective well-being requires that information on a relevant set of emotional experiences is collected. It should also be noted that understanding people's choices is not a prerequisite for NTA, just as understanding choices about work, consumption, and investment are not a prerequisite for the NIPAs.

Nonetheless, the evaluated time-use data provide a new opportunity to model people's allocation of time.

Finally, it is unclear how to fully integrate sleep and health into NTA. To some extent, both factors are reflected in our measures of affect. For example, people who are in poor health experience more pain during their daily lives (Krueger and Stone 2008). And a bad night sleep is associated with a bad mood and greater tiredness throughout the day (Kahneman et al. 2004). In other words, sleep and health both affect the process benefit of various uses of time. But if people learn to sleep half as much without lowering their average emotional experience during waking moments, our current summary measures would not credit an improvement in well-being. In addition, health surely has a direct effect on well-being independent of any effect on momentary emotional experience.

While these limitations of NTA are important, they are not insurmountable. We suspect that many of the current limitations of NTA are amenable to research, just as research helped to overcome some of the problems posed by changes in product quality in the NIPAs. Moreover, the choices that people make regarding their allocation of time, particularly labor supply, have long been subject to economic analysis. Research on the allocation and experience of nonwork time is less developed, but no less important for economics and policy. Evaluated time use also strikes us as a fertile area for research because most determinants of subjective well-being are not well captured by data on market transactions, and this will be even more so in the future as people live longer and spend a smaller share of their lives engaged in market work and home production.

Appendix

Linear probability multiple regression models for U-index, full sample, and by sex

	Full sample		Women		Men	
Explanatory variable	Coefficient	*t*-ratio	Coefficient	*t*-ratio	Coefficient	*t*-ratio
Female	0.024	1.96	—	—		
Black	0.052	1.84	0.042	1.18	0.065	1.42
Hispanic	0.033	1.26	0.057	1.62	0.010	0.25
Log income	−0.023	−2.31	−0.027	−2.15	−0.020	−1.21
< High school	−0.005	−0.21	0.006	0.17	−0.010	−0.27
Some college	−0.017	−0.96	0.006	0.27	−0.052	−1.98
College	−0.056	−3.27	−0.045	−1.99	−0.070	−2.76
College +	−0.045	−2.31	−0.020	−0.71	−0.082	−3.00
Age	0.003	1.67	0.009	3.11	0.000	−0.02
Age-squared	0.000	−1.95	0.000	−3.58	0.000	−0.07
Married	−0.017	−1.17	−0.051	−2.69	0.020	0.94
Tuesday	−0.012	−0.51	0.019	0.61	−0.043	−1.28
Wednesday	0.004	0.18	0.026	0.89	−0.022	−0.62
Thursday	0.005	0.22	0.035	1.13	−0.024	−0.68
Friday	−0.020	−0.86	0.000	0.00	−0.049	−1.42
Saturday	−0.009	−0.36	0.027	0.82	−0.055	−1.52
Sunday	−0.061	−2.62	−0.052	−1.79	−0.070	−1.87
June	−0.015	−0.92	−0.036	−1.66	0.010	0.41
July	−0.025	−1.67	−0.022	−1.01	−0.031	−1.50
August	0.046	2.32	0.030	1.16	0.065	2.14
No. of episodes	9,989		6,136		3,853	

Notes: All regressions also control for 15 "who with" dummies, 5 dummies indicating the order in which affect questions were asked, and an intercept. Heteroskedasticity consistency standard errors that allow for within-person correlated errors were calculated. Data are from the PATS. Dashed cells indicate there is no coefficient, since the gender variable is a constant for women and men.

References

Aguiar, M., and E. Hurst. 2007. Measuring trends in leisure: The allocation of time over five decades. *Quarterly Journal of Economics* 122 (3): 969–1006.

Alesina, A. F., E. L. Glaeser, and B. Sacerdote. 2002. Why doesn't the U.S. have a European-style welfare state? *Brookings Papers on Economic Activity* (Fall): 187–277.

Ashby, F. G., A. M. Isen, and A. U. Turken. 1999. A neuropsychological theory of positive affect and its influence on cognition. *Psychological Review* 106 (3): 529–50.

Becker, G. 1965. A theory of the allocation of time. *Economic Journal* 75 (299): 493–517.

Berk, L. S., D. L. Felten, S. A. Tan, B. B. Bittman, and J. Westengard. 2001. Modulation of neuroimmune parameters during the eustress of humor-associated mirthful laughter. *Alternative Therapies* 7 (2): 62–76.

Berkowitz, L. 1987. Mood, self-awareness, and willingness to help. *Journal of Personality and Social Psychology* 52 (4): 721–29.

Blair, E., and S. Burton. 1987. Cognitive processes used by survey respondents to answer behavioral frequency questions. *Journal of Consumer Research* 14 (2): 280–88.

Blanchflower, D. G. 2007. Is unemployment more costly than inflation? NBER Working Paper no. W13505. Cambridge, MA: National Bureau of Economic Research, October.

Brickman, P., D. Coates, and R. Janoff-Bulman. 1978. Lottery winners and accident victims: Is happiness relative? *Journal of Personality and Social Psychology* 36 (8): 917–27.

Clark, A., E. Diener, Y. Georgellis, and R. Lucas. 2003. Lags and leads in life satisfaction: A test of the baseline hypothesis. Working Paper 2003-14, DELTA (Ecole normale supérieure).

Clark, A., and A. Oswald. 1994. Unhappiness and unemployment. *The Economic Journal* 104 (424): 648–59.

Coghill, R. C., J. G. McHaffie, and Y. Yen. 2003. Neural correlates of interindividual differences in the subjective experience of pain. *Proceedings of the National Academy of Sciences* 100 (14): 8538–542.

Connolly, M. 2007. Some like it mild and not too wet: The influence of weather on subjective well-being. In *It's about time: Three essays on time use, weather and well-being,* PhD diss., Department of Economics, Princeton University.

Csikszentmihalyi, M. 1990. *Flow: The psychology of optimal experience.* New York: HarperCollins.

Csikszentmihalyi, M., J. D. Patton, and M. Lucas. 1997. Le bonheur, l'experience optimale et les valeurs spirituelles: Une étude empirique auprès d'adolescents (Happiness, the optimal experience, and spiritual values: An empirical study of adolescents). *Revue Quebecoise de Psychologie* 18: 167–90.

Cunningham, M. R., J. Steinberg, and R. Grev. 1980. Wanting to and having to help: Separate motivations for positive mood and guilt-induced helping. *Journal of Personality and Social Psychology* 38 (2): 181–92.

Danner, D. D., D. A. Snowdon, and W. V. Friesen. 2001. Positive emotions in early life and longevity: Findings from the nun study. *Journal of Personality and Social Psychology* 80 (5): 804–13.

Devins, G. M., J. Mann, H. P. Mandin, and C. Leonard. 1990. Psychosocial predictors of survival in end-stage renal disease. *Journal of Nervous and Mental Disease* 178 (2): 127–33.

Diener, E., and R. E. Lucas. 1999. Personality and subjective well-being. In *Wellbeing: The foundations of hedonic psychology,* ed. D. Kahneman, E. Diener, and N. Schwarz, 213–29. New York: Russell-Sage.

Diener E., R. E. Lucas, and C. N. Scollon. 2006. Beyond the hedonic treadmill: Revisions to the adaptation theory of well-being. *American Psychologist* 61: 305–14.

Diener, E., C. Nickerson, R. E. Lucas, and E. Sandvik. 2002. Dispositional affect and job outcomes. *Social Indicators Research* 59 (3): 229–59.

Diener, E., E. Sandvik, and W. Pavot. 1991. Happiness is the frequency, not the intensity, of positive versus negative affect. In *Subjective well-being,* ed. F. Strack, M. Argyle, and N. Schwarz, 119–40. New York: Pergamon Press.

Dillon, K. M., B. Minchoff, and K. H. Baker. 1985. Positive emotional states and enhancement of the immune system. *International Journal of Psychiatry in Medicine* 15 (1): 13–18.

Dow, G. K., and F. T. Juster. 1985. Goods, time, and well-being: The joint dependence problem. In *Time, Goods, and Well-Being,* ed. F. T. Juster and F. P. Stafford. Survey Research Center, Institute for Social Research 397–413. Ann Arbor, MI: University of Michigan Press.

Doyle, W. J., D. A. Gentile, and S. Cohen. 2006. Emotional style, nasal cytokines, and illness expression after experimental rhinovirus exposure. *Brain, Behavior, and Immunity* 20 (2): 175–81.

Ekman, P., and E. L. Rosenberg, eds. 1997. *What the face reveals.* New York: Oxford University Press.

Evans, P., M. Bristow, F. Hucklebridge, A. Clow, and N. Walters. 1993. The relationship between secretory immunity, mood and life-events. *British Journal of Clinical Psychology* 32 (2): 227–36.

Fogel, R. W. 1999. Catching up with the economy. *American Economic Review* 89 (1): 1–21.

———. 2001. *Simon S. Kuznets, Biographical memoirs, vol. 79.* Washington DC: The National Academy Press.

Frey, B., and A. Stutzer. 2002. *Happiness and economics.* Princeton, NJ: Princeton University Press.

Gershuny, J., and B. Halpin. 1996. Time use, quality of life and process benefits. In *In pursuit of the quality of life,* ed. 188–210. Avner Offer, Oxford: Clarendon Press.

Glorieux, I. 1993. Social interaction and the social meanings of action: A time budget approach. *Social Indicators Research* 30 (2–3): 149–73.

Graham, C., A. Eggers, and S. Sukhtankar. 2006. Does happiness pay? An exploration based on panel data from Russia. *Journal of Economic Behavior and Organization* 55 (3): 319–42.

Gross, J. J., L. L. Carstensen, M. Pasupathi, J. Tasi, C. G. Skorpen, and A. Y. Hsu. 1997. Emotion and aging: Experience, expression and control. *Psychol Aging* 12 (4): 590–99.

Harker, L., and D. Keltner. 2001. Expressions of positive emotions in women's college yearbook pictures and their relationship to personality and life outcomes across adulthood. *Journal of Personality and Social Psychology* 80: 112–24.

Heady, B. W., and A. J. Wearing. 1989. Personality, life events, and subjective well-being: Toward a dynamic equilibrium model. *Journal of Personality and Social Psychology* 57 (4): 731–39.

Howell, R. T., M. L. Kern, and S. Lyubomirsky. 2007. Health benefits: Meta-analytically determining the impact of well-being on objective health indicators. *Health Psychology Review* 1: 83–136.

Isen, A. M., and P. F. Levin. 1972. Effect of feeling good on helping: Cookies and kindness. *Journal of Personality and Social Psychology* 21: 384–88.

Juster, F. T. 1985. Preferences for work and leisure. In *Time, goods, and well-being.* ed. F. T. Juster and F. P. Stafford, 333–51. Ann Arbor, MI: Institute for Social Research, University of Michigan.

Juster, F. T., P. Courant, and G. K. Dow. 1985. A conceptual framework for the analysis of time allocation data. In *Time, goods, and well-being,* ed. F. T. Juster and F. P. Stafford. Ann Arbor, MI: Survey Research Center, Institute for Social Research, University of Michigan.

Juster, F. T., and F. P. Stafford, eds. 1985. *Time, goods, and well-being.* Ann Arbor: Institute for Social Research.

Kahneman, D. 2003. Maps of bounded rationality: Psychology for behavioral economics. *American Economic Review* 93 (5): 1449–75.

Kahneman, D., and A. Krueger. 2006. Developments in the measurement of subjective well-being. *Journal of Economic Perspectives* 20 (21): 3–24.

Kahneman, D., A. Krueger, D. Schkade, N. Schwarz, and A. Stone. 2004. A survey method for characterizing daily life experience: the Day Reconstruction Method. *Science* 306 (December): 1776–80.

Kahneman, D., P. Wakker, and R. Sarin. 1997. Back to Bentham? Explorations of experienced utility. *Quarterly Journal of Economics* 112 (2): 375–405.

Kiecolt-Glaser, J., L. D. Fisher, P. Ogrocki, J. C. Stout, C. E. Speicher, and R. Glaser. 1988. Marital quality, marital disruption, and immune function. *Psychosomatic Medicine* 49 (1): 13–34.

Kirschbaum, C., K. M. Pirke, and D. H. Hellhammer. 1993. The "Trier Social Stress Test"—A tool for investigating psychobiological stress responses in a laboratory setting. *Neuropsychobiology* 28 (1–2): 76–81.

Krueger, A. B. 2007. Are we having more fun yet? Categorizing and evaluating changes in time allocation. *Brookings Papers on Economic Activity* 2 (September): 193–215.

Krueger, A. B., D. Kahneman, C. Fischler, D. Schkade, N. Schwarz, and A. Stone. 2009. Comparing time use and subjective well-being in France and the U.S. *Social Indicators Research,* forthcoming.

Krueger, A., and A. Mueller. 2008. The lot of the unemployed: A time use perspective. IZA Discussion Paper no. 3490, Institute for the Study of Labor (IZA), Bonn, Germany.

Krueger, A. B., and D. Schkade. 2008. The reliability of subjective well-being measures. *Journal of Public Economics* 92 (8–9): 1833–45.

Krueger, A. B., and A. Stone. 2008. Assessment of pain: A community-based diary survey. *The Lancet* 371 (9623): 1510–25.

Kubey, R., and M. Csikszentmihalyi. 1990. *Television and the quality of life: How viewing shapes everyday experience.* Hillsdale, NJ: Lawrence Erlbaum.

Layard, R. 2005. *Happiness: Lessons from a new science.* London: Penguin.

Leonhardt, D. Obamanomics. *New York Times Magazine,* August 20, 2008. Available at: http://www.nytimes.com/2008/08/24/magazine/24Obamanomics-t.html ?pagewanted=all.

Levy, S. M., J. Lee, C. Bagley, and M. Lippman. 1988. Survival hazard analysis in first recurrent breast cancer patients: Seven-year follow-up. *Psychosomatic Medicine* 50: 520–28.

Lucas, R. E. 2001. Pleasant affect and sociability: Towards a comprehensive model of extraverted feelings and behaviors. *Dissertation Abstracts International* 61 (10-B): 5610 (UMI no. AAI9990068.)

Lucas, R. E., A. E. Clark, Y. Georgellis, and E. Diener. 2003. Reexamining adaptation and the set point model of happiness: Reactions to changes in marital status. *Journal of Personality and Social Psychology* 84 (3): 527–39.

Lykken, D. 1999. *Happiness: What studies on twins show us about nature, nurture and the happiness set-point.* New York: Golden Books.

Lyubomirsky, S., L. King, and E. Diener. 2005. The benefits of frequent positive affect: Does happiness lead to success? *Psychological Bulletin* 131 (6): 803–55.

Lyubomirsky, S., K. M. Sheldon, and D. Schkade. 2005. Pursuing happiness: The architecture of sustainable change. *Review of General Psychology* 9 (2): 111–31.

Maier, H., and J. Smith. 1999. Psychological predictors of mortality in old age. *Journal of Gerontology* 54B: 44–54.

March, J. 1978. Bounded rationality, ambiguity, and the engineering of choice. *Bell Journal of Economics* 9 (2): 587–608.

Marks, G. N., and N. Fleming. 1999. Influences and consequences of well-being among Australian young people: 1980–1995. *Social Indicators Research* 46: 301–23.

Marsland, A. L., S. Pressman, and S. Cohen. 2007. Positive affect and immune function. In *Psychoneuroimmunology, 4th ed., vol. 2,* ed. R. Ader, 761–779. San Diego, CA: Elsevier.

Michelson, W. 2005. *Time use: Expanding explanation in the social sciences.* Boulder, CO: Paradigm Publishers.

Nadal, J. I. G., and A. S. Sanz. 2007. A note on leisure inequality in the U.S.: 1965–2003. Oxford University, Department of Economics, Discussion Paper.

O'Malley, M. N., and L. Andrews. 1983. The effect of mood and incentives on helping: Are there some things money can't buy? *Motivation and Emotion* 7 (2): 179–89.

Oswald, A., and N. Powdthavee. Does happiness adapt? A longitudinal study of disability with implications for economists and judges. IZA Discussion Paper no. 2208, Institute for the Study of Labor (IZA), Bonn, Germany.

Palmore, E. B. 1969. Predicting longevity: A follow-up controlling for age. *Gerontologist* 9 (4): 247–50.

Perera, S., E. Sabin, P. Nelson, and D. Lowe. 1998. Increases in salivary lysozyme and IgA concentrations and secretory rates independent of salivary flow rates following viewing of humorous videotape. *International Journal of Behavioral Medicine* 5 (2): 118–28.

Polk, D. E., S. Cohen, W. J. Doyle, D. P. Skoner, and C. Kirschbaum. 2005. State and trait affect as predictors of salivary cortisol in healthy adults. *Psychoneuroendocrinology* 30 (3): 261–72.

Pollak, R., and M. L. Wachter. 1975. The relevance of the household production function and its implications for the allocation of time. *Journal of Political Economy* 83 (2): 255–77.

Ramey, V., and N. Francis. 2006. A century of work and leisure. NBER Working Paper no. 12264. Cambridge, MA: National Bureau of Economic Research, May.

Riis, J., G. Loewenstein, J. Baron, C. Jepson, A. Fagerlin, and P. A. Ubel. 2005. Ignorance of hedonic adaptation to hemo-dialysis: A study using ecological momentary assessment. *Journal of Experimental Psychology: General* 134 (1): 3–9.

Robinson, J., and G. Godbey. 1997. *Time for life: The surprising ways Americans use their time.* University Park, PA: Pennsylvania State University Press.

Robinson, M. D., and G. L. Clore. 2002. Belief and feeling: Evidence for an accessibility model of emotional self-report. *Psychological Bulletin* 128: 934–60.

Russell, J. A. 1980. A circumplex model of affect. *Journal of Personality and Social Psychology* 39: 1161–78.

Schwarz, N. 2007. Retrospective and concurrent self-reports: The rationale for real-time data capture. In *The science of real-time data capture: Self-reports in health research,* ed. A. A. Stone, S. S. Shiffman, A. Atienza, and L. Nebeling, 11–26. New York: Oxford University Press.

Schwarz, N., and G. L. Clore. 1983. Mood, misattribution, and judgments of well-being: Informative and directive functions of affective states. *Journal of Personality and Social Psychology* 45 (3): 513–23.

Schwarz, N., D. Kahneman, and J. Xu. 2009. Global and episodic reports of hedonic experience. In *Using calendar and diary methods in life events research,* ed. R. Belli, D. Alwin, and F. Stafford, 157–74. Newbury Park, CA: SAGE.

Schwarz, N., and F. Strack. 1999. Reports of subjective well-being: Judgmental processes and their methodological implications. In *Well-being: The foundations of hedonic psychology,* ed. D. Kahneman, E. Diener, and N. Schwarz, 61–84. New York: Russell-Sage.

Shapiro, D., L. D. Jamner, and I. B. Goldstein. 1997. Daily mood state and ambulatory blood pressure. *Psychophysiology* 34: 399–405.

Smith, D. M., K. M. Langa, M. U. Kabeto, and P. A. Ubel. 2005. Health, wealth, and happiness. *Psychological Science* 16 (9): 663–66.

Smyth, J., M. C. Ockenfels, L. Porter, C. Kirschbaum, D.C. Hellhammer, and A. A. Stone. 1998. Stressors and mood measured on a momentary basis are associated with salivary cortisol secretion. *Psychoneuroendocrinology* 23: 353–70.

Snowdon, D. 2001. *Aging with grace.* New York: Bentam.

Spanier, G. B., and F. F. Furstenberg. 1982. Remarriage after divorce: A longitudinal analysis of well-being. *Journal of Marriage and the Family* 44 (3): 709–20.

Stone, A. A. 1987. Event content in a daily survey differentially predicts mood. *Journal of Personality and Social Psychology* 52: 56–58.

Stone, A. A., D. S. Cox, H. Valdimarsdottir, L. Jandorf, and J. M. Neale. 1987. Evidence that secretory IgA antibody is associated with daily mood. *Journal of Personality and Social Psychology* 52 (5): 988–93.

Stone, A. A., S. M. Hedges, J. M. Neale, and M. S. Satin. 1985. Prospective and cross-sectional mood reports offer no evidence of a "blue Monday" phenomenon. *Journal of Personality and Social Psychology* 49: 129–34.

Stone, A. A., C. Marco, C. E. Cruise, D. S. Cox, and J. M. Neale. 1996. Are stress-induced immunological changes mediated by mood? A closer look at how both desirable and undesirable daily events influence sIgA antibody. *International Journal of Behavioral Medicine* 3 (1): 1–13.

Stone, A. A., J. E. Schwartz, N. Schwarz, D. Schkade, A. Krueger, and D. Kahneman. 2006. A population approach to the study of emotion: Diurnal rhythms of a working day examined with the Day Reconstruction Method (DRM). *Emotion* 6: 139–49.

Stone, A. A., and S. Shiffman. 1994. Ecological Momentary Assessment (EMA) in behavioral medicine. *Annals of Behavioral Medicine* 16 (3): 199–202.

Stone, A. A., S. Shiffman, A. Atienza, and L. Nebeling. eds. 2007. *The science of real-time data capture: Self-reports in Health Research.* London: Oxford University Press.

Stone, A. A., S. S. Shiffman, and M. W. DeVries. 1999. In *Well-being: The foundations of hedonic psychology,* ed. D. Kahneman, E. Diener, and N. Schwarz, 26–39. New York: Russell-Sage.

Stone, A. A., H. B. Valdimarsdottir, E. S. Katkin, J. M. Burns, D. S. Cox, S. Lee, J. Fine, D. Ingle, and D. H. Bovbjerg. 1993. Mitogen-induced lymphocyte responses are reduced following mental stressors in the laboratory. *Psychology and Health* 8: 269–84.

Sudman, S., and B. Wansink. 2002. *Consumer panels.* Chicago: American Marketing Association.

Ubel, P. A., G. Loewenstein, N. Schwarz, and D. Smith. 2005. Misimagining the unimaginable: The disability paradox and health care decision making. *Health Psychology* 24 (4, Supplement): S57–S62.

Urry, H. L., J. B. Nitschke, I. Dolski, D.C. Jackson, K. M. Dalton, C. J. Mueller, M. A. Rosenkranz, C. D. Ryff, B. H. Singer, and R. J. Davidson. 2004. Making a life worth living: Neural correlates of well-being. *Psychological Science* 15 (6): 367–72.

Vitaliano, P. P., J. M. Scanlan, H. D. Ochs, K. Syrjala, I. C. Siegler, and E. A. Snyder. 1998. Psychological stress moderates the relationship of cancer history with natural killer cell activity. *Annals of Behavioral Medicine* 20 (3): 199–208.

Wong, G. 2007. Be it ever so humble: Understanding housing using subjective well-being data. University of Pennsylvania, Wharton School, Working Paper.

Xu, J., and N. Schwarz. 2009. Do we really need a reason to indulge? *Journal of Marketing Research* 46 (1): 25–36.

Zuckerman, D. M., S. V. Kasl, and A. M. Ostfeld. 1984. Psychosocial predictors of mortality among the elderly poor. The role of religion, well-being, and social contacts. *American Journal of Epidemiology* 119 (3): 410–23.

2

That Which Makes Life Worthwhile

George Loewenstein

Too much and for too long, we seemed to have surrendered personal excellence and community values in the mere accumulation of material things. Our Gross National Product, now, is over $800 billion dollars a year, but that Gross National Product—if we judge the United States of America by that—that Gross National Product counts air pollution and cigarette advertising, and ambulances to clear our highways of carnage. It counts special locks for our doors and the jails for the people who break them. It counts the destruction of the redwood and the loss of our natural wonder in chaotic sprawl. . . . And the television programs which glorify violence in order to sell toys to our children. Yet the gross national product does not allow for the health of our children, the quality of their education or the joy of their play. It does not include the beauty of our poetry or the strength of our marriages, the intelligence of our public debate or the integrity of our public officials. It measures neither our wit nor our courage, neither our wisdom nor our learning, neither our compassion nor our devotion to our country, it measures everything in short, except that which makes life worthwhile. —Robert Kennedy, 1968 (quoted from Krueger et al., Chapter 1, this volume)

2.1 Introduction

Like Krueger and his collaborators, I find Robert Kennedy's words both compelling and moving. I share with Kennedy and Krueger et al., the view that gross national product (GNP) fails to fully capture that which makes life worthwhile, and Kennedy's list of what GNP fails to include comes close

George Loewenstein is the Herbert A. Simon Professor of Economics and Psychology at Carnegie Mellon University.

I thank Erik Angner and Alan Krueger for helpful comments.

to matching my own perspective on what makes life worthwhile. The issue I address in this commentary is the degree to which National Time Accounting (NTA) captures what makes life worthwhile, including, given the prominence they give to Kennedy's quote, the aspects listed by Kennedy.

The purpose of a scale, or an index such as NTA's U-index, is to measure an underlying construct. For the U-index, the underlying construct is welfare. As Krueger et al. express it, NTA provides "an alternative way of measuring society's well-being, based on time use and affective (emotional) experience." Ideally, the U-index could be used to determine whether one group of people (e.g., the citizens of a country) is better off than another, or whether a specific group is, or would be, better off under one set of circumstances than another.

In the language of research methodology, Kennedy's passage can be interpreted as a critique of GNP's *validity* as an index of welfare. Validity addresses the degree to which an index or scale measures the construct that it is intended to measure. (Reliability, in contrast, addresses the extent to which you get the same answer when you elicit the scale in different ways or at different points in time.)

Scales and indexes have low validity to the extent that they encompass dimensions that are not part of the construct they are intended to represent, and fail to encompass dimensions that are part of the construct. As summarized in table 2.1, Kennedy can be interpreted as having made the point that GNP has low validity as a measure of welfare because it includes a variety of things that do not belong in the construct of welfare (top right cell), and fails to encompass many important factors that are important aspects of welfare (bottom left cell).[1]

Beyond the specifics of what it should include that it does not, and what it does not include that it should, GNP embodies implicit assumptions that are questionable. For GNP to represent a reasonable proxy for welfare, the economic activity indexed by GNP must be allocated to purposes that people value. If people or their elected governments do a poor job of allocating wealth to activities that enhance their well-being, by whatever metric of well-being one adopts, then GNP will fall short of measuring welfare.

---

1. Kennedy does not mention material prosperity, but presumably he would agree that prosperity is a part of GNP and deserves to be considered as one dimension of welfare. Hence, I have included it in the on-diagonal (bottom right) cell of the table. I leave the top left cell blank because there are an infinite number of things that do not belong in GNP that are not included in it, such as the length of people's hair. Krueger et al. expand on Kennedy's list of things that are not accounted for (or accounted for improperly) in GNP, citing "near-market" activities (e.g., unpaid cleaning, cooking, and child care), social activities, consumer surplus (because economic activity is measured by prices, which reflect marginal valuations), prices distorted by imperfectly competitive markets, the distribution of income (which might matter in its own right and might also influence prices and marginal valuations in a fashion that could distort welfare calculations), and finally externalities (costs people impose on others that they do not internalize).

Table 2.1   **What makes life worthwhile: Kennedy versus National Income Accounts**

Kennedy	GNP	
	Not included	Included
Not included	(Infinite)	• Air pollution • Cigarette advertising • Ambulances to clear highway carnage • Special locks for doors • Jails • Destruction of redwood • Chaotic sprawl • Violent television programs
Included	• Health of children • Quality of their education • Joy of their play • Beauty of our poetry • Strength of marriages • Intelligence of public debate • Integrity of public officials • Wit, courage, wisdom, and learning • Compassion • Devotion to country	Material prosperity?

That is, indexing welfare by GNP assumes, implicitly, that people allocate resources in a fashion that promotes their welfare.[2]

2.1.1   Validity of NTA and the U-index

What about NTA? Is NTA and its instantiation in the U-index more successful than GNP in capturing what makes life worthwhile? National Time Accounting does have desirable qualities. Most fundamentally, NTA, unlike GNP, does not assume that people necessarily behave in a self-interest fashion. In the not-so-old (and definitely not-so-good-old) days of economics, when it was widely assumed that people were reliable pursuers of self-interest, measuring welfare was (comparatively) easy. Ignoring distributional issues, it could be assumed that increasing disposable income also increased well-being because it presumably gave people greater scope to pursue their own material and nonmaterial goals. The emergence of behavioral economics, with its multiple challenges to the view that people rationally pursue self-interest, complicated this tidy picture. Once one accepts that people are unreliable, and indeed often biased, pursuers of self-interest, it can no longer be assumed that increasing affluence will make them better off.

2. See Loewenstein and Ubel (2008) for a deeper discussion of this point.

As the economist Avner Offner (2006) points out in a recent book titled *The Challenge of Affluence,* if people make systematic mistakes when it comes to maximizing their own well-being, then increasing their income may not only not enhance their welfare; it may be tantamount to giving them more rope to hang themselves with. Offner cites research on well-being (albeit not using NTA methods) that he interprets as showing that well-being decreased in the United States and Britain not only as, but *because,* affluence increased. Perhaps NTA's greatest strength, then, is that it does not assume any particular relationship between income and happiness. Has the increase in income over the last century led to improvements in welfare? National Time Accounting would indicate that it has only if people spend a larger fraction of their time in a predominantly positive mood.

However, NTA and the U-index do have serious limitations. Krueger et al. acknowledge that "Like the National Income Accounts, NTA is also incomplete, providing a partial measure of society's well-being." NTA, they note, "misses people's general sense of satisfaction or fulfillment with their lives as a whole, apart from moment to moment feelings." Nevertheless, they argue, NTA "provides a valuable indicator of society's well-being, and the fact that our measure is connected to time allocation has analytical and policy advantages that are not available from other measures of subjective well-being, such as overall life satisfaction." As depicted in figure 2.1, Krueger et al.'s implicit perspective seems to be that, while NTA, like NIA (national income accounts) misses some important aspects of welfare, it is superior to NIA in terms of capturing "true" welfare.

My own perspective is somewhat more pessimistic. Contrary to figure 2.1, and more consistent with figure 2.2, I believe that much if not most of what makes life worthwhile is *not* captured by moment to moment happiness, but corresponds more closely, if not perfectly, to what Krueger et al. acknowledge to be absent from NTA, namely "people's general sense of satisfaction or fulfillment with their lives as a whole, apart from moment to moment feelings." In the remainder of this chapter, I provide a more detailed rationale for my misgivings about NTA, starting with the next section, which enumerates dimensions of welfare that are missing from NTA.

Table 2.2 summarizes Kennedy's perspective on what makes life worthwhile, classifying his specific items into broad categories. The two main categories that subsume the majority of his items are *wisdom* (with four items) and *values* (encompassing four or five items, depending on whether the "strength of our marriages" falls under this heading). Only one item ("the joy of [our children's] play"—in italics) is directly related to happiness.

It is possible that four other items (highlighted in bold) could be reflected in happiness in an indirect fashion. That is, it seems reasonable to assume that children and their parents are happier when children are healthy. Perhaps more controversially, it might be expected that people would be happier when marriages are stronger (although not if strong marriages means that

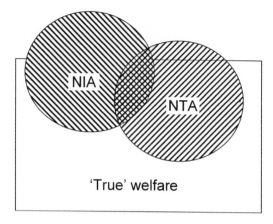

Fig. 2.1   Krueger et al.'s (implicit) perspective

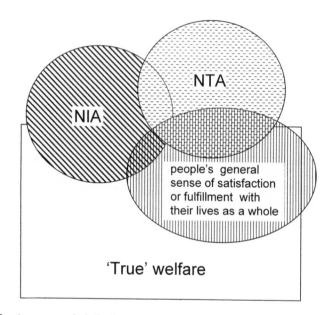

Fig. 2.2   A more pessimistic view

people are trapped in unhappy marriages), or when they are exposed to others' compassion or wit (although gratitude is not always such a pleasant feeling, and too much wit coming from others can be depressing for those lacking in it).

Even if health, social stability (a generalization of marital strength), wit, and compassion do have a positive impact on happiness, however, it seems unlikely that this impact adequately captures their full value. Thus, as I dis-

Table 2.2   **Kennedy's view of what makes life worthwhile**

	Health	Wisdom	Happiness	Culture	Values
Health of our children[b]	X				
Quality of their education[c]		X			
Joy of their play[a]			X		
Beauty of our poetry[c]				X	
Strength of our marriages[b]					?
Intelligence of our public debate[c]		X			
Integrity of our public officials[c]					X
Wit[b]		X			
Courage[c]					X
Wisdom and learning[c]		X			
Compassion[b]					X
Devotion to our country[c]					X

[a]Directly captured by NTA.
[b]Could be captured by NTA (indirectly).
[c]Unlikely to be captured by NTA.

cuss later, although people adapt to health problems as severe as quadriplegia and exhibit close to normal levels of happiness, most people, including quadriplegics themselves would be willing to make tremendous sacrifices to retain (or regain) the use of their limbs. This suggests that unhappiness does not capture the full (negative) value of quadriplegia. It is also *possible* that an improvement on any or all of the remaining seven items (those not italicized or highlighted in bold) might increase happiness, but the connection seems tenuous at best. Are societies that are more courageous happier? Perhaps, but on the face of it this seems no more likely than the opposite.

In sum, NTA does capture some aspects of welfare that are not part of NIA, but whether it constitutes an improvement or even that much of a useful complement, is unclear.

2.2   What's Missing from NTA?

One modern perspective on what can go wrong in survey design applies insights from research on conversational norms (e.g., Grice 1975; Clark and Clark 1977) to understanding how survey respondents make sense of the questions they are asked (Clark and Schober 1992; Schwarz 1999). According to this perspective, a survey can be viewed as a kind of "conversation" between the surveyor and the respondent in which the usual norms of conversation apply.

As an illustration, the "maxim of quantity" (Grice 1975), which enjoins speakers to provide information that is new and not redundant, can shed light on the results of a study on marital satisfaction and life-satisfaction (Schwarz, Strack, and Mai 1991). Some respondents to a survey were first asked how satisfied they were with their life as a whole and then were asked to report their satisfaction with their marriage. Others were asked the same questions in the reverse order, and still others had both questions introduced by a join lead-in designed to evoke the norm of nonredundancy by informing respondents that they would be answering two questions, one related to well-being and the other relating to their marriage. When the life satisfaction question was asked before the marital satisfaction question, the correlation between the two items was lower ($r = .32$) than when they were asked in the reverse order ($r = .67$), presumably the marital question brought the marital dimension of life to mind when people were reporting their overall life satisfaction. However, the correlation was lowest ($r = .18$, n.s.) in the third condition, presumably because, as Schwarz (1999) expressed it, "respondents interpreted the general life-satisfaction question as if it were worded, 'Aside from your marriage, which you already told us about, how satisfied are you with other aspects of your life?'"

Playing on the idea of a survey as a "conversation," I propose a new notion of validity: validity as *feeling understood* by a researcher—a concept that, I believe, has not previously been suggested in the literature. The criterion of feeling understood can be viewed as a high-level inference, on the part of the respondent, that the "conversation" with the surveyor has the capacity to answer the surveyor's question in a fashion that the respondent deems reasonable.

In the course of life I have been asked to complete myriad surveys that, it was apparent, were intended to measure a wide range of things: How happy was I with a class I had taken? Was I satisfied with my new car? Was giving blood a pleasant or unpleasant experience? Deducing the purpose of a scale from the questions I am being asked, I often find myself thinking that the designers of the scale have asked the wrong questions to address whatever they seemed to be interested in. I was once asked, for example, whether the telephone operator at a U.S. Airline was courteous, and my answer was affirmative; yet I suspected that the airline would have also been interested in whether I found the operator competent—whether he had been able to do for me what I needed done—and I knew that the answer to this question would have been much less favorable. The airline survey, therefore, would have fared poorly on the "feeling understood" measure of validity.

I introduce this new, and perhaps somewhat atheoretical notion of validity because, at different points in time after I had taken on the assignment of writing this commentary, I attempted to assess whether the U-index would successfully capture my own perception of the quality of a particular activity I was engaged in—that is, whether researchers who attempted to elicit my U-index using the Day Reconstruction Method (DRM) would come to the same conclusion as I would have about my quality of life in that period of time.

If there was a discrepancy, of course, it is possible that the U-index correctly assessed my well-being while I misestimated it. But this possibility actually goes to the heart of my main misgiving about the U-index. The U-index assumes that the quality of a person's life can be measured in terms of happiness, but individuals might have very different criteria for what makes their own life worthwhile. If an individual values something other than happiness, who is to say that happiness is the right measure of welfare? In the remainder of this section, I discuss a variety of dimensions of life other than happiness that I personally care about but that would not be fully picked up on by a measurement of happiness.

2.2.1   Meaning

If you asked men of my father's generation to relate their life story, a typical narrative would devote hours to the individual's experiences during the war, then devote little more than a sentence to the remaining bulk of their lives—for example, "When I got back from the war, I finished school, got married, had kids, retired, and here I am." Their experiences during the war may not have been pleasant, but they gave their lives meaning. My own father's case was especially extreme. He spent part of the war interned in a French prisoner of war camp, hungry to the point where he dug up worms for food and chewed on shoe leather. But he once reported to me that being in the camp was the peak experience of his life.

Of course memory has a way of blotting out the misery—the hunger, discomfort, and fear—and leaving an idealized residue of meaning. Yet it would be a mistake to entirely dismiss these retrospective evaluations. For my father, having to use his wits to survive in the camp and the feeling of camaraderie and interdependence with the small group he allied himself with were never matched by the comfortable suburban existence he eventually established for himself and his family. Not only is the U-index unlikely to pick up on the value from experiences such as war (or mountaineering[3]); it would be likely to encode as maximally negative many of the experiences that people recount as having been the most worthwhile because, while often difficult at the time, they conferred meaning.

Meaning can, of course, have many interpretations (see Karlsson, Loewenstein, and McCafferty [2004] for a discussion of the nonrole of meaning in economics[4]). However, many of the possible interpretations of the concept

---

3. The reports of mountaineers are similar. When they give a more complete response to the "why?" question than "because it is there," mountaineers often cite meaning as a major benefit they derive from their escapades (Loewenstein 1999).

4. We distinguish between four different possible definitions, which we discuss in order from the one that is easiest to assimilate with traditional economic theory to the one that is most difficult to assimilate:

- Meaning as a resolution of uncertainty about preferences: People are often uncertain about what they want from life. Finding meaning, in some cases, can entail learning about what one values or cares about.

are missing from NTA. For example, it could be argued that meaning entails having a range of emotional experiences; always being in an unchanging emotional state would entail a lack of meaning. Or, it could be argued that meaning arises from experiences that change one's self-concept or alter the story one would tell about one's life. National Time Accounting, and especially its instantiation in the U-index, which implicitly defines welfare as the absence of negative emotions, misses out on all of these notions of meaning, and especially interpretations that are associated with emotional range.

Tibor Scitovsky, one of a small number of economists who embraced psychology in the 1970s, would probably not have been a fan of this aspect of the U-index. In his classic, *The Joyless Economy* (1976), Scitovsky argued, much as do Krueger et al., that GNP is a poor measure of a society's welfare because societies often spend resources in ways that are not conducive to true well-being. However, he cautioned against the tendency for individuals and societies to expend their resources on things that bring bland "comfort," characterized mainly by an absence of risk, discomfort, or uncertainty, as compared with goods and activities that bring "pleasures," which he defined in terms of features such as challenge, risk, and variability. The U-index, which encodes only periods of net negative affect, and fails to give credit for the more dramatic ups and downs that give life much of its richness, would evaluate favorable exactly the kind of society and lifestyle that Scitovsky cautioned against.

Another likely skeptic of the U-index would have been Aldous Huxley, whose classic novel *Brave New World* presented a vision of a future distopia in which everyone was happy because society has been engineered (partly with the aid of a drug called Soma, eerily similar to modern antidepressants) to eliminate negative emotions. As a world leader going by the title of "The Controller" states, presumably referring to a historical period coming shortly after our own, "Our ancestors were so stupid and short-sighted that when the first reformers came along and offered to deliver them from those horrible emotions, they wouldn't have anything to do with them" (45).

- *Meaning as an extension of self either socially or temporally:* One's life can often seem insignificant and inconsequential when viewed in the context of the span of human (or even natural) history or of the vast numbers of people alive in the world. The quest for higher meaning may serve the function of expanding the self through time and across persons.
- *Meaning as an act of sense-making:* The brain is a sense-making organ, and one of its most important tasks is to make sense of the life of its owner. Such sense-making typically takes the form of a narrative—a "life story."
- *Meaning as an assertion of free will:* People derive personal meaning from the act of making autonomic choices. Hence, meaning-making can involve the assertion of free will.

To this list, perhaps should be added *"meaning as the experience of a range of emotions."* Part of what it means to be alive is to experience a range of emotions. Such a desire to experience a range of emotions may help to explain why we voluntarily expose ourselves to emotions that are normally seen as "negative" (such as the fear of a roller coaster or the sadness of a tragedy).

Huxley's implicit, although not too subtle point is that "those horrible emotions" actually have value; they are what protect us from an existence devoid of meaning. In one representative scene in the book, the two-person flying machine occupied by Henry and Lenina (both prototypical citizens of their time) suddenly rises, buoyed by a column of hot air from the chimney of a crematorium they have passed over. Huxley writes that "Henry's tone was almost, for a moment, melancholy. 'Do you know what that switchback was?' he said. 'It was some human being finally and definitely disappearing.' He sighed. Then, in a resolutely cheerful voice, 'Anyhow,' he concluded, 'there's one thing we can be certain of; whoever he may have been, he was happy when he was alive. Everybody's happy now'" (75). Huxley's Brave New World would achieve an almost perfect score on the U-index, despite his own intention to present it as the antithesis of true welfare.

2.2.2   Wisdom

One of the most common critiques of happiness as a measure of welfare involves the tension that often seems to exist between happiness and intelligence or wisdom. Most famously, John Stuart Mill, while embracing utilitarianism and its central assumption that happiness should be the goal of public policy, argued that the *quality* of happiness has to be considered as well as the quantity. According to Mill, although a pig might derive a great quantity of pleasure from wallowing in the mud, "it is better to be a human being dissatisfied than a pig satisfied; better to be Socrates dissatisfied than a fool satisfied" (Mill 1871, chapter 2). National Time Accounting accounts for wisdom in a positive fashion only to the degree that wisdom contributes to happiness (or, more precisely, subtracts from unhappiness), but, as suggested by the commonplace that "ignorance is bliss," a wiser society might well be a less happy one.

According to the empirical analysis presented in Krueger et al., education is among the least enjoyed activities measured by the U-index. It is the second-to-worst activity without controlling for individual fixed effects and third-to-worst after controlling for fixed effects. Yet people seem to value education tremendously. Education is a voluntary activity and is heavily subsidized by the state.

People do obtain education in part to secure professional goals, and societies certainly value education in part for economic reasons. Gross national product would be an appropriate index for capturing the economic value of education. People may also obtain education, in part, because they believe it will bring happiness in the long run. Indeed, there is suggestive evidence from one of the empirical studies presented by Krueger et al. (table 1.8 from their chapter) that this might be the case. Those with a college degree or greater have substantially lower U-indexes. Just as traditional income accounts can be a useful way of picking up on intertemporal tradeoffs of income, NTA could be a useful tool for picking up on these intertemporal tradeoffs of happiness.[5]

However, even if education makes people miserable while they are engaged in it, people seem to value education, or the wisdom it confers, for other than either purely economic or purely hedonic reasons. My own university, like many others, offers a whole program of education targeted at senior citizens that is so popular that it has a wait-list half as long as the number of active participants. Why are so many people who have little to gain in terms of either future economic returns or happiness engaged in so much education if it leads to so much negative affect? Like meaning, wisdom seems to be a quality that people value in themselves and others, regardless of its impact on happiness.

Wisdom adds an important dimension to life. Much as gaining sight for a blind person would allow the individual to perceive dimensions that he or she had not previously perceived, even if it did not enhance their happiness, wisdom adds dimensions to thought and perception. Thus, an individual who, by dint of education, gains a taste for and appreciation of the subtle differences between wines may end up enjoying the average bottle of wine less. However, gaining a taste in wine is like speaking a new language. Dimensions of wine that were not previously apparent come into focus, and perceiving these dimensions has value in its own right. I would argue that the same is true for most forms of wisdom.

Krueger et al. were certainly acutely aware of the problem posed by Mill's objection to Bentham's utilitarianism, which may be why they included "interest" as one of only two positive affects in the short list of six affects that they measured (with pain, happy, tired, stressed, and sad being the others), even though "interest" is rarely treated as an affect by emotion researchers, seems difficult to compare to the other affects, and is not even necessarily positive. For example, I might be very *interested* to hear the details of a referee report that my coauthors have informed me is negative, yet not derive much pleasure from that interest or from the information when I obtain it. Wisdom is an important component of what makes life worthwhile, but including "interest" in the list of affects is unlikely to value wisdom appropriately.

2.2.3   Values

My wife and I spent last Thanksgiving vacation with her family, in Florida, with much of the family's time devoted to taking care of her ailing father. If

---

5. Of course, it is unclear which way the causality runs, or whether the benefits of higher education might come through income, which would be captured by traditional national income accounting. Without conducting extended longitudinal research, and without randomly assigning people to get different levels of education (which is probably impossible), these issues are unlikely to get resolved.

the quality of our days during that vacation had been elicited using DRM or PARS, our vacation would have come out very unfavorably. Much of the caregiving elicited strong negative emotions, whether it was because of the specifics of what the care involved or because of the contrast we were forced to confront between her father's current condition and his past vitality. Yet our low U-index during the vacation would fare badly on the *feeling understood* criterion of validity. By caring for their aging parent, my wife and her siblings were displaying their humanity, sharing their love for their father and their sense of the family as an integral unit. None of these values would have been picked up by ratings of momentary happiness.

In one of the empirical studies reported in Krueger et al., the single activity that comes out worst on the U-index, whether or not one controls for fixed effects, is adult care. Does this mean that we could improve welfare by spending less time taking care of our parents? We would, of course, need to take account of the happiness of the people being taken care of, but it seems unlikely that their welfare gains compensate for the losses of those doing the caretaking.[6] Indeed, for many of those receiving care, it is difficult to discern if they are even aware of the fact that they are being taken care of. Should we dismiss caretaking of other people if the U-index fails to show commensurate benefits to those being taken care of? Clearly, this would be a mistake. I can easily imagine Kennedy having included "care for our elderly" in his list of what makes life worthwhile, but assuming it comes from family members instead of professionals, neither GNP nor NTA value it positively.

2.2.4 Capabilities

In a recent study, my coauthors and I (Smith, Loewenstein, and Ubel, forthcoming) asked seventy-one patients who had received a colostomy (an operation in which the bowels are surgically diverted to empty into a bag) to report two measures of happiness (a five-item satisfaction with life scale (Diener et al. 1985), and a "ladder scale" (Cantril 1967) at three points in time: (a) one week after they were released from the hospital; (b) one month after release, and (c) six months after release. The critical variable of interest was whether the colostomy was of a type that is permanent (can never be reversed) or was potentially reversible at some point in the future. Based on prior, albeit more anecdotal, evidence, we anticipated that those who had reversible colostomies would fare worse happiness-wise than those who had irreversible ones. As shown in figure 2.3, our prediction was strongly supported. Those with permanent colostomies got progressively happier over time. Those with reversible ones got less happy according to

---

6. Another, I believe, implausible account of why we take care of parents is to set a good example for children in the hope they will take care of us and improve our U-index when we ourselves age. It would be easy to examine whether children who do not themselves have children are less dutiful caretakers of their parents. I doubt this is the case.

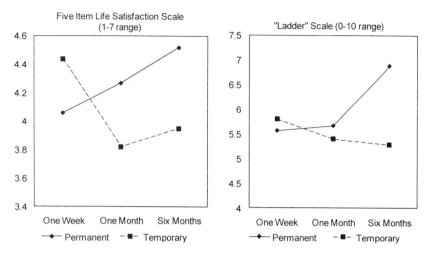

Fig. 2.3   Happiness over time: Permanent versus reversible colostomy

one measure, or remained at a roughly constant level of happiness according to the other.

Should physicians react to these results (assuming they were confirmed by additional research) by ceasing to perform potentially reversible colostomies? Obviously not. Not having a colostomy is better than having a colostomy—much better—even if those with permanent colostomies are no less happy.

The improvement in happiness of the permanent colostomy group is emblematic of a large body of research showing that people adapt to a wide range of conditions—including conditions that most people would classify as extremely adverse—and come to achieve close-to-normal levels of happiness. Yet, as Peter Ubel and I discuss in a paper devoted to the point (Loewenstein and Ubel 2008), there is widespread agreement, not only by the general public, but also by people who currently have these health conditions as well as people who had them in the past, that these health conditions are extremely undesirable—a distaste that is reflected in all of these groups' stated willingness to make various types of sacrifices (e.g., willingness to pay money or to risk a chance of death) to maintain or regain health. The research showing that people powerfully dislike health conditions that they fully adapt to poses a serious challenge to measures of welfare based on happiness.

Amartya Sen (1985, 1992) and Martha Nussbaum (2000) have proposed an approach to measuring welfare that is designed to avoid exactly this problem. Their "capabilities" approach was designed to deal with the problem that people may adapt to, and hence be content with, poor social and physical conditions or injustice, because they have experienced them for a prolonged period of time or have never experienced anything else. As Nussbaum (2000, 114) expresses it, aspirations for a better life can be squelched by "habit, fear, low expectations, and unjust background conditions that deform people's choices and even their wishes for their own lives." The capabilities approach delineates a series of central human capabilities, such as health, freedom from assault, political voice, property rights, equal employment, and access to education that are seen as central to welfare regardless of their connection to happiness. Several of these capabilities would be likely to be undermined by disability; hence the capabilities approach would view adverse health conditions as negative outcomes, even if those experiencing them displayed normal levels of happiness.

It is interesting to note that very few, if any, of the quality of life indicators used to rate, for example, the best city to live in or to visit, measure time use. Instead, consistent with the capabilities perspective, they tend to involve some kind of crude weighting of desiderata such as income, health, freedom, political stability, absence of crime, education, opportunities for advancement, culture, and so on.[7] And although different quality of life measures use somewhat different criteria, they tend to produce fairly similar rankings that, at least to my eye, often seem quite reasonable, given my experience with cities.

2.3   Other Problems with NTA

2.3.1   Does National Time Accounting Get the Accounting Right?

One of the most important empirical investigations of the U-index presented in Krueger et al. is a comparison of well-being among women in a French and American city (Rennes, France and Columbus, Ohio). A major difference between French and American life, salient to anyone with a passing familiarity with the two cultures, is that the French take much more vacation than Americans (twenty-one more vacation days, on average, according to Krueger et al.). Krueger et al. are concerned with this, since, as they relate, their empirical methodology severely undersamples vacation days. However, the authors reassure the reader that

> this is not a large bias. The twenty-one day difference in vacations amounts to only 5.8 percent of the year. If the U-index is 10 points lower on vacation days than nonvacation days, which is almost double the difference on weekdays and weekends, then the French U-index would be an additional 0.58 percentage points lower than the American U-index.

7. The UN Human Development Index (HDI) is a cross-national measure of well-being that, somewhat consistent with a capabilities approach, is based on normalized measures of life expectancy, literacy, education, standard of living, and GDP per capita. Among other applications, the index is used to measure the impact of economic policies on quality of life.

Although this "back of the envelope" calculation does provide reassurance that failing to monitor well-being during vacations is not a major problem, it highlights what I believe to be a more fundamental problem: national time accounting fails to properly account for time. Half of a percentage point is simply too small a marginal impact for an effect as large as a twenty-one day difference in vacation time.[8] (Note that in contrast, the impact of moving from being a student to a nonstudent is ten times as large, and the impact of moving from the worst day of the week [Monday] to the best [Sunday] is fourteen times as large.)

National time accounting assumes that the importance of an experience is exactly proportionate to the time spent on it. However, people do not account for time in such a fashion, and for good reason. Part of the reason has to do with the attributes previously discussed, such as meaning and values, which are only crudely related to time allocation. National Time Accounting also fails to properly account for the importance of peak experiences. Episodes of strong positive and negative affect tend to be rare in most lives (see Frederickson 2000). But, while rare, such episodes tend to be significant in terms of meaning. As Kahneman's own work on retrospective evaluation suggests, when people evaluated extended experiences, they tend to put disproportionate weight on moments of peak intensity. Kahneman views this tendency as a bias, but people themselves view it as natural. For example, people will evaluate a trip to the Grand Canyon as wonderful even if the vast majority of the time was spent on mundane, often uncomfortable, transportation—getting there, then returning home.

In fact the DRM implicitly succumbs to, and is in part rescued by, the tendency to encode experiences in terms of meaning. It divides the day into meaningful "episodes" (e.g., eating dinner, commuting to work, etc.) and then has people rate their affect during each episode. Dividing the day into such episodes reflects an implicit, if unintended, understanding that people make sense of their lives in terms of meaningful episodes and not in terms of raw numbers of minutes and hours spent in different ways. Moreover, it seems likely that what people are reporting for a particular episode is not their average affect during the episode, but some function of extremes and meaning. If, while biking to work, I get into an argument with a driver (as happens about every other week), I would evaluate the overall commute as negative, even if the altercation took place in the last few minutes of my commute and the remainder of the commute was quite pleasant. If one took

---

8. The problem of accounting for time would be even more serious if sleep were counted as part of the day. Currently, the denominator of the U-index does not include time spent sleeping (David Schkade, personal communication). On the one hand, this seems reasonable. If the denominator of the U-index included time spent sleeping, and one allows for an average of eight hours of sleep a day, then the .58 percentage point maximum impact of the twenty-one vacation days French-American difference would be reduced to an even more paltry .39 percentage point difference. If sleep were added to the denominator, everything other than sleep would matter even less.

time accounting seriously and did the same type of time-weighting within episodes that NTA does between episodes, it is likely that the same calculus that renders twenty-one days of additional vacation almost imperceptible would imply that such a commute was in fact a positive experience. In fact, if one really accounted for time the ways that NTA dictates, I suspect that almost everything that people care about would end up having an imperceptible impact on estimated welfare. Ironically, the validity of NTA is rescued to some extent by its failure to take its architects' own time-proportionate time accounting too seriously.

2.3.2   The Problem of Retrospection

While working on this commentary, I asked my jogging partner to report on his momentary affect. We jog together practically every day, so presumably this is an activity that we both find worthwhile. If asked to retrospectively evaluate how much we enjoy jogging, we would both rate it very highly. Indeed, when I asked him whether he was enjoying our jog *while we were jogging* his immediate response was affirmative. However, the reality of jogging is not that pleasant, and when we probed the issue more deeply he recognized that his momentary affect was really not all that positive— that he had actually been reporting his gestalt sense of the jog as meaningful, not his momentary feelings, which were quite negative. Although we usually start our jogs feeling comfortable, by the middle of the run we are almost inevitably exhausted and either too hot or too cold. And the truth is that we do not start out comfortable. I have a permanently torn hamstring that causes acute discomfort until the endorphins kick in, and my jogging partner suffers from mild asthma that is especially bad in the winter and the spring and when it is cold and when it is muggy—in short, most of the time. So why do we do it? Companionship? Health? Poor memory for pain? Probably all of these reasons and more. All I know is that I want to continue jogging with my friend, and am convinced that it is often the high point of my day, despite the misery. The Day Reconstruction Method would, in fact, reveal jogging to be a positive activity for me, but only because I would report the meaning of the activity rather than the "true" momentary affect.

Although I have no hard evidence to back the assertion, I suspect that child care is similar. Child care comes out as the second most positive activity according to the U-index, second only to socializing. Yet, again I suspect that this is because child care is meaningful and not because it is so conducive to positive emotions in the moment. Indeed, it is perhaps instructive that child care comes out *second worst* with the PATS data collection scheme. Child care comes out so inconsistently probably because the reality is not really all that wonderful most of the time but, as Krueger suggested to me in an e-mail, "no one wants to sound like they are a bad parent who doesn't enjoy being with their kids."

2.3.3   Loss of Information with the U-Index

By encoding an activity as either negative or positive, with no finer gradations, the U-index discards a lot of potentially useful information. The stated reason for throwing out all this seemingly valuable information, according to Krueger et al., is to allow for interpersonal comparability. Summing total happiness across people is not a meaningful task, but estimating the average percent of time that people are in negative affective states is, at least in theory, meaningful. However, this implies that the U-index is effective in distinguishing between affectively negative and positive experiences, which seems questionable to me, as suggested by my anecdote about jogging.

Also, the U-index would seem to depend substantially on what specific emotions are included in the list. The U-index requires people to assess the intensity of emotions in a fashion such that intensities can be compared with one another, but it is not clear how one should compare the intensity of "happy" and "stressed." If one is moderately happy and a bit more than moderately stressed, is that a net negative emotional state? Not to my thinking. And what if the word "happy" were replaced by "ecstatic"? As a result of this change in wording, almost certainly more events would be encoded as negative. Should the U-index depend on the implied intensity of the affective terms included in the list? Moreover, the current U-index list of six emotions includes two—"tired" and "interested"—that not only do not seem like emotions, but are not even unambiguously positive or negative.

In contrast to the coarse treatment of happiness, the U-index is very fine-grained in its treatment of time. If one takes a negative activity and makes it much more negative—for example, changing a 10 volt electric shock to a 110 volt shock, this will have no impact on the U-index, which simply encodes whether the experience is positive or negative. However, if one increases the duration of the shock by 10 percent, its contribution to the U-index will increase by 10 percent. This raises questions about the validity of decompositions presented in the chapter, such as the one that addresses the question of why older people are happier. According to this decomposition, 60 percent of the difference is due to time usage, but this conclusion seems dubious given the much greater sensitivity of the U-index to time use than to intensity of affect.

The insensitivity of the U-index to the intensity of affect is also problematic from a policy perspective. Many policies one could imagine implementing are likely to change the intensity of negative affect, but are unlikely to move people over the positive/negative line. Thus, for example, one might respond to the high U-index for adult care, not by attempting to reduce the time spent on it, but by attempting to provide assistance that would make giving such help less onerous. But, if such assistance raised negative affect from –9 to –3, this would have no impact on the U-index, whereas reducing the amount of time spent on adult care would have an impact exactly proportionate to the time reduction.

2.4   A Proposed Revision to NTA

The greatest strength of NTA, in my opinion, is that it evaluates well-being in terms of how people actually use their time. Although, as I have discussed, not all of well-being can be captured in such terms, how one uses time is clearly important; a life spent doing things one did not want to do is a life not worth living. The main limitation of NTA, in my opinion, is its focus on happiness, which elevates a particular hedonic feeling to an all-important role at the expense of a wide range of other things that matter, such as meaning, wisdom, and values. The specific implementation is also problematic because, as just discussed, it discards valuable information while not really achieving the interpersonal comparability that is the motivation for doing so.

There is no reason why NTA could not be improved by retaining its strengths while eliminating its weaknesses. Krueger, in an e-mail response to my verbal commentary at the meeting devoted to NTA, asked whether I thought that NTA could be improved by asking people to report whether a particular use of their time was "a waste of time." I think it would, dramatically. Moreover, the same idea could be approached more positively by asking whether a particular use of time was a "valuable use of time." These more general questions, I believe, come closer to measuring what makes life worthwhile than do questions that measure affect. Taking care of one's parent may not be enjoyable, nor climbing a mountain nor jogging with a friend. But if the individuals engaging in these activities report that they are worthwhile, I believe that those individuals' assessments of what matters to them should be accepted.[9] Although I don't think that such an index of whether people spend their time doing things that they want to do would be the best imaginable unitary measure of well-being, I do believe that such an index would do a better job of complementing GNP—of measuring important aspects of well-being that are not captured by GNP.

2.5   Conclusion

During the winter break of 2007, my family and I had been planning to fly to Los Angeles to go hiking in Joshua Tree National Park. However, we

9. Of course every method of elicitation has its problems, and these are almost always underestimated before one starts thinking deeply. For example, if someone makes a lot of money at a job they hate, should they respond that their work is worthwhile or a waste of time? If you are in the hospital to get needed treatment, is that worthwhile or a waste of time? Accounting is tricky, and accounting for happiness or meaning is especially so.

all felt exhausted by the prior semester and ended up staying home (and incidentally, conforming to the dictates of economic rationality by walking away from the sunk costs represented by our tickets). We had a very comfortable, relaxed holiday, catching up on sleep, friends, movies, and novels, and also work—including writing this commentary. During the entire period when we had been planning to be away, I felt happy and relieved that we had not gone to Los Angeles. I had images of changing planes, missing flight connections, looking for hotel rooms during a peak holiday season, realizing we were in the wilds without some critical piece of camping equipment, and so on. At some point, however, the irony hit me that, while I had devoted part of the vacation to writing a commentary critical of NTA, we had made exactly the choice that NTA, and particularly the U-index, would have favored—and were all very glad to have made it.

Was it the right choice? As friends returned from exotic destinations— Europe, a Caribbean cruise, Egypt—I did start to wonder. Though we had a wonderfully relaxed time, and they returned with exactly the types of horror stories the contemplation of which had helped to sustain my contentment with having stayed home, none of them regretted their decisions. In fact, I had the impression that several of them pitied us for having stayed put.

Did we make the right decision? Even if we were happier on average, I'm not sure. Moreover, I do know that if we made the same decision every time it would be a mistake, even if we spent more time in a state of happiness. Holding all else constant, it is generally better to be happy than to be unhappy. But happiness is only one of many things that make life worthwhile, and many of the other things, such as meaning, wisdom, values, and capabilities often come at the expense of happiness. Next time, I hope, we'll go hiking.

References

Cantril, H. 1967. *The pattern of human concerns.* New Brunswick, NJ: Rutgers University Press.

Clark, H. H., and E. V. Clark. 1977. *Psychology and language.* New York: Harcourt, Brace, Jovanovich.

Clark, H. H., and M. F. Schober. 1992. Asking questions and influencing answers. In *Questions about questions,* ed. J. M. Tanur, 15–48. New York: Russell Sage Foundation.

Diener, E., R. A. Emmons, R. Larsen, and S. Griffin. 1985. The satisfaction with life scale. *Journal of Personality Assessment* 49 (1): 71–75.

Frederickson, B. 2000. Extracting meaning from past affective experiences: The importance of peaks, ends, and specific emotions. *Cognition and Emotion* 14 (4): 577–606.

Grice, H. P. 1975. Logic and conversation. In *Syntax and semantics: Vol. 3. Speech acts,* ed. P. Cole and J. L. Morgan, 41–58. New York: Academic Press.

Huxley, A. 1932. *Brave new world.* New York: Harper and Row. (Perennial Library Edition, 1969.)

Karlsson, N., G. Loewenstein, and J. McCafferty. 2004. The economics of meaning. *Nordic Journal of Political Economy* 30 (1): 61–75.

Loewenstein, G. 1999. Because it is there: The challenge of mountaineering . . . for utility theory. *Kyklos* 52 (3): 315–44.

Loewenstein, G., and P. Ubel. 2008. Hedonic adaptation and the role of decision and experience utility in public policy. *Journal of Public Economics* 92 (8–9): 1795–1810.

Mill, J. S. 1871. *Utilitarianism, 4th ed.* London: Longmans, Green, Reader, and Dyer.

Nussbaum, M. 2000. *Women and human development: The capabilities approach.* Cambridge: Cambridge University Press.

Offner, A. 2006. The challenge of affluence: Self-control and well-being in the United States and Britain since 1950. Oxford: Oxford University Press.

Schwarz, N. 1999. Self-reports: How the questions shape the answers. *American Psychologist* 54 (2): 93–105.

Schwarz, N., F. Strack, and H. P. Mai. 1991. Assimilation and contrast effects in part-whole question sequences: A conversational logic analysis. *Public Opinion Quarterly* 55 (1): 3–23.

Scitovsky, T. 1976. *The joyless economy: The psychology of human satisfaction.* Oxford: Oxford University Press.

Sen, A. 1985. *Commodities and capabilities.* Amsterdam: North-Holland.

———. 1992. *Inequality reexamined.* Cambridge, MA: Harvard University Press.

Smith, D., G. Loewenstein, and P. Ubel. Forthcoming. Happily hopeless: Lack of adaptation to temporary versus permanent colostomy. *Health Psychology.*

3

Measuring National Well-Being

David M. Cutler

The chapter by Alan Krueger and colleagues (chapter 1, this volume) is an ambitious attempt to measure the well-being of the population. The chapter is nominally about how we spend our time, but it is really about how we live our lives. Are we better off than we used to be? That is the ultimate motivation for a set of time accounts.

There is much to discuss in the well-being chapter. I focus my comments on three areas.

The distinction between time accounting and well-being accounting
What is missing conceptually in the U-index
Possible answers to the puzzle of the United States and the French

3.1   Time Accounts and Well-Being Accounts

Krueger and colleagues place their analysis in the history of time accounting. But much of the genesis of their work is in the measurement of well-being. We care about what we do, after all, because we want to know what we get for our efforts. Market activity is only one measure of well-being; time allocation promises to open a window on the remainder.

I assume for my comments that our ultimate goal is to measure national well-being. I ask how well the U-index does in that regard.

A historical development shows some of the limitations. While Krueger and colleagues give many antecedents to their work, they miss one of the most important ones: Jeremy Bentham in the 1840s. Bentham is best known as the founder of utilitarian analysis. He also tried to quantify how

David M. Cutler is the Otto Eckstein Professor of Applied Economics at Harvard University and a research associate of the National Bureau of Economic Research.

happy people were. Bentham laid out his felicity calculus in *An Introduction to the Principles of Morals and Legislation,* published in 1823. In that work, Bentham delineated fourteen simple pleasures and twelve simple pains (complex pleasures and pains involved combinations of the simple pleasures and pains). The list of pleasures and pains is detailed in table 3.1.

There is clearly some overlap between Bentham's pleasures and pains and those in Krueger et al. Pleasures of the sense are (somewhat) captured in the Krueger et al. analysis. Pleasures of expectation, relief, and those dependent on association are also captured to some extent. But many of the pleasures and pains are missing. Pleasures of wealth, skill, amity, a good name, piety, and benevolence are generally missing, for example.

A bit of inspection suggests the difference. The U-index proposed by Krueger and colleagues is about the process of consuming goods, not about the enjoyment of the actual consumption. Thus, time spent preparing a meal counts as valuable or not, but the quality of the meal is not valued. Similarly, work is counted as a disamenity, but the goods that the work buys are not included on the good side of the ledger.

This distinction between process measures and existential measures is key to resolving one of the major puzzles highlighted by the Krueger et al. work: why do Americans spend so much of their time—nearly 20 percent—engaged in activities that they do not find pleasurable? Clearly, they do that so that they can afford other pleasures: better food and clothes, more gadgets, and so on. But those other pleasures are not counted as improving welfare. Thus, we appear more miserable than we are.

Existential happiness is not just about material goods consumption. Consider the example of a smoker who gives up smoking so that he can live a

Table 3.1   **Jeremy Bentham's simple pleasures and pains**

Simple pleasures	Simple pains
1. The pleasures of sense.	1. The pains of privation.
2. The pleasures of wealth.	2. The pains of the senses.
3. The pleasures of skill.	3. The pains of awkwardness.
4. The pleasures of amity.	4. The pains of enmity.
5. The pleasures of a good name.	5. The pains of an ill name.
6. The pleasures of power.	6. The pains of piety.
7. The pleasures of piety.	7. The pains of benevolence.
8. The pleasures of benevolence.	8. The pains of malevolence.
9. The pleasures of malevolence.	9. The pains of the memory.
10. The pleasures of memory.	10. The pains of the imagination.
11. The pleasures of imagination.	11. The pains of expectation.
12. The pleasures of expectation.	12. The pains dependent on association.
13. The pleasures dependent on association.	
14. The pleasures of relief.	

Source: Bentham (1823).

longer, healthier life. The loss of pleasure from the foregone cigarettes will show up in lower happiness for some period of time. But the psychic enjoyment that comes with knowing that one has done the right thing will not.

Krueger and colleagues limit their analysis to time allocation, because they want to avoid these existential valuations. But that strikes me as too limiting. The major problem that needs to be addressed is how to measure the well-being of the population. Time allocation is most useful if it can contribute to that analysis.

3.2   The Formation of the U-Index

Let me leave aside the conceptual issues about well-being and turn to the formation of the U-index. How shall we measure the amount of time a person spends doing unpleasant activities? The index that Krueger and colleagues propose is generally reasonable, but I have a few amendments to offer.

One issue is the treatment of the family. Krueger and colleagues consider the unit to be the individual. But the family might be more appropriate. Consider the example of a wife who goes to work so that her husband does not have to work as much. The disamenity of working will be noted on the wife's account. The husband will have fewer hours of unhappiness, but still some. It may be that reported unhappiness is the same (equal hours increase for her as a reduction for him). Or perhaps more hours are worked in total (if the wage of the wife is not high), leading to an increase in U. But because the family made the decision to maximize joint welfare, the family is happier overall.

A second major conceptual issue on which I would like to see more work is the separability of the utility function. Krueger and colleagues note that their index only makes sense if utility is independent across activities. If utility is interdependent, the authors cannot analyze each activity separately. At some ultimate level, separability cannot be true. Consider health. At very low levels of health—for example, death or near death—there is no utility from any other activity. Thus, utility cannot be independent. A less extreme case might be work. If people do not work and thus have extremely low income, the unpleasantness associated with most any activity will be high. What is pleasurable about leisure if one has no money at all?

One way that Krueger and colleagues might examine this is by relating overall satisfaction to happiness in different domains, and interactions of domain-specific happiness. If the interactions are significantly related to overall health, that would suggest possible nonlinearities to examine.

I do not have the Krueger et al. data to do this, but I do have some information that can be brought to bear on this. Danny Blanchflower kindly made available to me data from the General Social Survey (GSS) from 1972 through 2006. In many years, the GSS asked people an overall level of happiness (not too happy, pretty happy, and very happy), and questions about their satisfaction with different aspects of their life: family, friends, health, job, and financial. Satisfaction is coded on a 1 to 7 basis: none; a little; some; a fair amount; quite a bit; a great deal; and a very great deal. I sample adults in all years who are asked overall happiness and the five domains of satisfaction. The sample is 19,029 people.

The first column of table 3.2 relates overall happiness to satisfaction in each of the five domains. Because happiness is an ordered variable with three responses, I use an ordered probit regression. To control for time trends, I also include year dummy variables (not reported). Satisfaction in each domain of life is associated with greater happiness. The largest coefficient is for financial satisfaction; job and family satisfaction are next, and health and friend satisfaction are least important.

The second column of the table includes those five satisfaction variables and two-way interactions between each of them—ten in total. While the standard errors on each interaction are large, the χ-squared test rejects the null hypothesis that the interaction coefficients are all insignificant. Most of the interaction terms are positive; being more satisfied in one domain increases the impact of satisfaction in other domains on overall well-being. To the extent there is a hierarchy, satisfaction with family and friends is most basic. People who are not satisfied with family and friends find that satisfaction in other areas of life translates little into overall happiness.

There are clearly significant issues associated with the interpretation of happiness measures, which I do not discuss. Rather, I want to use take from these results that happiness in different domains is unlikely to be independent, and thus that unhappiness with time allocation is unlikely to be independent of what else a person is doing. Using the rich data in the surveys that Krueger and all collect, they could do a detailed analysis of how overall time allocation affects well-being.

3.3 Cross-Country Comparisons

I address the third part of my comments to the most interesting substantive finding in the Krueger et al. work—the fact that the French are so much happier than Americans. The reason for this is not hard to divine: the French work less than Americans. But why do Americans work so much? American workers are just as productive as French workers; thus, we could be as happy as the French are, by working less and enjoying leisure more. Why do we not do this?

One possibility is that Krueger et al. are wrong—we are not less happy than the French. It is true that the French spend less time at work, but our additional income buys us more material goods: bigger houses, more food, flat screen TVs, and the like. Since consumption values are not well captured by the index, it appears we are less happy, when in fact we are not.

Table 3.2   **Explaining overall happiness**

	(1)	(2)
Satisfaction with		
Family	.201	.124
	(.007)	(.073)
Friends	.105	−.084
	(.008)	(.079)
Health	.125	.016
	(.007)	(.067)
Job	.264	.064
	(.011)	(.099)
Financial	.337	.059
	(.012)	(.109)
Interactions between satisfaction		
Family and friends	—	.008
		(.005)
Family and health	—	.008
		(.005)
Family and job	—	.002
		(.009)
Family and financial	—	−.004
		(.010)
Friends and health	—	.008
		(.005)
Friends and job	—	.002
		(.009)
Friends and financial	—	.015
		(.011)
Health and job	—	−.001
		(.008)
Health and financial	—	.004
		(.009)
Job and financial	—	.031
		(.015)
N	19,029	19,029
ln(Likelihood)	−15,396.929	−15,381.947

Notes: Ordered probit model for "not too happy," "pretty happy," "happy." All regressions contain year dummy variables. Dashes indicate that the variable was not included in the regression model.

There is no perfect way to test this. One type of test is to see whether revealed preference is at all useful in predicting what people do. The most basic test of revealed preference is that people who like work less should work fewer hours. If this is true, it suggests that people are optimizing, and perhaps there is some truth in this explanation. If people who dislike work more work the same or additional hours, it suggest that people are in a suboptimal time allocation.

One possible reason for this is my second theory about the continental differences in happiness: we think we know what will make us happy, but we are continually wrong. In this theory, Americans are led to believe that working long and hard is good, because it allows us money to live in the suburbs and raise our families. What we forget to take into account, though, is that living in the suburbs involves long commutes, and working more means more interaction with the boss. Something else is needed to close this theory; we do learn, after all, that work is stressful and commutes are unpleasant. But one could imagine a situation where people are deluded for a period of time, and thus we are less happy than people in other countries.

A final theory is that leisure is complementary across people, and thus that no single American could be happy if they chose the French lifestyle. Vacation might be more fun because everyone is on vacation; when others are at work, relaxation may be difficult.

The types of regressions I suggested previously might be used to test this. In particular, it suggests that work might be more satisfying when one has many close friends who work, or when friends and family work many hours. Krueger or others might test this.

3.4   Conclusion

Alan Krueger and colleagues have written a chapter designed to provoke. It certainly does that. I hope they will continue on the path, to pull together the well-being of the U.S. population. To do that, however, the analysis will need to expand beyond what we do and get into the issue of how well we like the results. The data and conceptual needs involved could be quite substantial.

References

Bentham, J. 1823. *An introduction to the principles of morals and legislation.* London: W. Pickering.
National Opinion Research Center (NORC). 1972–2006. *General social survey.* The University of Chicago. Available at: http://www.norc.org/GSS+Website/.

4

National Time Accounting and National Economic Accounting

J. Steven Landefeld and Shaunda Villones

The National Time Accounts (NTAs) are a major step forward in the measurement of well-being. Since the inception of national economic accounting, it has been recognized that using Gross Domestic Product (GDP) per capita was an incomplete measure of social welfare. Over time there have been numerous proposals for developing a broader measure, but the basic data and concepts needed were not available to produce a comprehensive, consistent, objective, and useful measure of well-being. Recent developments in the form of official time-use data and advances in concepts and methods in economics and psychology have made the National Time-Use Accounts possible, as presented in Chapter 1 of this volume by Krueger, Kahneman, Schkade, Schwarz, and Stone (henceforth, KKSSS). This chapter compares the NTAs to the U.S. national economic accounts—the National Income and Products Accounts (NIPAs). It first examines the NTAs in terms of the basic characteristics of the NIPAs and then in terms of how the NTAs might be used in conjunction with the NIPAs.

4.1 National Economic Accounts

The U.S. National Economic Accounts were developed to address both a gap in measurement and a related policy need. Prior to the national accounts, there was only fragmentary and sometimes duplicative data on the state of the economy. As a result, Presidents Hoover, Roosevelt, and their advisers had no comprehensive information on the state of the economy and were left to develop economic policy during the Great Depression with

J. Steven Landefeld is the director of the Bureau of Economic Analysis, U.S. Department of Commerce. Shaunda Villones is an economist at the Bureau of Economic Analysis.

such business indicators as building contracts, manufacturing production, sales of 10-cent chains, industrial and railroad stock price indexes, and rail car shipments.[1]

In response to this critical gap in data, the Department of Commerce worked with Simon Kuznets of the National Bureau of Economic Research to develop a comprehensive and consistent measure of economic activity based on national income in the aggregate and by industry (Kuznets 1934). These national income accounts were delivered to the Congress in 1935 and were used by President Roosevelt in his State of the Union address in January of 1936. Wartime planning needs led to the extension of the accounts to a measure of production in the aggregate and by type of spending. These national product accounts were introduced in 1942 and immediately used in war and then postwar planning activities. Over time, the National Income and Product Accounts expanded in response to business and policymakers' needs to a rich set of integrated national, international, regional, and industry accounts.

National economic accounts are one of the most successful analytical measures used in the United States and around the world. The national accounts, in combination with better informed policies and institutions, have contributed to a reduction in the severity of business cycles and a postwar era of strong economic growth. This success and the tendency for policymakers to use GDP per capita as a shorthand measure of improvements in standards of living and welfare have also been one of the sources of calls for a broader measure of welfare than GDP.

Therefore, it is instructive to look at the characteristics of the NIPAs and use those characteristics to examine the NTAs to see how they measure up and might be used by policymakers and the public.

4.1.1 Comprehensiveness

The first characteristic of the NIPAs is that they are a comprehensive measure of all economic activity. The total not only gives a picture of the overall economy, but because it is built up as an unduplicated total from its components, it is possible to examine the effects of a policy change or economic event on the total as well as to trace through its effects on the various parts of the economy.

The NIPAs provide an unduplicated count by measuring GDP in one of three ways. The first is GDP, which is measured by final spending on each type of good or service. By measuring only final sales, GDP avoids the double-counting that would occur if one not only counted the sales of bread to consumers by retailers, but also the sales of bread by bakers to retailers,

---

1. See, for example, the *Survey of Current Business,* May 1930, p. 2, "Monthly Business Indicators."

the sales of flour by millers to bakers, and the sale of wheat by farmers to millers. The second is gross domestic income (GDI), which is measured by the incomes earned in the form of wages and salaries, rents, interest, and profits, which is equal to GDP. The third measure is value-added by industry, which is measured by taking the gross sales of each industry and subtracting intermediate inputs (goods and services purchased from other industries for further processing), which yields value-added. Value-added is by definition equal to both GDI and GDP.

4.1.2   Market Valuation and Aggregation

The various transactions in the National accounts are valued using market values. These market values provide consistent weights for aggregating expenditures across types of expenditures, incomes, and industries. The use of market values avoids the use of explicit subjective or implicit weights used in other indexes. Market valuation provides comparability across components, and when combined with deflators, (and purchasing power parity measures) comparability over time and across countries. Market-based accounts are useful in scorekeeping and analysis of events and programs with multiple effects across industries, commodities, incomes, regions, and countries (United Nations et al., 2003). They can be used in comparisons of impacts of differing programs.

Real inflation-adjusted estimates are based on well-developed index number literature. Data based on market prices also have the advantage of coming from business records, thereby avoiding many of the problems of recall and bias present in household surveys.

The sum of final sales in the economy can also be regarded as a cardinal measure of economic activity valued at market prices. If consumers allocate their consumption so that the marginal utility of the last dollar spent on each product is equal, the prices will represent consumers' relative valuation of goods and services. Weitzman (1976) has shown that under certain conditions, maximizing net domestic product (GDP less depreciation) will maximize welfare. (Net domestic product is sometimes described as the amount of production necessary to maintain consumption while putting aside a sufficient amount to replace the capital stock used up in production.)

4.1.3   Double-(or Triple) Entry Accounting

The national accounts are a double-entry set of accounts, with final expenditures equaling incomes earned in production (which is also equal to value-added by each industry). These double-entry accounts are useful for statistical purposes, as inconsistencies present in individual series are apparent in reconciling each of the three aggregates. As a former Commerce Under Secretary described it, the national accounts are the "mineshaft canary" for the U.S. statistical system.

The double-entry accounts are also used as a set of supply and use tables. These tables are useful in tracing effects of tax changes and other economic events and across the three measures of economic activity.

4.1.3 Timeliness and Relevance

To be useful for public and private decision makers, the accounts have to provide timely information on the state of the economy and accurately measure the changing U.S. economy. Frequent updating of the accounts is necessary for accurately depicting trends and providing useful estimates for decision makers.

Fortunately, the NIPAs have always used data collected for other purposes. These data, combined with the double-entry structure of the NIPAs, allow for relatively low cost and accurate estimates extrapolated from benchmark data.

The advanced GDP estimates (the early estimates for a quarter) are intended to present an accurate general picture of economic activity: is the economy expanding or contracting; is growth high or low relative to trend; is growth accelerating or decelerating; what are the main components contributing to growth; and what are the trends in the main components such as saving and investment or government? The early estimates are revised as more accurate data become available, but the general picture—as defined by these characteristics—is little changed. In a sense, the early GDP estimates are more like an ordinal than cardinal measure.

One of the most important functions of the NIPAs is providing the rigor of a comprehensive and consistent framework for evaluating the overall impact of alternative policies and economic events.

4.2   Why National Economic Accounts Are Not a Measure of Welfare

All these attributes notwithstanding, there are significant limitations to their use as a broad measure of welfare. As Kuznets (1934) noted in introducing the first set of accounts in the 1930s, the prices used to value and aggregate to GDP are based on the existing distribution of income. The prices also do not reflect the impact of both positive and negative externalities. And many near-market inputs to production are excluded, as outlined in the National Academies reports, *Nature's Numbers* (Nordhaus 1999) and *Beyond the Market* (Abraham and Mackie 2005). The NIPAs exclude: natural resources and environmental inputs; investments in human capital and health; household production; and investments in R&D and other intangibles.

More broadly, many determinants of utility are not included. As Nordhaus and Tobin (1972) pointed out, measuring "Net Economic Welfare" involves a wide range of activities beyond the marketed transactions included in GDP. Subsequent efforts have focused on "adjusting" GDP to reflect the costs imposed by economic growth, such as the depletion of natural resources, the costs of pollution, or the costs of crime, and adding the value of household production.

4.3   National Economic Accounts: Nonmarket Production Accounts

Efforts to broaden the scope of the NIPAs have focused on near-market production activities in satellite accounts, or supplementary accounts. For example, Landefeld and McCulla (2000) developed household production accounts that are a combination of market and nonmarket inputs (utilizing ATUS data) to produce output and are valued at market value or proxy for market value. They are a double-entry set of accounts, and include detailed input-output tables for household production.

Household production or environmental accounts provide a more complete picture of sources of growth. For example, the increasing labor force participation resulted in a larger increase in measured economic growth than overall production, including household production. Household production accounts provide a more comprehensive picture of the determinants of demand for goods and services (the trade off between market versus nonmarket). They also highlight the shift from market to nonmarket production over the course of the business cycle.

Such accounts are useful for a number of scorekeeping, analytical, and policy activities. Examples include analyses of the sources of growth and the business cycle; the impact of tax incentives, changes in prices, relative wages, the provision of child care, and investments in health.

The difficulty with these expanded satellite accounts for household production, the environment, and other items omitted from conventional accounts is that they really do not address the core issue, exemplified by Robert Kennedy's eloquent critique of GNP: "It measures everything in short, except that what makes life worthwhile . . . beauty, integrity, wit, strength, courage, joy, wisdom, learning, compassion, and devotion."[2]

4.4   How NTAs Compare to NEAs

Like the NIPAs, the National Time Accounts clearly address a long-standing measurement gap. Kuznets (1934) warned of the misuses of the economic accounts in the analysis of welfare and urged that the market-based accounts be expanded to account for the "disamenities of modern life" and the use of "natural resources."

The problem has been in developing a comprehensive, consistent, and objective index that goes beyond GDP to a broad-based measure of welfare.

2. To access a transcript of the speech, go to: http://www.jfklibrary.org/Historical+Resources/Archives/Reference+Desk/.

The subjectivity and uncertainty inherent in broader measures of welfare developed in the 1970s and 1980s resulted in such efforts being abandoned. The Bureau of Economic Analysis' experience with environmental accounting in the 1990s also suggest that political decision makers are skeptical of quantitative measures for nonmarket phenomena based on imputed market prices.[3]

The lack of acceptance for broader measures of welfare also may relate to the urgency of the need for welfare accounts. Unlike the demand for national economic accounts created by the depression and World War II, the policy need for, and applicability of, NTAs estimates may be perceived as longer-term and less pressing. However, the need for an accepted measurement framework and a clearer definition of the need for such statistics underlines the importance of building professional and public support for the NTAs.

4.4.1   Comprehensiveness

Like the NIPAs, which are a comprehensive measure of market activity and its components, the NTAs are designed as a comprehensive measure of total utility and its parts. It covers all activities over the waking hours of the day. It is designed to cover the range of utility emotions from "happy" to "unhappy" with a broad variety of emotions. The NTAs present an unduplicated count of activities and associated emotions that allow analysis of how the parts affect the total U (unhappiness) index.

However, focusing on the U-index rather than the "net affect" of the full range of emotions may limit the perceived and actual usefulness of the NTAs. It might be useful to feature both the overall "net affect" and U-index. The net effect might be thought of as analogous to GDP and the U-index as analogous to the poverty, with both providing an important perspective on social welfare.

Use of both the net affect and the U-index help to provide a more comprehensive measure of happiness, but it is not clear how utility that does not quite fit into the episode-based happiness-unhappiness index is covered. In particular, how are meritorious—rather than hedonic, or happiness—measures on Kennedy's list captured by the NTAs? One would imagine, for example, that beauty, wit, and joy are captured by the NTAs, but it is less clear how integrity, courage, wisdom, learning, compassion, and devotion are captured. Given the sacrifices and effort involved in attaining an education, fighting a battle, or caring for a parent with Alzheimer's, many of these experiences that we value as life experiences may indeed be scored as unhappy—tired, stressed, sad, or painful—by respondents in the episode-based happiness index.

It is also unclear how external factors, such as a war or an economic down-

---

3. For more information on BEA's experience in environmental accounting see the *Survey of Current Business,* April 1994, p. 33.

turn, are reflected in the episode-based index. Do they affect each episode's happiness equally, or are they unaffected by such events?

All of these factors may help to explain the source of the differences between subjective and episode-based measures. The higher rating of the value of child care and work by the subjective "Juster" index relative to the "DRM" index may reflect the inclusion of the value of meritorious emotions captured by the subjective "Juster" index, but not the episode-based "DRM" index. During the episode, when your child is screaming in your ear, and/or you are changing their diaper, your score of that experience at that moment is likely to be more negative than positive. Whereas, in reflection, your subjective evaluation of your experience in caring for your children is one of the most satisfying you experience.

This difference in what the subjective and episode-based indexes illustrate may simply indicate that they are measuring different things, rather than that one or the other is wrong. Or that consumer behavior—ranging from the large investments households make in child care or luxury cars relative to their relatively low episodic rating of the value of time spent with their children or commuting in their luxury cars—is irrational. As Krueger et al. note, the NTAs—like the NIPAs—are a subset of a broader measure of utility.

4.4.2 Valuation and Aggregation

By using individuals' own evaluations of activities during specific blocks of time and aggregating using those blocks of time, the NTAs avoid the long-standing problem of many well-being indicators that put a subjective value, or weight, on the various indicators used to develop an index of well-being. The Genuine Progress Indicator, an often cited index in the 1990s, determined that time children spent watching TV was a negative event and was subtracted as a subjective negative value associated with that time from an adjusted GDP estimate.[4]

In two respects, the NTAs differ from the NIPAs. The first relates to what time aggregation implies about extreme emotions. With valuation and aggregation using prices, there is lots of room to express different valuations of different goods and services. The NTAs, on the other hand, are limited to just a few emotions that are equally weighted based on the time elapsed during each period in the time-use diary, including happy, neutral (interested), and unhappy (tired, stress, sad, pain). The ordinal ranking of the NTAs and time aggregation do not seem to adequately distinguish the sadness, for example, that one feels from watching a tearjerker and the emotions one feels on hearing about the loss of a spouse in the 9-11 terrorist attack. Such events

---

4. The latest report (2007) and more information on the Genuine Progress Indicator is available from Redefining Progress Org.: http://www.rprogress.org/publications/2007/GPI%202006 .pdf.

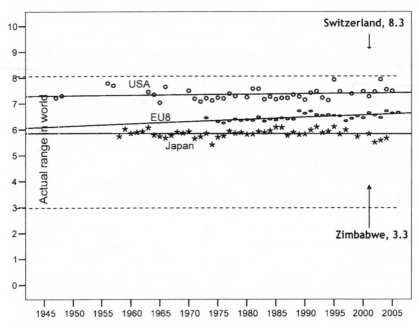

Fig. 4.1   Trend happiness in the EU8, United States, and Japan
Source: (Veenhoven 2007).

are simply off the chart. Now, the NIPAs do not adequately distinguish such strong "disutility" but through insurance and other means, life-saving health expenditures or the replacement of houses and personal property are at least given a heavy weight.

The second issue relates to what time aggregations of happiness/unhappiness imply about comparisons over time. Real GDP and GDP per capita show changes over the course of business cycles and growth over time in standards of living as measured by GDP. However, as KKSSS point out in their chapter, individuals are able to adapt to a wide range of circumstances. Existing evidence from cross-section, cross-country, and time series measures suggest a lot of adaptation toward some common level of happiness/well-being. (See fig. 4.1.)

This lack of variation over time may inhibit their usefulness for analytical purposes. However, it may be that this lack of variability is the result of using subjective, "Juster-like," measures of well-being and that time-series data using the DRM method will show more variation over time.

4.4.3   Double-Entry Accounting

Although the NTAs are not a double-entry accounting system one can imagine them being combined with a set of household production accounts to produce a set of input-output accounts. These tables could use the household production accounts to record the supply of goods, services, and time that are inputs into the production of happiness by activity. The NTAs could be used to measure the "output" of these activities. Such input-output accounts could be used for the analysis of economic changes that affect happiness or by changes in tax incentives, regulations, or investments in infrastructure (child care).

One of the most intriguing aspects of the NTAs would be the possibility of integrating them, along with the American Time Use Survey (ATUS) and the Consumer Expenditure Survey (CES). The ATUS and the CES both are drawn from the same household survey (a follow-up survey from the Census Bureau's Current Population Survey). Such integration would be a major advance in analysis of consumer demand and economic policy (health care, etc.). Adding time inputs and relative satisfaction to estimates of consumer spending would significantly expand understanding of the determinants of consumer behavior.

4.4.4 Timeliness and Relevance

If the U-index or net affect indexes change slowly, then the NTAs probably do not need to be constructed or released in as timely a manner as the NIPAs. As noted previously, constructed average happiness indexes shows very little change over time (see fig. 4.2). However, the changes over time in the constructed U-index presented in the Krueger et al. chapter (table 1.18) suggest that there may be more variation using the DRM method. The changes in the constructed U-index over time only reflect changes in the composition of time use over time. If the evaluation of episodes of

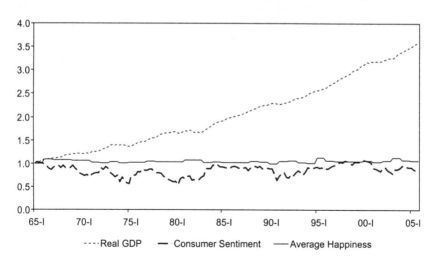

Fig. 4.2 GDP and other welfare indexes over time
Sources: BEA, University of Michigan, Veenhoven (2007), World Database of Happiness, Distributional Findings in Nations.

time spent in different activities also changes over time, the DRM-based U-indexes and net affect may show more variation over time than the subjective measures.

Even if the U-index moves relatively slowly, it might be useful to construct "snapshots" for major events like downturns, war, and elections. Although the NTAs are relatively expensive to construct, users would be particularly interested in any information that the U-index could supply in answering the election year question: "are you better off today than you were eight years ago?"

The U-index will undoubtedly be endlessly fascinating for scorekeeping, but if the index is relatively stable over shorter periods of time—with limited response to key events—its uses for public policy or in forming public opinions may be limited. The usefulness of the NTAs might be expanded if a hybrid model of satisfaction could be prepared and presented to the public. This hybrid could present both an overall measure of subjective well-being and evaluated time-use measure by activity. Also, as previously suggested, the NTAs could be combined with existing and expanded national accounts and other data series.

However, like the NIPAs, one of the most important aspects of the NTAs will be their framework. They are a carefully constructed set of estimates based on people's use of their time and their own evaluations of the time spent in different activities. As demonstrated by KKSSS, the NTAs are a conceptual framework built on a large body of economic and psychological research and the resulting estimates are robust across different samples and countries. Armed with this framework, analysts and policymakers can examine how different events and policies may affect the nation's overall well-being as well as the individual components affecting that overall well-being.

References

Abraham, K. G., and C. Mackie, eds. 2005. *Beyond the market: Designing nonmarket accounts for the United States.* Washington, DC: The National Academies Press.

Kuznets, S. 1934. National Income 1929–1932. Senate Document no. 124, 73rd Congress, 2nd Session. Washington, DC: Government Printing Office.

Landefeld, J. S., and S. H. McCulla. 2000. Accounting for nonmarket household production within a national accounts framework. *Review of Income and Wealth* 46 (3): 289–307.

Nordhaus, W. D. 1999. *Nature's numbers: Expanding the national economic accounts to include the environment.* Washington DC: National Academy Press.

Nordhaus, W. D., and J. Tobin. 1972. Is growth obsolete? In *Economic research: Retrospect and Prospect vol. 5: Economic growth,* ed. W. D. Nordhaus and J. Tobin, 1–80. New York: Columbia University Press.

United Nations, Commission of the European Communities, International Monetary Fund, Organization for Economic Cooperation and Development, and World Bank. 1993. *System of national accounts 1993,* Series F, no. 2, rev. 4. New York: United Nations.

Veenhoven, R. 2007. Measures of gross happiness. Paper presented at the OECD conference on measurability and policy relevance of happiness. 2–3 April, Rome, Italy.

Weitzman, M. L. 1976. On the welfare significance of national product in a dynamic economy. *Quarterly Journal of Economics* 90 (1): 156–62.

Measuring Real Income with Leisure and Household Production

William Nordhaus

5.1 Different Approaches to Evaluating Time Use

5.1.1 The Central Role of Time in Augmented Accounting

Our economic accounts center primarily on market transactions. But much of economic activity, and in all likelihood much of economic welfare, depends upon activities outside of the marketplace. Moreover, although we do not yet have economic accounts that incorporate the use of time, it is plausible that the economic value of time is the most important single nonmarket input, and perhaps also nonmarket output.

I will consider three issues relating to the use of time in this chapter. First, how might we integrate time into our economic accounts? Second, are attempts to use hedonic psychology likely to be a fruitful way of valuing time in our economic accounts? Third, do measures of emotions have the property of "interpersonal cardinality" that is required to construct quantitative social indicators?

To begin with, it is worth reflecting on the importance of time use for nonmarket economic activity. Nonmarket activity consists of activities like education, recreation and other uses of leisure time, babysitting, home production of laundry and similar services, and work-related activities like commuting. The inputs into these activities consist of nonmarket and market labor, capital services, and material inputs. By far the largest inputs for nonmarket activity are labor (time). Indeed, virtually the entire value added of the nonmarket sectors comes from time inputs, while most of the nontime inputs are purchased in the market economy.

William Nordhaus is the Sterling Professor of Economics at Yale University, and a research associate of the National Bureau of Economic Research.

Consider the cost of home production (such as doing the laundry). The total value of such activities consists of the value of purchased market inputs (soap, washing machines, electricity, and the like) plus the value of the time spent in the activities. For example, doing the family laundry might have a total cost of $21, of which $20 (one hour × $20 per hour) is the value of the time, while one dollar is the cost of the soap and washing-machine services. Virtually all the nonmarket inputs are likely to be time.

The same story holds for virtually every nonmarket activity: the major nonmarket input is labor. The one important exception might be the inputs of nonmarket environmental capital (clean air, clean water, public beaches) that enter into recreation and health activities. These examples suggest that measuring and valuing time use may be the most important single component of nonmarket accounts.

Up to recently, the United States had been particularly laggard with respect to generating comprehensive and periodic time-use statistics. Fortunately, beginning in 2003, the Bureau of Labor Statistics (BLS) began the collection of a large time-use survey for the United States (the American Time Use Survey, or ATUS).[1] In the latest survey year, 2006, this survey interviewed 13,000 households annually from the out-rotating panel of the Current Population Survey. It is currently the only time-use survey in the world to be conducted on a continuous basis. The ATUS will be an important addition to the U.S. statistical system and a crucial ingredient in the future construction of augmented accounts. In addition, there are now harmonized historical data on time use, such as the American Heritage Time Use Study (AHTUS).[2] The time of time-use studies has arrived.

5.1.2   Two Approaches to Quantitative Indicators on Time Use

In developing quantitative social indicators to integrate time use, we can consider two fundamentally different approaches. The first approach would be to use the methodology of national economic accounting. This approach, which has been considered in the literature on augmented and nonmarket accounts, would add the consumption and production of time to the accounts. To implement this strategy, we would need to develop a set of prices or values to weight the time consumptions, after which time could be added to apples and pears using the standard methodology of economic accounts. As I will indicate in the first part of this chapter, while this approach would conform to standards of national economic accounting, the data requirements are both theoretically and practically far beyond what is currently available.

A second approach, which has developed along a parallel track with an entirely different approach to valuation, is in the spirit of emotions re-

---

1. A review of the BLS time-use survey is available at http://www.bls.gov/tus/.
2. The Web page containing a description is available at http://www.timeuse.org/ahtus/.

search. This would include overall measures of emotions, such as happiness and misery; it might also attach emotions to particular activities, such as unemployment or the time spent watching television. This approach was pioneered by F. Thomas Juster and is followed in the study by Alan B. Krueger et al. (hereafter KKSSS).[3] This strategy uses a completely different approach to measuring the values associated with time uses—one based on surveys or other psychometric measurements. The second part of this chapter addresses the potential for use of hedonic psychology and emotions research in constructing quantitative social indicators.

5.2 Time Accounts Using the Approach of National Economic Accounting

This section examines the incorporation of time use into the standard national economic accounts. It derives equilibrium conditions for consumer behavior with market and nonmarket consumption, along with process or intrinsic values of time in different activities. (Process values and intrinsic values are terms that are used to represent the preference value of the time itself rather than the things produced by time.) Using a standard index-number approach, we show that a full set of accounts has data requirements that are far beyond those that are currently or prospectively available, with problems particularly arising for the valuation of time and for measuring technological change for nonmarket consumption and use of time. However, in a simplified case, we show that the growth of real income can be approximated by a weighted average of productivity growth rates in market and nonmarket productivity and that the valuation of hours drops out of the formula. We examine the case of a representative consumer. Further difficult issues, such as aggregation of diverse individuals or households, are discussed briefly.

5.2.1 Consumer Preferences and Equilibrium Conditions

I begin with a standard analysis of how consumers allocate their time and choose consumption. For this purpose, I assume that preferences are time separable and examine the *ith* consumer deciding at time *t*. The consumer can choose to work in the market and buy market goods, to work at home and produce home goods, and to use time to enjoy leisure or nonwork activities. In general, we separate time used in home production from leisure by the definition that the time used in home production can be substituted for the time of others (such as washing dishes), while the activities in leisure cannot be produced by others (such as playing golf).

We begin with the determinants of consumer choice as represented by a standard ordinal preference function. (I call this a preference function instead of a utility function to reserve the latter for the psychological hedo-

3. See Juster (1985) and Krueger et al. (chapter 1 of this volume).

nics that follow.) The variable W is an ordinal index that represents more preferred combinations of bundles as higher values, while U is a standard preference function for individual i at time t.

$$(1) \qquad W_{i,t} = U(c_{i,t}^m, c_{i,t}^{nm}, B_{i,t}^m, h_{i,t}^m, B_{i,t}^{nm}, h_{i,t}^{nm}, B_{i,t}^l, h_{i,t}^l),$$

where $c_{i,t}^m$ = market consumption, $c_{i,t}^{nm}$ = home consumption, $h_{i,t}^m$ = market hours, $h_{i,t}^{nm}$ = home work hours, $h_{i,t}^l$ = leisure and nonwork time, $B_{i,t}^m$ = technological change in market time, $B_{i,t}^{nm}$ = technological change in nonmarket time, and $B_{i,t}^l$ = technological change in leisure.

This formulation is unusual in the literature on time use in specifically incorporating a process value or intrinsic value of time. It is also novel in allowing for the possibility of technological change that makes time spent more or less pleasant. This specification recognizes that leisure time is generally an input into a technology that produces the desired experience. For example, listening to music involves not only time but also complementary inputs such as equipment, space, background noise, and performance quality. Some time may be experienced as unpleasant (such as in dental surgery), but these are nowhere as unpleasant as surgery before anesthetics. Some examples would be the development of technologies that make work more pleasant (such as ventilation or air conditioning of factories), that make home work more pleasant (such as dishwashers), and that make leisure more pleasant (such as improved television sets). The point is that technologies can make nonmarket time more productive (e.g., by using machines rather than washing by hand), but technologies can also make the experiences themselves more preferred. Of course, as in the case of air travel or airline food, time spent can also become more unpleasant.

Note that the preference function in equation (1) is not separable over activities. Most work on estimating the process value of time, going back to Juster and continuing with KKSSS, assumes that the preference function is to be separable across different time uses.[4] This assumption has been viewed as inappropriate and incompatible with empirical evidence in preference theory for many decades and is especially objectionable for time use (we discuss this point further next).[5]

The consumer has three constraints: an income constraint relating to market consumption, a home production function relating to home work and home consumption, and a time budget. The analysis uses a skeletal model that strips away inessential elements. The first constraint is that market consumption equals a fixed element (fringe benefits plus property income plus net transfers) plus market hours multiplied by the marginal wage:

$$(2) \qquad c_{i,t}^m = I_{i,t} + w_{i,t}^m h_{i,t}^m.$$

4. Ibid.
5. See Stigler (1950).

We simplify the analysis by assuming that there are no lump-sum elements and that marginal compensation is proportional to the average productivity of market labor for that individual, $w_{i,t}^m = A_{i,t}^m$, so:

$$(3) \qquad\qquad c_{i,t}^m = A_{i,t}^m h_{i,t}^m.$$

Home production is given by the home production function:

$$(4) \qquad\qquad c_{i,t}^{nm} = A_{i,t}^{nm} h_{i,t}^{nm},$$

where $A_{i,t}^{nm}$ is the productivity per hour worked of home production.

Finally, we have the time budget constraint:

$$(5) \qquad\qquad \overline{h}_{i,t} = h_{i,t}^m + h_{i,t}^{nm} + h_{i,t}^l.$$

Total time is $\overline{h}_{i,t}$.

We assume that preferences and resources are intertemporally separable. This assumption is purely for expositional convenience and does not change the measurements or analysis. Maximizing the preference function subject to the budget constraints yields the following two first-order conditions. In the balance of this discussion, we suppress the i subscript where it is unnecessary.

$$(6) \qquad\qquad \frac{\partial U}{\partial h_t^m} = w_t + B_t^m \pi_{3,t} - B_t^l \pi_{5,t} = 0.$$

$$(7) \qquad\qquad \frac{\partial U}{\partial h_t^{nm}} = \pi_{2,t} A_t^{nm} + B_t^{nm} \pi_{4,t} - B_t^l \pi_{5,t} = 0.$$

For notational convenience, $\pi_{k,t} = U_{k,t}/U_{1,t}$ is the marginal rate of substitution between the kth argument of the preference function in equation (1) and market consumption; $U_{k,t} = \partial U/\partial x_k$ is the derivative of U with respect to the kth elements; and the marginal rates of substitution are time dated to recognize that the marginal preferences change over time.

Equation (6) states that the marginal preference value of leisure should equal the net value of an hour in the market in producing goods. Equation (7) states that the marginal preference value of leisure should equal the net value of an hour of home work in producing home goods.

These conditions differ from standard practice in one major respect: each equilibrium condition recognizes that there may be process or intrinsic values of time in different activities (market work and home work) and that these values therefore need to be netted out in the calculation. Most analyses of time use assume that the marginal preference value of work is equal in the market and at home and further assume a homogeneous output. From these assumptions, we get the standard condition that the productivity of home production equals the marginal post-tax wage. There are also many unobservable variables in this approach, which will come back to haunt us when we attempt to construct an empirical measure reflecting the underlying preference function.

5.2.2   Measuring Real Income with Apples, Pears, and Hours

We now consider the question of how to measure real income when we include the consumption of time along with the consumption of goods and services—we want to add apples, pears, and hours, so to speak. In developing an index in the absence of complete data, the equilibrium conditions are necessary for developing the theory.[6]

In this section, we are interested in devising a measure of real income that is the analog of real income in the theory of income and prices. The concept underlying the approach is Becker's concept of whole income.[7] We begin by transforming the preference function in equation (1) into an index of real whole income for individual i at time t:

$$(8) \qquad R_t = R(c_t^m, c_t^{nm}, B_t^m h_t^m, B_t^{nm} h_t^{nm}, B_t^l h_t^l).$$

The function R is an ordinal transformation of U such that, along the equilibrium path, R is locally homothetic. This implies that the rate of growth of real income is measured as:

$$(9) \qquad g(R_t) = s(c_t^m)g(c_t^m) + s(c_t^{nm})g(c_t^{nm}) + s(h_t^m)g(B_t^m h_t^m)$$
$$+ s(h_t^{nm})g(B_t^{nm} h_t^{nm}) + s(h_t^l)g(B_t^l h_t^l).$$

In this equation, $g(\cdot)$ is the proportional rate of growth of the element, and $s(\cdot)$ is the elasticity of the real income function with respect to that element. In a market context, the elasticities are the expenditure shares of each element in whole income using the market or preference prices of each element. The expenditure shares are defined as $s(x_{k,t}) = \pi_{k,t} x_{k,t} / \sum_{k=1}^{5} \pi_{k,t} x_{k,t}$. In this expression, $x_{k,t}$ is the kth element; $\pi_{k,t} = R_{k,t}/R_{1,t} = U_{k,t}/U_{1,t}$ is the marginal rate of substitution between item k and market consumption; item k represents the kth element in the preference or real-income function; and subscripts $k = 1$ through $k = 5$ represent market consumption, nonmarket consumption, market time, nonmarket time, and leisure time.

Note that for globally homothetic U functions, R is uniquely defined. Moreover, this procedure assumes that U is a smooth function. If the U function is not globally homothetic, R will depend upon the path of consumption and prices. This property is shared with all superlative indices.

There are different alternatives to aggregating indices over individual consumers to construct a social index. The usual index, following Robert Pollak, uses the approach of the plutocratic index in which each (real) dollar

---

6. The approach utilized here follows the standard approach to the development of indices of real income and expenditures. See, for example, Diewert (1987).

7. See Becker (1965).

is equally weighted.[8] This then yields a growth rate in the total or national index that is simply the sum of the individual indices, where the individual indices are weighted by each individual's share of total consumption. We will omit this step for brevity, and because it adds nothing important in the current context.

5.2.3 The Fundamental Measurement Problem

Our theory now collides with a fundamental measurement difficulty. Our measure of the growth of real whole income requires measures of both the items in the preference function as well as the marginal preference values. Only one of these, market consumption, has comprehensive measures, although we now have reasonably complete measures of hours for the United States since 2003. We have no reasonably accurate measures of home consumption. Furthermore, we have no measures at all of the marginal rates of substitution between time and market consumption (the $\pi_{k,t}$). And we have no measures of any of the technological variables outside the marketplace (the B_t^k). In other words, any attempt to measure whole income is doomed to fail for lack of critical data.

5.2.4 A Simplified Measure of Income Growth

We can develop a substitute for the ideal growth index with some further assumptions. First, we assume that there is no technological change in the technology of time use. In other words, the $B_t^k = 1$ for all k. Second, we assume that it is possible to measure the productivity of nonmarket work. We denote variables with dots over them as time derivatives, then rewrite equation (9) as:

$$(10) \qquad \dot{R} = \dot{c}_t^m + \pi_{cnm,t}\,\dot{c}_t^{nm} + \pi_{hm,t}\dot{h}_t^m + \pi_{hnm,t}\dot{h}_t^{nm} + \pi_{hl,t}\,\dot{h}_t^l.$$

We take the time derivatives of equations (3) and (4), obtaining:

$$(11) \qquad \dot{c}_t^m = \dot{w}_t h_t^m + w_t \dot{h}_t^m,$$

$$(12) \qquad \dot{c}_t^{nm} = \dot{A}_t^{nm} h_t^{nm} + A_t^{nm}\dot{h}_t^{nm}.$$

Substituting these into equation (10) yields

$$(13) \qquad \dot{R}_t = \dot{w}_t h_t^m + \pi_{cnm,t}\dot{A}_t^{nm}h_t^{nm} + \Psi_t,$$

where

$$\Psi_t = \dot{h}_t^m(w_t^m + \pi_{hm,t}) + \dot{h}_t^{nm}(\pi_{cnm,t}\,A_t^{nm} + \pi_{hnm,t}) + \pi_{hl,t}\,\dot{h}_t^l.$$

---

8. The concepts are discussed in Pollak (1998).

From the first-order conditions in equations (6) and (7) and the time budget constraint in equation (4), we have $\Psi_t = 0$, which reduces the expression in equation (13) to

(14)
$$\dot{R}_t = \dot{w}_t h_t^m + \pi_{cnm,t} \dot{A}_t^{nm} h_t^{nm}.$$

We then make one further simplification. We take the shares in equation (9) to be the shares of whole consumption rather than whole income, where whole consumption is equal to market plus nonmarket consumption. Substituting from equation (4) that the growth in market income is $\dot{w}_t^m / w_t^m = \dot{A}_t^m / A_t^m$, this implies that the growth in real income is:

(15)
$$g(R_t) = \dot{R}_t / R_t = g(A_t^m)\sigma(c_t^m) + g(A_t^{nm})\sigma(c_t^{nm}),$$

where $g(A_t^m)$ and $g(A_t^{nm})$ are the rates of productivity growth in the market and the nonmarket consumption sectors, and the weights are the shares of the two items in whole consumption, $\sigma(c_t^m) = c_t^m / (c_t^m + \pi_t^{nm} c_t^{nm})$ and $\sigma(c_t^{nm}) = \pi_t^{nm} c_t^{nm} / (c_t^m + \pi_t^{nm} c_t^{nm})$.

We can get a slightly more intuitive result if we simplify further. Assume that the marginal preference value of market work is equal to the marginal preference value of home work and that the marginal product of home work is equal to the marginal compensation of market work. These assumptions imply that the weights in equation (15) are proportional to h^m and h_t^{nm} which yields:

(16)
$$g(R_t) = g(A_t^m)\left(\frac{h_t^m}{h_t^m + h_t^{nm}}\right) + g(A_t^{nm})\left(\frac{h_t^{nm}}{h_t^m + h_t^{nm}}\right).$$

Equations (15) and (16) are the fundamental results. The simpler expression in equation (16) states that the growth in real income is equal to the weighted growth of market and home productivity, where the weights are the relative importance of market time and home work time. This is completely intuitive in emphasizing that the productivity of nonmarket time is a key ingredient in economic welfare. The important and nonintuitive result in equations (15) and (16) is that the valuation of hours can be eliminated from the equation for the growth of real income. Only the growth rates of productivity in the two consumption sectors and their shares enter into the growth equation.

The correct growth rate would be slightly different if we made different assumptions about differences in marginal preference values or relative productivities of home production, but equation (16) provides the basic intuition. Note that the only difference between equation (15) and equation (16) is the relative size of the weights.

The results depend upon strong assumptions, however. They require not only that the consumer equilibrium conditions in equations (6) and (7) hold, but also that there is no technological change in the enjoyment of time. While we might worry that these are unrealistic, it is hard to imagine any series of measurements that could shed much light on these issues.

How much does the growth in real income given in equation (16) differ from conventional measures? According to the ATUS, time devoted to market and nonmarket work were approximately the same from 2003 to 2006 (3.5 hours per day for market work versus 3.8 hours per day for nonmarket work). This indicates that the welfare significance of productivity growth in nonmarket work is of the same order of importance as productivity growth in market work. We have virtually no serious research on the relative importance of market productivity growth as compared to home productivity growth, so the relative importance of the two terms in the welfare equation (16) is currently unknown.

5.2.5 Graphical Approach

We can show the results graphically as follows. To derive the graphical results, we simplify by assuming that the preference function is additively separable, so

(17) $W_t = U_{cm}(c_t^m) + U_{cnm}(c_t^{nm}) + U_{hm}(h_t^m) + U_{hnm}(h_t^{nm}) + U_{hl}(h_t^l).$

The U functions in equation (17) are separable preference functions for each of the time elements in equation (1) (note that this is a simplification and should not be used in practice). We define the net marginal preference value of an hour of market work, home work, and leisure, respectively, as

$$N(h^m) = U_{cm}'(c_t^m)w_t + U_{hm}'(h_t^m),$$

$$N(h^{nm}) = U_{cnm}'(c_t^{nm})A_t + U_{hnm}'(h_t^{nm}),$$

$$MU(h^l) = U_{hl}'(h_t^l).$$

The equilibrium conditions are then

(18) $N(h^m) = N(h^{nm}) = MU(h^l).$

Figure 5.1 shows a Jevons stick diagram for the allocation of time using separable utility and only two activities, market work and leisure. The downward sloping line shows the net marginal preference value of market work, while the upward sloping line shows the marginal preference value of leisure, with leisure measured leftward from the right axis. At the equilibrium, E, the net marginal preference value of market work is equalized to the marginal preference value of leisure time, with market work being the segment WE and leisure time being the segment EZ.

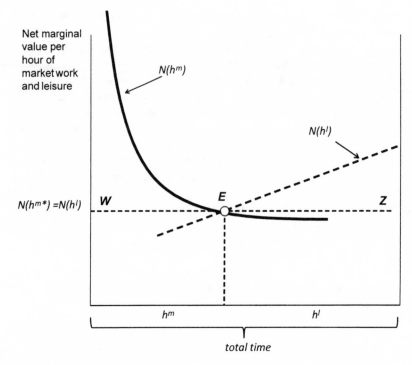

Fig. 5.1   Time-use equilibrium

5.3   Valuation Using Direct Measurement via Hedonic Psychology

5.3.1   What Are We Attempting to Measure?

The first part of this analysis examined the development of quantitative valuation of time use using the standard approach of national economic accounting and determined that the standard account appears to have excessively demanding requirements for valuation. We now examine the potential of the techniques of emotions research and hedonic psychology to value time in different activities and to develop quantitative social indicators.

Before discussing different approaches, we begin with some definitions of different kinds of variables. Most functions in standard preference theory in economics are *individually ordinal*. This indicates that these functions can be transformed by a monotonic function and yield the same observable outcomes. In some economic applications, such as behavior toward risk, functions are *individually cardinal*. This indicates that the variable or function is unique up to a linear monotonic transformation for each person. Both are *individual* in the sense that there is no method by which levels can be compared across different individuals.

To serve as a quantitative social indicator, a function or variable must have a cardinal scale that is meaningfully defined across individuals. I will call this characteristic *interpersonally cardinal*. This means that the variable must have a uniquely defined zero and a well-defined unit of increment and that there must be a method to compare the values across individuals. This implies that the zero and the increment must be stable across time, people, and countries.[9] Consumption is an interpersonally cardinal variable because my personal consumption expenditures can be added to yours, as long as we respect the convention of using the same prices and commodities; consumption has a natural zero and a natural unit of increment, and these are comparable across individuals. Interpersonal cardinality has much tighter constraints than personal cardinality, which in turn is stricter than ordinality.[10]

The development of quantitative social indicators using measures of emotions—such as happiness using hedonic psychology—could take three potential paths. We can think of these as proceeding from least demanding to most demanding of the data and analytical constructs.

A first approach, which is the spirit of the macrohappiness studies, including the development of the U-index by KKSSS, has been to develop measures of the instantaneous or average flow of emotions such as happiness, pain, and the like. These are analogous to estimates of global mean temperature. They are measurements that are not attached to particular causes or activities. A significant body of research is devoted to this strategy, as is summarized by Kahneman, Diener, and Schwartz in their overview of a compendium of studies in their edited volume, *Well-Being*.[11]

> We are particularly hopeful that a scientific understanding of hedonic experience will allow for the development of valid hedonic indicators that reflect the pleasantness of life in the everyday experiences of people. . . . To this end, we propose that nations should begin monitoring

9. This point can be illustrated with a simple example. Assume that we are interested in comparing the happiness of two groups, calculated as the average happiness of each group. (a) Under an ordinal measure, there is no meaningful way of taking averages of indices that simply provide greater than or less than rankings. We might make Pareto rankings, as is done in welfare economics, but these would continue to be ordinal measures. (b) Assume that the happiness scales are individually cardinal but not interpersonally cardinal across groups. The happiness measures of group A are (1, 7) for an average of 4, while those of group B are (2, 4) for an average of 3. Under the original scaling, group A is happier than group B. By individual cardinality, we can add, say, 5 to each value in group B and maintain all observable functions of the variable. After the rescaling, group B is happier than group A. (c) Finally, assume that the scale is interpersonally cardinal and can be transformed only by a common scale variable, k. Then the average value for A is always $k4$, which is always greater than group B's $k3$.

10. These definitions from economics differ from those used in other areas. In psychology, a cardinal scale is referred to as an interval scale. What is called interpersonally cardinal in this chapter is referred to as ratio measurement in psychology. The terminology in psychology originated with Stevens (1946). The related theory of measurement has, over the last half-century, sparked a fierce controversy in psychology with virtually no counterpart in economics.

11. See Kahneman, Diener, and Schwartz (1999, xi).

pleasure and pain through on-line experience recording among samples of respondents to complement existing social indicators, and to provide a more direct assessment of the final outcome about which people are most concerned.

The second approach attempts to attribute emotions to particular causes or activities. This is analogous to saying that global warming is due to the accumulation of greenhouse gases. This brand of emotions research associates well-being with attributes or activities such as inflation, unemployment, or per capita income. The KKSSS study, like the work of Thomas Juster and John Robinson before it, attempts to associate emotions with particular time-use activities. For example, the U-index of KKSSS relates to whether the maximum of the negative emotions exceeds the maximum of the positive emotions. The following discussion points to several difficulties that arise in attribution; for example, the studies assume separability of time values over time and activities.

The third approach, which imbeds the analysis in the framework of national economic accounts developed in the first part of this chapter, would aim to estimate the value of time as compared with other components of economic activity. The accounting framework values the time using the marginal rates of substitution or marginal values of time. This approach might be devoted to measuring the growth of whole income in equation (9). This method is the most demanding of the three because it requires estimating marginal valuations of time relative to other economic activities such as consumption of goods and services. It is possible that the psychometric approach could estimate the marginal rates of substitution, but this approach has not been pursued, partly because of lack of interest and partly because of lack of data.

5.3.2   Some Difficulties with the Hedonic Approach

Most of the measures developed in the three approaches previously described assume that the magnitudes are interpersonally cardinal. Economists have come to regard cardinal measures of utility with suspicion. As Paul Samuelson summarized:[12]

> With ever fewer exceptions, modern economic theorists believe that . . . everything of interest and relevance in [the nonstochastic theory of consumer preference] can be expressed in purely *ordinal* terms.

I review several issues that arise in the application of hedonic measurements in the construction of quantitative indicators, both generally and specifically as applied to time use. The fundamental problem can be easily summarized. Most measures in emotions research can best be described as ordinal, and few or none would seem to be interpersonally cardinal in the

---

12. See Samuelson (1952, 137).

sense previously defined. Statistical operations (such as averages over space or time) on ordinal variables are not invariant to monotonic transformations of the variables. Therefore, we will get different answers depending upon the scaling of our measures. This implies that these variables are not useful as quantitative social indicators.

Difficulties in Measuring Marginal Values

The first issue arises when we attempt to put valuations on time in the context of utility analysis or preference analysis. What are we attempting to measure with our indices of emotion or happiness? Are we trying to test whether the equilibrium conditions for utility maximization are met? Or, are we attempting to estimate the total or the average of the emotional values for each activity? (The total is the area under the different marginal value curves and above some zero level of time in figure 5.1).

We begin with the question of using hedonic measures to measure the equilibrium values of time, such as those that are needed for equations (5) and (6). (It should be emphasized that this has not been the objective of much of the psychometric literature.) This approach would be necessary to value the impact of policies or shocks that shift time use among different activities. The problem, as shown in figure 5.2, is that it is difficult to ensure that we are capturing equilibrium valuations in a slice-of-time sampling methodology. The value of a time slice will be given by the point on the net marginal value curves where the time slice is taken. We show four different slices: *A* and *B* are ones where market work is sampled, while *C* is one where leisure is sampled, and *E* is an hour that is just at the indifference point.

Even in the situation where we have perfectly resolved the issues of how to measure process value—we have the perfect hedonimeter—we are almost certain to capture above-equilibrium slices of time. It is very unlikely that we would get a slice at exactly point *E*, which is the point at which the values of the marginal hours are equalized. While many studies do not attempt to measure the equilibrium value, these measures are the standard approach for evaluating policies or shocks that reallocate hours among different uses for individuals who are making purposive use of their time.

The Zero Problem for Total Utility

Many studies of happiness are concerned with measuring total or average value or utility from different uses of time. Attempting to measure total utility falls into the conceptual morass called the zero problem.[13] Suppose that we want to measure the total consumer surplus of water consumption in the national accounts. We then need to integrate the marginal surpluses between some zero level and current consumption. But what do we mean by zero? Is it literally zero water consumption (in which case consumer surplus is equal

13. See Nordhaus (2006).

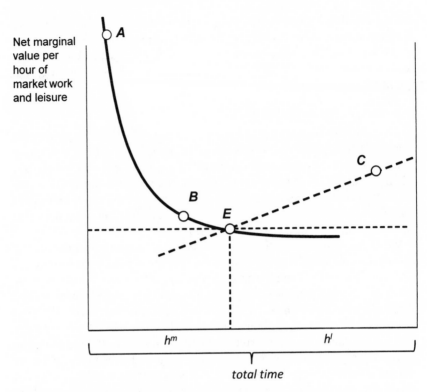

Net marginal value per hour of market work and leisure

A

B

C

E

h^m h^l

total time

Fig. 5.2   Valuation with the time-slice methodology

to the value of life itself)? Or is it the level of consumption in preindustrial times? If the latter, should preindustrial times relate to the 1700s, when water in the United States was plentiful; or to the time when humans first crossed the Bering land bridge, when ice was plentiful but water was scarce? In time-use studies, should we consider the surplus of time spent breathing? If so, would this include the first minute as well as the marginal minute? If we attempt to measure total surpluses for necessities in too many areas with low zeroes, we will undoubtedly find ourselves with multiple infinities of the value of time.

Difficulties Due to Nonstorability of Time

While some studies of happiness and time use might limit themselves to pure measurement, virtually every study goes on to attribute well-being to particular activities or other determinants. The KKSSS study, for example, associates the U-index with different time-use activities.

The next set of issues revolves around the difficulties of attributing time to particular time-use activities because of an oversimplified set of assumptions. One concern revolves around the fact that time is a nonstorable commodity. In the previous analytical section, we assumed that time could be allocated to different activities without regard to the time of day, week, or year. In reality, time is a heterogeneous commodity rather than a homogeneous lump that can be allocated continuously over tasks. For example, I have an implicit contract with Yale University that I will teach intermediate macroeconomics from 11:35 AM to 12:50 PM on a particular day. There is an important seminar going on at the same time, but I cannot both teach in one place and be in the seminar room at the same time. Some activities can be shifted over time, so that I can record *News Hour* on my DVR and move it over time. But I cannot move my time over time.

If we consider time as a nonstorable commodity, we would need to estimate the time-use stick diagrams for each slice of time. In this respect, time is like electricity, which also cannot be cheaply stored. We see wide variations in hourly electricity prices, and there is no reason why time prices should not vary greatly as well. For individuals facing rigid schedules (for work, school, meetings, and so forth), we could easily find that marginal valuations are all over the map, depending on the extent of time crunch or time glut.

Treatment of nonstorable time will lead to substantial complications in the analysis. The activities need to be represented with the appropriate time-stamped constraints. For example, work must start at 8:30 AM, and commuting must take place in the time just prior to the start of work. Peak times will have a higher shadow price. This implies that any activity that is observed during peak times must have a high valuation. By contrast, off-peak times will have a low valuation. We may see that something—like watching TV—occurs in off-peak times and conclude that this is a low-value activity, whereas the truth is that it is simply occurring in off-peak periods.

Difficulties Due to Simultaneous Uses of Time

A similar difficulty in attributing well-being to activities arises because time is very often devoted to multiple purposes. We frequently encounter people talking on their cell phone while walking; these are clearly two distinct and inseparable activities—communicating while traveling. We might be listening to the radio while driving to work. These are not isolated examples—simultaneous time use is pervasive.

Since little time-use research to date has been economic in its orientation, little attention has been given to the problem of joint production in time use. We can introduce simultaneous activities easily in the analytical apparatus of section 5.2. Assume that there is no technological change in time use and that there are n different kinds of simultaneously enjoyed leisure time. Denote $\pi_{5,k,t}$ as the marginal preference value of the kth component of leisure time, where $\pi_{5,1,t}$ is the marginal preference value of the primary activity (perhaps measured by hedonic psychologists). The equilibrium condition in equation (6) for the simultaneous time uses becomes:

$$(19) \qquad w_t + \pi_{3,t} = \pi_{5,1,t} + \sum_{k=2}^{n} \pi_{5,k,t}.$$

This shows that if we identify only a single activity (activity $k = 1$), we might misestimate the marginal value of the hour. The general supposition is that we exclude many valuable nonmarket time-use activities, which would lead to biased estimates of the value of nonmarket time.

Difficulties Arising from Nonseparability of Hedonic Values

A final issue relating to separability—which can be thought of as the general case involving time separability and activity separability—is that the emotional effects of experiences have deep and potentially unfathomable patterns of substitution and complementarity. So here again, attempting to attribute emotions to particular activities may prove impossible.

For example, when we observe someone who reports "eating and drinking," the reported pleasures and pains are likely to depend upon the context and history, as well as companions and quality of the food. The following summary by Rozin provides a cautionary note on the difficulties of attaching experiential values to different activities:[14]

- Sensory pleasure (especially culinary and sexual) is extremely context dependent.
- Most sensory pleasure is experienced in the remembered or anticipated domains, as opposed to the on-line (experienced) domain.
- Combinations of sensory pleasures do not obey any simple, hedonic algebra. It is not clear what we would even want to say about the pleasure of listening to Beethoven while eating our favorite food (and having a massage).
- There is a large effect of experience on sensory pleasure. Hedonic shifts and reversals are common.

Note in particular the difficulty of defining the pleasure of simultaneous activities such as eating and listening to music.

This finding is critical to the interpretation of time-use data. As previously noted, most studies examining the value of time, including the KKSSS study, rely centrally on the assumption of separability of the preference function for different time uses. This assumption is clearly unwarranted on the basis of empirical studies of the psychology of sensory experiences. While additive utility was standard in the early years of the development of demand theory, it was Edgeworth—an early proponent of psychometric studies—who "destroyed this pleasant simplicity and specificity" when he wrote the general nonseparable utility function that we used in equation (1) and that is now common currency in economics.[15]

---

14. See Rozin (1999).
15. The quotation is from Stigler (1950, 322).

It will be useful to recall why additive utility functions fell out of favor in economics. To begin with, they were seen to be an unnecessary restriction. Moreover, on careful examination, we see complements and substitutes everywhere—such as left shoes and right shoes for the former, or beef and chicken for the latter. Addictions are examples of strong intertemporal complementarities that are well established in economics and psychology. People are often embarrassed about eating alone in a restaurant, while Robert Putnam has classified the activity of bowling alone as symptomatic of the decline of social capital. While understanding dependences over time, space, and activities is a challenging task for time-use research, measuring these relationships will be necessary for the accurate attribution of emotions to particular activities.

5.3.3   The Lack of Interpersonal Cardinality

The ambitious program of hedonic psychology is to construct measures of pain and pleasure to complement existing quantitative social indicators. Can an index of happiness (or misery, or more generally of emotions) be constructed that would be a meaningful social indicator? Is this even theoretically possible? I think not.[16]

The basic difficulty is that measures of emotions are conceptually individually ordinal, while interpersonal cardinality is needed to qualify as a meaningful quantitative social indicator. Assume for purposes of discussion that we have developed a perfect hedonimeter based on brain scanning, and further that we have accurate techniques to map how brain images correspond to reported pain, pleasure, sadness, sweetness, or other features of reported emotions. Perhaps we can even calibrate the level of pain or frustration that would make me frown or grind my teeth. Would it make any sense to add these together or to average these emotions?

It makes no sense to use such measures of emotions as quantitative social indicators because they are not interpersonally cardinal. We point to three difficulties in existing approaches.[17] To begin with, it seems unlikely that we can define a condition that would represent an unambiguous zero or neutral emotional state (other than being dead, which is not appealing in this context). Because emotions are so contingent, the zero point will vary with mood, circumstances, genetics, context, history, and culture. Therefore, there is unlikely to be a natural zero point for happiness, misery, pain, or other emotions.

Secondly, it is difficult to conceive of a natural unit of increment for emo-

16. I do not discuss here whether such measures would be worthwhile social indicators, whether this view of human aspirations is too impoverished to be interesting, or the many paradoxes that arise in its interpretation. These issues have been widely debated in philosophical discussions of utilitarianism, such as in Sen and Williams (1982).

17. The discussion that follows is hardly original with the present author. It goes back at least to Isaiah Berlin, "Utilitarianism" [1937?].

tions that would apply across people. We cannot say how the incremental pleasure that Sam experiences in eating a "delicious" cheeseburger compares with the incremental pain that Helen experiences when she has a "bad" headache.[18] Therefore, it is difficult to see how the increment of emotions can be calibrated across different individuals.

Third, many if not all measures of emotions do not have the characteristic of cardinality; rather, they are ordinal in the sense that a state is identified as being "more painful" or "happier." These are ordinal measures because any numerical index that we construct based on the reported emotions can be stretched by a monotonic transformation and provide the same information. Can we really say that Sam's second cheeseburger makes him twice as happy as the first, rather than four times as happy or log(2) times as happy? Moreover, they are likely to be individually ordinal in the sense that we can stretch Sam's cardinal emotion scale arbitrarily relative to Helen's. Since the individual-reported emotions can be each mathematically stretched or transformed and maintain the property of more pleasant or less pleasant, the increment and level of any aggregate index will be arbitrary depending upon what individual transformations are applied. This implies that we cannot generally construct either aggregate indices of emotions over individuals or even indices of emotions over time of the same individual in a way that meaningfully represents the changes of individuals.

An example will illustrate the point. Constructing an index of aggregate pain or pleasure is similar to creating an aggregate index of the blueness of the Danube River. I do not doubt that in some ideal world we can make measurements of the spatially averaged wavelength of the light coming off the water. We might be able to measure the physiological responses to particular wavelengths of light in different people. Moreover, we could potentially correlate these physiological responses with how people describe their experience: whether the river is "blue" or "deep blue," or even so pleasurable as to inspire a song about "the beautiful blue Danube." However, it would make no sense to construct a national index of "Blueness of the Danube River" that involved adding up how individuals on a particular day report the experience of looking at the Danube River. Nor would it make sense to have an index of "Blueness" that would go up or down from day to day depending upon unemployment, inflation, or per capita income. Neither blue rivers nor blue moods constitute a meaningful index of emotions because they are not based on interpersonally cardinal variables.

The force of these criticisms will differ depending upon the exact details of the index that is created. The most problematical indices are ones that attempt to attribute differences in happiness over time and people to par-

---

18. The proponents of hedonic psychology are sensitive to this issue and make a case for a natural zero point. The psychological evidence against a universal neutral point is reasonably compelling, however. For example, whether a blue light is perceived as blue or green or neither blue nor green will depend upon what the person saw just before the blue light.

ticular causes. These would appear to suffer from many of the criticisms discussed here.

The U-index of KKSSS would appear to avoid the difficulties of some happiness indices by its creation of an ordinal index. But, their procedure simply pushes the difficulty into the background. To illustrate their procedure, we can simplify by assuming that we measure a pain subindex, P, and a happiness subindex, H. Then construct a net misery index, M, which equals one if $P > H$ and equals zero if $H > P$. While this looks ordinal, it actually makes very strong assumptions about the subindices. This approach is equivalent to assuming that there are interpersonally cardinal subindices in an underlying preference function, $U(P,H)$. The subindices assume interpersonal cardinality in the sense that the zeros must be the equivalent for each subindex (that is, $U[0,H] = U[P,0]$ for all P and H), and that the utility increments must be equal for each numerical increment for each emotion (i.e., $\partial U/\partial H = \partial U/\partial P$ for every point of the function where $P = U$). Even with these strong assumptions, there is no reason to assume that the U-indices would be interpersonally comparable, either across persons or over time for individuals.

We leave the last word to the philosopher who launched the utilitarian revolution, Jeremy Bentham. He expressed his own reservations about utility measurement as follows:[19]

> 'Tis in vain to speak of adding quantities which after the addition will continue to be as distinct as they were before; one man's happiness will never be another man's happiness; a gain of one man is no gain to another; you may as well pretend to add 20 apples to 20 pears, which after you had done that could not be 40 of anything but 20 of each just as there was before.

References

Becker, G. S. 1965. A theory of the allocation of time. *The Economic Journal* 75 (299): 493–517.

Berlin, I. [1937?]. Utilitarianism. Available at http://berlin.wolf.ox.ac.uk/lists/nachlass/index.htm.

Diewert, W. E. 1987. Index numbers. In *The new Palgrave: A dictionary of economics,* vol. 2, ed. J. Eatwell, M. Milgate, and P. Newman, 767–80. London: Macmillan.

Juster, F. T. 1985. Preferences for work and leisure. In *Time, goods, and well-being,* ed. F. T. Juster and F. P. Stafford, 333–51. Ann Arbor: University of Michigan.

Kahneman, D., E. Diener, and N. Schwartz. 1999. Preface to *Well-being: The foundations of hedonic psychology,* ed. D. Kahneman, E. Diener, and N. Schwartz. New York: Russell Sage Foundation.

Nordhaus, W. 2006. Principles of national accounting for nonmarket accounts. In

19. Quoted in Stigler (1950, 309–10).

A new architecture for the U.S. national accounts, ed. D. W. Jorgenson, J. S. Landefeld, and W. D. Nordhaus, 143–60. Chicago: University of Chicago Press.

Pollak, R. A. 1998. The Consumer Price Index: A research agenda and three proposals. *The Journal of Economic Perspectives* 12 (1): 69–78.

Rozin, P. 1999. Preadaptation and the puzzles and properties of pleasure. In *Wellbeing: The foundations of hedonic psychology,* ed. D. Kahneman, E. Diener, and N. Schwartz, 129. New York: Russell Sage Foundation.

Samuelson, P. A. 1952. Probability, utility, and the independence axiom. *Econometrica* 20 (4): 670–78.

Sen, A., and B. Williams, eds. 1982. *Utilitarianism and beyond.* Cambridge: Cambridge University Press.

Stevens, S. S. 1946. On the theory of scales of measurement. *Science* 103 (2684): 677–80.

Stigler, G. 1950. The development of utility theory: I. *The Journal of Political Economy* 58 (4): 307–27.

6

Well-Being Measurement
and Public Policy

Richard Layard

Chapter 1 of this volume represents an excellent use of time by its five authors. It is a high point in an important program that has provided major insights into what people enjoy and do not enjoy in their daily lives. Equally important, intensive study of the experience of daily living provides an important way of assessing the *overall* quality of an individual's life. This method of overall assessment can provide a valuable addition to the answers to the global questions now routinely asked about life satisfaction and happiness.

My comments will focus mainly on this latter issue and will be concerned only with the ways in which well-being data can best contribute to public policy debate. I shall begin by questioning whether the U-index is the best way to represent the overall quality of a day lived. I shall then discuss how far data on enjoyment in different activities can contribute to policy debate. Finally, I shall report on some parallel developments in Britain.

6.1 The U-Index and Public Policy

6.1.1 Public Policy Usefulness

A major reason for much social science is to illuminate the public debate. It is not, of course, the only reason, but in the end much of social science gets used in policy debate. Given this, it is best to set up the inquiry so that its findings are as explicitly helpful for policymaking as possible.

Among economists, the standard approach to public policy is to think of social welfare (W) as an additive aggregate of individual happiness, H_i,

Richard Layard is the director of the Well-Being Programme in the Centre for Economic Performance, London School of Economics.

perhaps with diminishing marginal social welfare attaching to increments of individual happiness:[1]

$$W = \sum_i f(H_i) \qquad (f' > 0, f'' \le 0),$$

where H_i is an empirically measurable value, but $f(\ )$ reflects the ethical perspective of whoever uses these data in public debate. There are two extreme versions of the $f(\ )$ function. In the Benthamite version, we just add up everyone's happiness:

$$W = \sum_i H_i,$$

and in the Rawlsian version, we just look at the happiness of the least happy person:

$$W = \underset{i}{\text{Maximin}}\ (H_i).$$

If we want to compare two situations, corresponding, for example, to two different policies, we examine the sign of the change in welfare, given by:

$$(1) \qquad \Delta W = \sum_i \frac{\partial f}{\partial H_i} \cdot \Delta H_i.$$

Clearly this involves comparing the magnitude of the changes in happiness experienced by different people.[2] So, we must be able to measure happiness in a cardinal fashion, on an interval scale, where a change of one unit in happiness means the same at different points of the scale. And these units need to be comparable between people. To the economist who objects to these ideas, I would say that we all use these ideas regularly in how we describe the world:

Cardinality: we say A's mood improved a lot today, but much less than it did yesterday.
Comparability: the bad news upset A much more than it upset B.

However, there is still the ethical issue about the function $f(\ )$. A strong egalitarian might say that we can ignore changes affecting any but the least happy people, on the grounds that public policy mainly exists to protect the weak (its equity function). But this, of course, is quite wrong: much public policy exists to improve the efficiency of society, since externalities, information problems, or economies of scale raise problems that require collective action for the benefit of all. In fact, most policy actions involve equity and efficiency considerations simultaneously, which is why the perspective provided by equation (1) is important.

---

1. See, for example, Atkinson and Stiglitz (1980, part 2).
2. The exception is the Rawlsian case, where a purely ordinal measure of H will suffice if it is comparable across people. But most people find the Rawlsian function too extreme.

6.1.2 Properties of the U-Index

How well would changes in the U-index provide a proxy for what is needed according to equation (1)? For egalitarians, one attraction might be the focus on the lower end of the happiness distribution (though not, of course, going as far as Rawls). But even over this part of the range, much information is discarded—we do not record *how* miserable an episode was, but only whether it was miserable or not. And again, if the experience was not miserable, we do not record how good it was, but simply that it was not miserable.

So, one might think that the most natural measure for each episode would be a scalar measure of how happy the person was. However, the authors claim that these affect measures (as reported) are purely ordinal and vary between individuals, so they cannot readily be used in that way. However, they say that by comparing two of the measures, something can be learned. For example, let us take a simple example (simpler and perhaps more intuitive than the one they use). Suppose we compare the answers on the Happy scale and the Blue scale and set U equal to one iff

$$Happy < Blue,$$

and otherwise zero. The argument is that if person A is more emotional in his reporting than person B, he will use higher values of both "Happy" and "Blue" to report the same state when compared with B. Thus, if we put the true ordinal measures on the horizontal axis and the reported measures on the vertical axis, we get the position shown in figure 6.1.

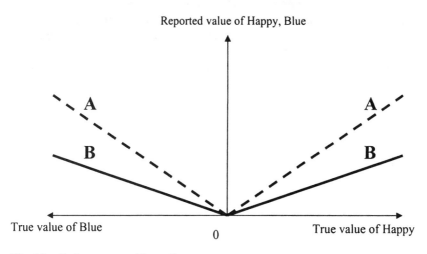

Fig. 6.1   Pattern assumed by authors

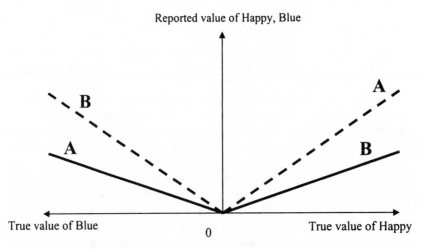

Reported value of Happy, Blue

True value of Blue   0   True value of Happy

Fig. 6.2   Alternative pattern

Thus, any given state will lead to the same value of U, whether it is reported by A or B.

But the reporting pattern shown in figure 6.2 is just as likely. Here, A is more optimistic than B: he overreports "Happy" and underreports "Blue." Now the two people may have different U values for the same state. Indeed, the chapter has in table 1.3 an illustration of this opposite mechanism: when H is asked about before Pain (rather than the other way around), the mean of H is higher and of Pain is lower.

So, if all the affect measures are truly ordinal, I do not see that the U procedure overcomes the problem. (Moreover, the procedure also requires that a person can compare on a scale of zero to six how "Happy" he is with how "Angry" he is. This is asking quite a lot. And how bad is extreme righteous anger if a person is at the same time quite high on the happiness scale?)

So, if the measures are truly ordinal, the procedure only partly handles the problem. Moreover, by comparing two numbers, it adds to problems of measurement error, while it loses so much of the information along the whole scale of H.

6.1.3   Is Happiness Purely Ordinal?

However, if we do want to use the whole scale, it cannot be purely ordinal in the sense that economists use the word—meaning that it can be arbitrarily subjected to any increasing monotonic transformation. Such a scale cannot be used to compare the magnitude of a change at one point of the scale with that at another. To do that we need a cardinal scale, which can be subjected only to an increasing *linear* transformation.

If we look at the ways in which people use the scales, they are surely not *perfectly* cardinal nor perfectly comparable,[3] but they do approximate to those conditions. The basic evidence, much of which is quoted in section 1.3, is that if H_i is treated as a scalar variable and is regressed on possible causal factors, the size of many causal effects is well determined. This is inconceivable with a purely ordinal scale that varies widely across individuals. Again, if we compare different studies of different populations, the effect of different experiences (like unemployment) is very similar across studies once we adjust for the length of the scale between "Very Happy" and "Very Unhappy." It certainly looks as if respondents try to divide up that range into intervals reflecting a standard difference in intensity.

This applies not only to estimates of the first order effect of a causal variable but also to some (second order) estimates of the curvature of an effect. An example of this is a recent study by Layard, Mayraz, and Nickell (2008b). The aim of the study was to see how quickly the marginal utility of income falls as income rises—a key parameter for all public policy (including cost-benefit analysis and optimal taxation). The six surveys used are shown in table 6.1 and cover fifty countries and thirty-three years. The happiness or life-satisfaction variable in each study was put through a linear transformation to fit into a scale from zero to ten. All the analyses included (besides income) country × year dummies, as well as sex, age, education, marital status, and employment status. The estimated equation was

$$(2) \qquad H_{it} = \alpha_{ct} \frac{y_{it}^{1-\rho} - 1}{1 - \rho} + \sum_j \beta_j x_{jit} + y_{ct} + \varepsilon_{it},$$

where i is individual, t is time, c is country, j is characteristic, and ρ is the elasticity of marginal utility with respect to real income.

Table 6.2 shows the estimated values of ρ. The results of the very different surveys are remarkably close, and they do not differ significantly between subgroups of the population. Since ρ is not so far from unity, the following logarithmic formulation is a reasonably accurate approximation:

$$(3) \qquad H_{it} = \alpha \log y_{it} + \sum_j \beta_j x_{jit} + y_{ct} + \varepsilon_{it}.$$

Table 6.2 shows the values of α obtained from the different surveys. The estimates are less similar than for ρ, but still remarkable, given the diversity of sources.

Clearly the finding about ρ is influenced by the assumption that people use the happiness scales in a truly cardinal way. This is not easy to check. We do ordered logit and probit analysis and obtain almost identical estimates of ρ, but this procedure depends crucially on the assumption of symmetrical cardinal errors.

---

3. Moreover, if we are wanting an aggregate measure of happiness across a number of time periods (episodes), there are further requirements that the scale be a ratio scale (Kahneman, Wakker, and Sarin 1997). We have no evidence that people's replies satisfy that requirement.

Table 6.1   Surveys used by Layard et al. (2008b)

Survey	Countries	Years	Observations	Happiness variable	Income variable
General Social Survey	United States	1972–2004	17,603	Happiness (3 levels)	Yearly gross
World Values Survey	Worldwide	1981–2003	37,288	Life satisfaction (1–10)	Varies
European Social Survey	Europe	2002, 2004	26,687	Both (0–10)	Monthly net
European Quality of Life Survey	Europe	2003	8,175	Both (1–10)	Monthly net
German Socio-Economic Panel	Germany	1984–2005	78,877	Life satisfaction (0–10)	Monthly net
British Household Panel Survey	Britain	1996–2004	43,484	Life satisfaction (1–7)	Monthly net

Table 6.2   Parameter estimates for equations (1) and (2)

	ρ	α
General Social Survey	1.20 (0.91–1.48)	0.70 (0.61–0.80)
World Values Survey	1.25 (1.05–1.45)	0.62 (0.57–0.66)
European Social Survey	1.34 (1.12–1.55)	0.60 (0.55–0.64)
European Quality of Life Survey	1.19 (0.87–1.52)	0.82 (0.73–0.91)
German Socio-Economic Panel	1.26 (0.90–1.63)	0.55 (0.51–0.59)
British Household Panel Survey	1.30 (0.97–1.62)	0.35 (0.30–0.40)
Overall	1.26 (1.16–1.37)	
Subgroups		
Men	1.22 (1.06–1.39)	
Women	1.26 (1.11–1.40)	
30–42	1.27 (1.12–1.42)	
43–55	1.26 (1.10–1.41)	
Low education	1.13 (0.85–1.40)	
Mid education	1.21 (1.01–1.42)	
High education	1.26 (1.16–1.37)	
Couples	1.27 (1.11–1.43)	
Never married	1.44 (1.13–1.77)	
Others	1.34 (1.12–1.55)	

Note: Ninety-five percent confidence intervals in brackets.

The better approach is to ask what one would mean by a true interval scale of happiness. One might suppose that each unit on the scale should be proportional to a Just Noticeable Difference (JND). If this were the case and people were retested on their replies, people who scored low on the scale should have the same degree of difference between their two replies as do people high on the scale. In other words, a regression of test 2 values on test

1 values should exhibit homoscedastic errors. In a test-retest study of net affect, Krueger and Schkade (2008) did not reject homoscedasticity.

6.2   The Role of Time Use

It is also extremely interesting to know how happy people are when they are doing different things. It can aid reflection on lifestyle, and it can help with public policy.

6.2.1   Work-Life Balance

But as Chapter 1 correctly says, there are no simple public policy conclusions. For example, if people do not much enjoy their work, it does not follow that they should work less, since the marginal money they earn may justify the comparative disutility.

In discussing optimal work-life balance, the more important information would be about distortions affecting choice: that is, about externality and misforecasting. If we can show that people's happiness depends on relative income as well as on absolute income, then there is a negative externality. A number of studies have investigated the impact of other people's income upon individual happiness,[4] but the estimates are not yet precise enough to yield estimates of optimal tax. Similarly, there is evidence that people under-predict the (negative) effect of current consumption on future happiness (Loewenstein et al. 2000). Again, the parameter estimates are not yet well defined. But studies of these issues are at least as relevant for public policy as studies of time use are.

6.2.2   Explanatory Power

But what about the explanatory power of time-use patterns in explaining the average happiness of different people or groups? I had expected the explanatory power to be greater. For example, the U-index is 2.8 points higher for Americans than for the French. But only one point of this is due to time use. Similarly, changing patterns of time use in the United States have predicted a one point fall in the U-index since the 1960s. But did it happen? And how much do differences in time use explain the differences between individuals in the sample?

One fascinating aspect of the France and United States comparison (Rennes, France versus Columbus, Ohio) is that while the U-index is higher for Americans, so is average life satisfaction. But these apparent differences are readily reconciled once we look at the *distribution* of life satisfaction (see table 6.3).

So, to explain the life satisfaction results, it does not seem necessary to

---

4. See Layard, Mayraz, and Nickell (2008a) and Layard (2005); see also Annex 2.5, available at http://cep.lse.ac.uk/layard/annex.pdf.

Table 6.3   **Results reported in Krueger et al.**

	United States (%)	France (%)
% not very satisfied or not at all satisfied	23.0	17.2
U-index (average)	18.8	16.0
U-index for bottom quartile	58.0	48.0

invoke differences in reporting habits, since in both types of data, the United States has a bigger tail of unhappy people. It would, however, be interesting to see how this looked if we used not the U-index, but instead used numbers below a certain level of happiness.

As table 1.21 shows, the bigger U.S. tail of unhappy people is not mainly due to greater income inequality.[5] It must be due to other aspects of inequality, perhaps more closely related to human relationships.

6.3   Britain

In Britain, it has become a matter of practical urgency to resolve these issues of measurement, because policymakers are demanding it. There are four main clients.

The Office of National Statistics has chosen well-being as one of the three main areas for statistical development over the next year. If successful, this would put measures of well-being at the center of national government. Meanwhile, the central government department that has so far been responsible for coordinating the Whitehall approach to well-being is the Department of the Environment (because opponents of gross domestic product [GDP] maximization are either promoters of well-being or promoters of the environment). This year, the department included in its annual Indicators of Sustainable Development the results of a well-being survey covering overall life satisfaction, domain satisfaction, "feelings experienced every day or most days in last two weeks," social activity, physical activity, and cultural activity. The measures "are presented on a provisional basis and as a starting point for possible future development." A regular national survey of positive mental health will also be done by the Department of Health.

Finally, local governments are demanding ways of measuring well-being locally—partly to monitor trends, and equally important, to identify where the real problems are in their communities.

All this reflects, of course, the policy interest in well-being. At least three departments have a policy-making section called "X and Well-Being," where

---

5. It is interesting that here, income does affect feelings measured by the U-index (see also table 6.1). This contrasts with the finding in Kahneman et al. (2006) for the Columbus sample, where feelings are measured by net affect and are broadly unrelated to income.

X includes health, work, or education. Major spending commitments have already resulted—for example, $600 million to provide evidence-based psychological therapy in the National Health Service (NHS). Similarly, local government is responding to a statutory duty put on them to promote the well-being of their population. The interest is bipartisan, and Conservative leader David Cameron has proposed General National Well-Being (GNW) as an alternative national goal to the gross national product (GNP).

6.4   Conclusion

Let me list a few bald conclusions.

1. Detailed measurement of affect over the day provides excellent information for monitoring well-being and its distribution in the population. Both the Day Reconstruction Method (DRM) and the Princeton Affect and Time Survey (PATS) can play a great role. The team has performed a service to the world in developing these tools, and I hope the U.S. government will adopt one of them.

2. The most useful analytical measures for each individual would be scalar averages over the day, especially of happiness.

3. The feeling that well-being is fuzzy is similar to the feeling that once prevailed that depression is fuzzy. But clinical psychology has successfully developed scales (like the Beck Depression Inventory) that are no longer controversial. I have no doubt that the same can be achieved for well-being, even using scalar variables. If we worry about the measurement error involved in single questions, we should bring in other closely related questions (as in the measurement of depression). Questions about anger and stress remain interesting but may not be near enough to the basic concept of well-being to be included in the scale.

4. Determined and repetitive presentation of results from these scales will eventually result in popular understanding of the scales, just as people now understand Fahrenheit and Celsius.

5. Congratulations on a fascinating study.

References

Atkinson, A. B., and J. E. Stiglitz. 1980. Household decisions, income taxation and labour supply. In *Lectures on public economics,* lecture 2. London: McGraw-Hill.

Kahneman, D., A. Krueger, D. Schkade, N. Schwarz, and A. Stone. 2006. Would you be happier if you were richer? A focusing illusion. *Science* 312 (5782): 1908–10.

Kahneman, D., P. Wakker, and R. Sarin. 1997. Back to Bentham? Explorations of experienced utility. *Quarterly Journal of Economics* 112 (2): 375–405.

Krueger, A., and D. Schkade. 2008. The reliability of subjective well-being measures. Special issue, *Journal of Public Economics* 92 (8/9): 1833–45.

Layard, R. 2005. *Happiness: Lessons from a new science.* New York: Penguin Press.

Layard, R., G. Mayraz, and S. Nickell. 2008a. Does relative income matter? Are the critics right? London School of Economics. Discussion Paper no. 918. London: Centre for Economic Performance.

———. 2008b. The marginal utility of income. Special issue, *Journal of Public Economics* 92 (8/9): 1846–57.

Loewenstein, G., T. O'Donoghue, and M. Rabin. 2000. Projection bias in predicting future utility. CBDR Working Paper no. 258. Pittsburgh: Center for Behavioral Decision Research.

7

International Evidence
on Well-Being

David G. Blanchflower

National Time Accounting (NTA) as propounded by Krueger et al. (see chapter 1 of this volume)—henceforth K2S3—is a way of measuring society's well-being based on time use. It is a set of methods for measuring, comparing, and analyzing the way people spend their time: across countries, over historical time, or between groups of people within a country at a given time. The arguments for NTA build on earlier work in Kahneman et al. (2004a, 2004b) and Kahneman and Krueger (2006). Krueger et al. argue that NTA should be seen as a complement to the National Income Accounts, not a substitute. Like the National Income Accounts, K2S3 accept that NTA "is also incomplete, providing a partial measure of society's well-being." However, National Time Accounting, as K2S3 note, "misses people's general sense of satisfaction or fulfillment with their lives as a whole, apart from moment to moment feelings" (see chapter 1 of this volume).

Krueger et al. propose an index, called the U-index (for "unpleasant" or "undesirable"), which is designed to measure the proportion of time an individual spends in an *unpleasant* state. The first step in computing the U-index is to determine whether an episode is unpleasant or pleasant. An episode is classified as unpleasant by K2S3 if the most intense feeling reported for that episode is a negative one—that is, if the maximum rating on any of the negative affect dimensions is strictly greater than the maximum rating of the positive affect dimensions. Once they have categorized episodes as

David G. Blanchflower is the Bruce V. Rauner Professor of Economics at Dartmouth College and a research associate of the National Bureau of Economic Research.

I thank Andrew Clark, Dick Easterlin, Richard Freeman, Alan Krueger, Andrew Oswald, Jon Skinner, Alois Stutzer, Justin Wolfers, and participants at the NBER Conference on National Time Accounting for helpful comments and suggestions.

unpleasant or pleasant, the U-index is defined by K2S3 as the fraction of an individual's waking time that is spent in an *unpleasant* state. The U-index can be computed for each individual and averaged over a sample of individuals. There do seem to be some differences in chapter 1 on how the U-index is actually calculated. For example, in K2S3's table 1.8, the U-index is defined as where "stressed, sad, or pain exceeded happy," whereas in table 1.21 it is defined as the "maximum of tense, blue, and angry being strictly greater than the rating of happy."

It is apparent that K2S3 believe their index is an improvement on the use of data on life satisfaction and happiness, which they suggest has a number of weaknesses. In Kahneman et al. (2004a), these same authors have criticized the use of such data because they argue that there are (a) surprisingly small effects of circumstances on well-being (e.g., income, marital status, etc.), and (b) large differences in the level of life satisfaction in various countries, which they regard as "implausibly large." They go on to argue that

> reports of life satisfaction are influenced by manipulations of current mood and of the immediate context, including earlier questions on a survey that cause particular domains of life to be temporarily salient. Satisfaction with life and with particular domains (e.g., income, work) is also affected by comparisons with other people and with past experiences. The same experience of pleasure or displeasure can be reported differently, depending on the standard to which it is compared and the context. (430)

Indeed, Kahneman and Krueger (2006, b) argue that well-being measures are best described as "a global retrospective judgment, which in most cases is constructed only when asked and is determined in part by the respondent's current mood and memory, and by the immediate context." Frey and Stutzer (2005) have a rather different view:

> As subjective survey data are based on individuals' judgments, they are, of course, prone to a multitude of systematic and non-systematic biases. The relevance of reporting errors, however, depends on the intended usage of the data. Often, the main use of happiness measures is not to compare levels in an absolute sense, but rather to seek to identify the determinants of happiness. For that purpose, it is neither necessary to assume that reported subjective well-being is cardinally measurable, nor that it is interpersonally comparable. Higher reports of subjective well-being for one and the same individual has solely to reflect that she or he experiences more true inner positive feelings. (208–9)

In the same vein Di Tella and MacCulloch (2007, 17) note, "One would expect that such small shocks can be treated as noise in regression analyses." Consistent with this, however, Krueger and Schkade (2007) have reported that overall life satisfaction measures . . . exhibited test-retest correlations in the range of .50–.70. While these figures are lower than the reliability ratios typically found for education, income and many other common micro economic variables, they are probably sufficiently high to support much of the research that is currently being undertaken on subjective well-being, particularly in cases where group means are being compared (e.g. rich vs. poor, employed vs. unemployed) and the benefits of statistical aggregation apply. (23)

In their earliest empirical analysis, Kahneman and Kruger (2006) calculated a U-index using data from a sample of 909 working women in Texas and showed that those who report less satisfaction with their lives spend a greater fraction of their time in an unpleasant state. Of the respondents who reported they were "not at all satisfied," 49 percent of their time was spent in an unpleasant state, compared with 11 percent who said they were "very satisfied." The authors also found that those who score in the top third on a depression scale spent 31 percent of their time in an unpleasant state, whereas those who score in the bottom third on the depression scale spent 13 percent of their time in an unpleasant state. Krueger et al. extend this work and report a comparison of the U-index based on data they collected in the United States and France—and I understand that results from Denmark are coming shortly. They sampled 810 women in Columbus, Ohio, and 820 women in Rennes, France, in the spring of 2005 and obtained information on both their life satisfaction and their U-index. The American women were *twice* as likely to say they were very satisfied with their lives as were the French women (26 percent versus 13 percent). Furthermore, assigning a number from one to four indicating life satisfaction also showed that the Americans are significantly more satisfied, on average. In contrast to reported life satisfaction, the U-index is 2.8 percentage points *lower* in the French sample (16 percent) than in the American sample (18.8 percent). Thus, the French, according to K2S3, appear to spend less of their time engaged in unpleasant activities (i.e., activities in which the dominant feeling is a negative one) than do the Americans in their samples. Moreover, national time-use data examined by K2S3 indicated that the French spend relatively more of their time engaged in activities that tend to yield more pleasure than do Americans.

The U-index relates to a relatively short period of time. Hence, there are a number of things the U-index does not measure—it appears to miss more general factors likely to impact a citizen's overall well-being. Examples, by country, include the fact that young people have been rioting in the streets of Paris (the U.K. *Daily Telegraph* headline read "Test for Sarkozy as Paris riots continue," November 27, 2007); the French soccer team has won the World Cup and the English team has been knocked out of Euro 2008; the United States is at war in Iraq and Afghanistan; and there has been a terrorist attack, a hurricane, and even forest fires in Malibu and floods in New Orleans. These may well be missed by the U-index while likely being picked up in happiness or life satisfaction measures, which relate to a more general feeling of happiness. It remains unclear whether an increase in unemployment, inflation, or inequality; a decline in growth; a drop in the stock market; or a rise in the possibility of recession the following year would raise the U-index. Does the U-index predict the outcomes of elections, or migration flows, or anything at all for that matter? As I will outline in more detail, it certainly seems that these factors impact our measures of well-being.

In what follows I provide a somewhat selective review of evidence on well-being using cross-country data, and I try to provide a framework for reconciling the findings from this work with those from the U-index. I present the main findings from responses on both happiness and life satisfaction, as well as on unhappiness, hypertension, stress, depression, anxiety, and pain from a considerable number of cross-country data sources. I also explore the results when happiness questions are based on what happened over the preceding week and find slightly weaker results. I then move on to look at how macro variables, such as the national unemployment rate, inflation, and output, impact life satisfaction. I find evidence that a 1 percentage point increase in unemployment lowers happiness more than an equivalent increase in inflation and that the highest level of inflation experienced as an adult lowers happiness further. Also, I show that life satisfaction levels in Eastern European countries predict the flow of workers to the United Kingdom and Ireland. Finally, I examine individual's expectations and show that happy people are particularly optimistic about the future, both for themselves and the economy. Subjective well-being data are clearly correlated with observable phenomena (Oswald 1997).

7.1 Happiness and Life Satisfaction

Data on happiness and life satisfaction in particular are now available for many countries and for a large number of time periods. As with the U-index, it is possible to average these already-existing data across individuals and countries to form a National Happiness Index (NHI) to generate a measure of national well-being, which would be a simple and cheap alternative to K2S3's proposed NTA. A crucial question is whether or not K2S3's proposed U-index is an improvement over an NHI. As I lay out in detail, there are many similarities between the two indices in terms of their determinants. The main differences relate to country rankings.

Before presenting data on happiness and life satisfaction in seminars to the many skeptical economists who do not believe you can, or even should, *measure* well-being—although there are less of that ilk these days—I explain that the data have been validated by researchers in other disciplines. The answers to happiness and life satisfaction questions are well correlated with a number of important factors (for references, see Di Tella and Mac-Culloch [2007]).

1. Objective characteristics such as unemployment.
2. Assessments of the person's happiness by friends and family members.
3. Assessments of the person's happiness by his or her spouse.
4. Heart rate and blood pressure measures of response to stress.
5. The risk of coronary heart disease.
6. Duration of authentic or so-called Duchenne smiles. A Duchenne smile occurs when both the zygomatic major and obicularus orus facial muscles fire, and human beings identify these as genuine smiles (see Ekman, Friesen, and O'Sullivan [1988]; Ekman, Davidson, and Friesen [1990]).
7. Skin-resistance measures of response to stress.
8. Electroencephelogram measures of prefrontal brain activity.

Happiness and life satisfaction data are easy to obtain at the macro level, as the data are downloadable from the World Database of Happiness for over one hundred countries. Most surveys now use a common format for the questions. In general, economists have focused on modeling two fairly simple questions: one on life satisfaction and one on happiness. These are typically asked as follows.

Q1. Three-step happiness—example from the U.S. General Social Survey (GSS): *"Taken all together, how would you say things are these days— would you say that you are very happy, pretty happy or not too happy?"*

Q2. Four-step life satisfaction—example from the European Eurobarometer Surveys: *"On the whole, are you very satisfied, fairly satisfied, not very satisfied, or not at all satisfied with the life you lead?"*

The microdata on happiness are easily obtained from most data archives, including the Interuniversity Consortium for Political and Social Research (ICPSR) for the GSS, and the Data Archive at the University of Essex and ZACAT, a social science data portal, in Germany (for the Eurobarometers, International Social Survey Programme [ISSP], European Social Survey [ESS], British Household Panel Survey [BHPS], German Socio-Economic Panel [GSOEP], European Quality of Life Survey [EQLS], etc.). Life satisfaction data are also now available annually from the Latinobarometers, while happiness data is available annually in the Asianbarometers (Blanchflower and Oswald 2008b). Several of the data series extend back at least to the early 1970s. Many of the data sets cover several countries.

Economists like to run regressions, so by now the standard econometric approach taken by economists is to use microdata on happiness or life satisfaction to estimate an ordered logit or an Ordinary Least Squares (OLS) regression, with the coding such that the higher the number, the more satisfied an individual is (e.g., Blanchflower and Oswald 2004a). Generally, it makes little or no difference if you use an OLS or an ordered logit. The results are similar—but not identical—for happiness and life satisfaction. The main, ceteris paribus, findings from happiness and life satisfaction equations across countries and time are as follows.

Well-being is higher among:
Women
Married people
The highly educated
Those actively involved in religion
The healthy
Those with high income
The young and the old—U-shaped in age
The self-employed
Those with low blood pressure
The sexually active, and especially those who have sex at least once a week
Those with one sex partner
Those without children

Well-being is lower among:
Newly divorced and separated people
Adults in their mid to late forties
The unemployed
Immigrants and minorities
Those in poor health
Commuters
People with high blood pressure
The less educated
The poor
The sexually inactive
Those with children

There have been a number of recent surveys of the happiness literature, including Clark, Fritjers, and Shields (2007); Frey and Stutzer (2002a, 2002b); and Di Tella and MacCulloch (2006), which provide discussions of the relevant issues. Recent findings from the statistical happiness research include the following.

1. For a person, money does buy a reasonable amount of happiness, but it is useful to keep this in perspective. Very loosely, for the typical individual, a doubling of salary makes a lot less difference than do life events like marriage or unemployment.

2. For a nation, things are different. Whole countries, at least in the West where almost all the research has been done, do not seem to get much happier as they get richer.

3. Happiness is U-shaped in age. Women report higher well-being than men. Two of the biggest negatives in life are unemployment and divorce.

Education is associated with high reported levels of happiness even after controlling for income.

4. Happy people are less likely to commit suicide (Koivumaa-Honkanen et al. 2001).

5. The structure of a happiness equation has the same general form in each industrialized country (and possibly in developing nations, though only a small amount of evidence has so far been collected). In other words, the broad statistical patterns look the same in France, Britain, and the United States. As Di Tella and MacCulloch note, " 'well-being equations,' (where happiness and life satisfaction scores are correlated with the demographic characteristics of the respondents) are broadly 'similar' across countries, an unlikely outcome if the data contained just noise" (2007, 9).

6. There is some evidence that the same is true in panels of people (that is, in longitudinal data). Particularly useful evidence comes from looking at windfalls like lottery wins.

7. There is adaptation. Good and bad life events wear off, at least partially, as people get used to them.

8. Relative things matter a great deal. First, in experiments, people care about how they are treated compared to those who are like them, and in the laboratory will even pay to hurt others to restore what they see as fairness. Second, in large statistical studies, reported well-being depends on a person's wage relative to an average or comparison wage, as found in Blanchflower and Oswald (2004a); Ferrer-i-Carbonell (2005); Di Tella, MacCulloch, and Haisken-DeNew (2005); and Luttmer (2005). Third, wage inequality depresses reported happiness in a region or nation (controlling for many variables), but the effect is not large (Alesina, Di Tella, and MacCulloch 2004). Some of these patterns are visible in raw data alone. Strong correlations with income, marriage, and unemployment are noticeable.

For the United States there seems to be relatively little evidence that despite rising affluence, happiness or life satisfaction have trended up much over time (Blanchflower and Oswald 2004a). For example, in the 2006 GSS, 13.1 percent of respondents said they were not too happy, 56.1 percent said they were pretty happy, and 30.8 percent said they were very happy. In 1972, the first year happiness data are available, the numbers were 16.5 percent, 53.2 percent, and 30.3 percent, respectively. As can be seen from figure 7.1, average happiness levels for the United States are flat, while real gross domestic product (GDP) per capita has risen. It is also apparent from table 1.18 of K2S3 that their U-index based on time in various activities each year is also flat over time, as seen in table 7.1. The picture is more mixed among European countries. For example, in figure 7.2, panels A and B, there is some sign of a strong long-run upward trend in Italy, and to a lesser extent in Denmark and France, while the data are relatively flat in the Netherlands, Germany, the United Kingdom, and Ireland. In contrast,

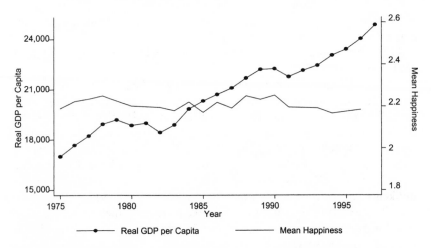

Fig. 7.1   **Average happiness and real GDP per capita for repeated cross-sections of Americans**

Table 7.1   Happiness averages: General Social Surveys, U.S.

	1965–1966 (%)	1975–1976 (%)	1985 (%)	1992–1994 (%)	2003 (%)	2005 (%)
All	20.1	19.5	19.5	20.0	19.3	19.6
Men	20.9	20.4	20.1	20.2	19.6	19.9
Women	19.4	18.7	19.0	19.8	19.2	19.4

Belgium and Portugal have significant downward trends (results not re-ported). Note that happiness levels are generally high in Denmark and low in Italy and France. In addition, Frey and Stutzer (2002b) have shown that the time trend in life satisfaction in Japan was flat between 1958 and 1991, the period when GDP per capita rose by a factor of six.

There is evidence, however, of *upward* trends in Eastern European coun-tries, Turkey, and South American countries over the recent past. Table 7.2 reports the distribution of life satisfaction scores over the recent past for countries from Western and Eastern Europe and from Latin America. Among the seventeen Western European countries, since the turn of the century, five have seen satisfaction broadly flat (Denmark, Greece, Ireland, Spain, and the United Kingdom); five have seen increases (Belgium, Finland, France, Luxembourg, and Sweden); and seven have seen declines (Austria, Germany, Italy, Japan, the Netherlands, Portugal, and the United States). In contrast, with the exception of Hungary, all of the Eastern European countries and Turkey have all seen increases, as is the case for all the Latin

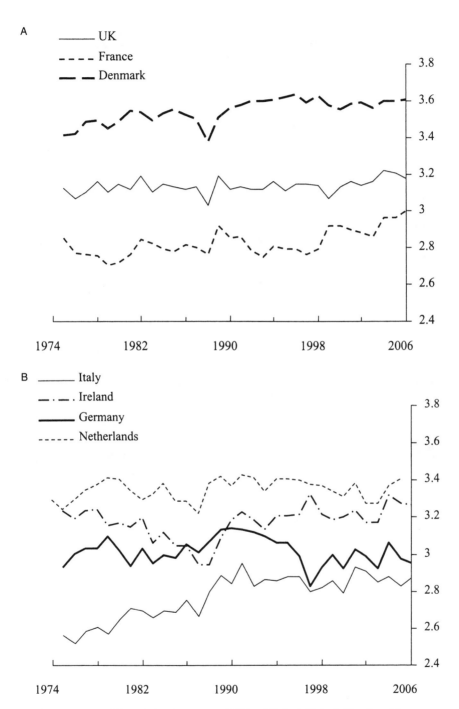

Fig. 7.2   Mean life satisfaction scores, 1975 to 2006: *A*, **United Kingdom, France, and Denmark;** *B*, **Italy, Ireland, Germany, and the Netherlands.**

Table 7.2   **4-step life satisfaction: Europe, the United States, Japan, and Latin America**

	2001	2002	2003	2004	2005	2006
		Western countries				
Austria	3.18	3.13	3.08	3.05	3.04	3.08
Belgium	3.06	2.96	3.04	3.18	3.16	3.19
Denmark	3.60	3.61	3.57	3.59	3.62	3.61
Finland	3.11	3.14	3.15	3.29	3.26	3.23
France	2.94	2.88	2.85	2.95	2.96	3.00
Germany	2.94	2.86	2.75	2.96	2.93	2.87
Greece	2.66	2.66	2.66	2.73	2.66	2.67
Ireland	3.26	3.18	3.15	3.32	3.29	3.28
Italy	2.93	2.95	2.86	2.86	2.83	2.85
Japan	2.71	2.61	2.59	2.74	2.58	n.a.
Luxembourg	3.31	3.30	3.25	3.44	3.42	3.39
Netherlands	3.42	3.31	3.28	3.33	3.41	3.36
Portugal	2.71	2.63	2.49	2.49	2.48	2.44
Spain	3.07	3.02	3.01	3.13	3.03	3.08
Sweden	3.35	3.32	3.28	3.40	3.42	3.39
U.K.	3.21	3.18	3.17	3.23	3.20	3.19
U.S.	3.35	3.33	3.37	3.42	n.a.	n.a.
		East Europe + Turkey				
Bulgaria	2.08	2.04	2.05	2.06	2.04	1.99
Czech Republic	2.84	2.84	2.73	2.82	2.93	2.92
Estonia	2.44	2.52	2.48	2.74	2.72	2.74
Hungary	2.54	2.63	2.53	2.44	2.53	2.50
Latvia	2.54	2.47	2.54	2.52	2.62	2.62
Lithuania	2.29	2.46	2.52	2.55	2.56	2.62
Poland	2.65	2.71	2.67	2.81	2.77	2.80
Romania	2.12	2.20	2.10	2.32	2.35	2.33
Slovakia	2.48	2.54	2.47	2.59	2.64	2.70
Slovenia	3.04	3.03	3.04	3.17	3.10	3.09
Turkey	2.26	2.43	2.71	2.87	2.90	2.84

	1997	2000	2001	2003	2004	2005
		Latin America				
Argentina	2.14	2.21	2.82	2.91	2.92	2.94
Bolivia	1.97	1.89	2.54	2.77	2.42	2.57
Brazil	2.34	2.61	2.71	2.71	2.67	2.73
Colombia	2.50	2.40	3.06	3.16	3.14	3.17
Costa Rica	2.82	2.65	3.34	3.46	3.29	3.34
Chile	2.32	2.84	2.82	2.92	2.80	2.85
Ecuador	2.06	1.86	2.74	3.03	2.48	2.68
El Salvador	2.49	2.34	2.90	3.34	2.88	2.90
Guatemala	2.40	2.64	3.01	3.15	3.03	3.13
Honduras	2.41	2.62	3.28	3.21	3.17	2.98
Mexico	2.61	2.71	2.95	3.13	2.96	3.06
Nicaragua	2.67	2.16	2.96	3.18	2.77	2.94
Panama	2.38	2.78	2.64	3.17	3.13	3.21

Table 7.2   (continued)

	1997	2000	2001	2003	2004	2005
Paraguay	2.16	2.14	2.93	3.26	2.84	2.95
Peru	1.70	1.72	2.48	2.74	2.49	2.50
Uruguay	2.40	2.36	2.91	2.88	2.73	2.90
Venezuela	2.45	2.82	3.26	3.36	3.26	3.45

Source: Blanchflower and Shadforth (2007), plus Eurobarometers, Latinobarometers, and the World Database of Happiness.

American countries from 1997.[1] There is also some consistent evidence that the well-being of the young (less than thirty years old) has risen over time in both the United States and Europe (Blanchflower and Oswald 2000). The rise is mostly among the unmarried. We found that this upward trend is not explained by changing education or work, falling discrimination, or the rise of youth-oriented consumer goods.

There is some evidence of convergence over time in the happiness of men and women in the United States, as women have become less happy (Blanchflower and Oswald 2004a). Stevenson and Wolfers (2007) find that the relative decline in women's well-being holds for both working and stay-at-home moms, for those married and divorced, for the old and the young, and across the education distribution. The relative decline in well-being holds across various data sets, regardless of whether one asks about happiness or life satisfaction. Stevenson and Wolfers find that the exception to this is that African American women have become happier over this period, as have African American men, and there has been little consistent change in the gender happiness gap among African Americans over this period. As with U.S. women, Stevenson and Wolfers find that the well-being of European women has declined relative to men. However, while U.S. women also experienced an absolute decline in well-being, the subjective well-being of European men and women has risen over time.

There is also intriguing new evidence that *high frequency* happiness data yields information about preferences. Kimball et al. (2006), for example, showed that happiness dipped significantly in the first week of September 2005, after the seriousness of the damage caused by Hurricane Katrina started to become apparent. The dip in happiness lasted two or three weeks and was especially apparent in the South Central region, closest to the devastated area.

---

1. Easterlin and Zimmermann (2008) suggest that the observed increases in happiness in East Germany have arisen following a noticeable drop in life satisfaction at the time of unification (Blanchflower 2001), so the rise is largely a recovery to pretransition levels. In private communication, Dick Easterlin has further suggested that based on his recent work, the collapse and recovery of life satisfaction is *typically* the case for the European transition countries.

7.2 The U-Index

The first column of table 7.3 is taken from K2S3 and reports their U-index, which should be thought of as the inverse of a subjective well-being or happiness index. The higher the U-index, the more unhappy the person is. There is little difference by gender, and blacks are especially unhappy, as are the poor and the least educated. Unhappiness declines with age and is particularly low for the married and high for the widowed. How do these findings compare with those found using happiness and life satisfaction data? Column (2) presents the proportion of people in the United States from the GSS of 2000 to 2006 who say they are very happy (on a one to three scale), while column (3) presents the proportion of Europeans from the 2000 to 2006 Eurobarometers who say they are very satisfied (on a one to four scale). The final column reports the proportion of Latin Americans from the 2005 and 2006 Latinobarometers who say they are very satisfied (on a one to four scale).[2] Here a larger proportion means happier people, which is the inverse of the U-index. Interestingly, the results are very similar in all four columns. Happiness is higher for the more educated, for married people, for those with higher incomes, and for whites.

Happiness does rise with age in the United States, but once controls are included, happiness is U-shaped in age (Blanchflower and Oswald 2008b). It is U-shaped in age in both the European and Latin American countries, even in the raw data and even when controls are included (Blanchflower and Oswald 2007b).[3] This result is confirmed by K2S3 in their table 1.19, where unhappiness seems to follow an inverted U-shape.[4] We explore this

2. The countries covered in these Eurobarometers are Austria, Belgium, Bulgaria, Croatia, Cyprus, Czech Republic, Denmark, Estonia, Finland, France, Germany, Greece, Hungary, Ireland, Italy, Latvia, Lithuania, Luxembourg, Malta, the Netherlands, Norway, Poland, Portugal, Romania, Slovakia, Slovenia, Spain, Sweden, Turkey, and the United Kingdom. The Latinobarometer covers Argentina, Bolivia, Brazil, Chile, Colombia, Costa Rica, Dominican Republic, Ecuador, El Salvador, Guatemala, Honduras, Mexico, Nicaragua, Panama, Paraguay, Peru, Uruguay, and Venezuela.

3. As Clark (2007) notes, this finding is repeated in happiness equations in Blanchflower and Oswald (2004a); Clark (2005); Clark and Oswald (1994); Di Tella, MacCulloch, and Oswald (2001); Frey and Stutzer (2002a); Frijters, Haisken-DeNew, and Shields (2004); Gerdtham and Johannesson (2001); Graham (2005); Helliwell (2003); Kingdon and Knight (2007); Lelkes (2007); Oswald (1997); Powdthavee (2005); Propper et al. (2005); Sanfey and Teksoz (2007); Senik (2004); Shields and Wheatley Price (2005); Theodossiou (1998); Uppal (2006); Van Praag and Ferrer-i-Carbonell (2004); and Winkelmann and Winkelmann (1998).

4. Blanchflower and Oswald (2008b) find that a robust U-shape in age in happiness and life satisfaction is found in seventy-two countries—Albania, Argentina, Australia, Azerbaijan, Belarus, Belgium, Bosnia, Brazil, Brunei, Bulgaria, Cambodia, Canada, Chile, China, Colombia, Costa Rica, Croatia, Czech Republic, Denmark, Dominican Republic, Ecuador, El Salvador, Estonia, Finland, France, Germany, Greece, Honduras, Hungary, Iceland, Iraq, Ireland, Israel, Italy, Japan, Kyrgyzstan, Laos, Latvia, Lithuania, Luxembourg, Macedonia, Malta, Mexico, Myanmar, the Netherlands, Nicaragua, Nigeria, Norway, Paraguay, Peru, Philippines, Poland, Portugal, Puerto Rico, Romania, Russia, Serbia, Singapore, Slovakia, South Africa, South Korea, Spain, Sweden, Switzerland, Tanzania, Turkey, Ukraine, the United Kingdom, the United States, Uruguay, Uzbekistan, and Zimbabwe.

Table 7.3   **U-index, happiness, and life satisfaction for various demographic groups**

	U-index (%)	GSS (%)	EB (%)	LB (%)
Sex				
Men	17.6	30.9	27.0	30.5
Women	19.6	31.3	26.8	30.1
Race/ethnicity				
White	17.5	32.7		
Black	23.8	26.6		
Hispanic	21.9	24.8		
Household income				
<$30,000	22.5	31.8		
$30,000–$50,000	18.6	23.6		
$50,000–$100,000 ($110k)	18.6	38.2		
>$100,000	15.7	46.8		
Education				
<High school/<16 years	20.5	28.9	19.3	28.0
High school/16–19 years	21.3	31.2	25.1	31.6
Some college/20+ years	19.6	31.7	34.8	32.4
College/still studying	15.6	37.2	32.5	
Masters	16.6	36.6		
Doctorate	11.3	36.4		
Men				
15–24	18.8	23.4	28.0	34.1
25–44	17.1	29.2	25.7	30.8
45–64	18.7	33.0	25.9	27.6
65+	15.6	39.8	30.5	28.0
Married	17.4	39.0	29.3	33.6
Divorced/separated	24.3	17.5	18.6	27.1
Widowed	20.2	22.1	21.6	
Never married	16.9	20.3	23.3	29.1
Women				
15–24	18.9	29.5	28.9	33.7
25–44	20.5	32.0	28.1	30.5
45–64	20.9	33.5	25.4	26.6
65+	16.1	33.6	24.6	28.7
Married	17.4	41.6	29.4	32.9
Divorced/separated	24.5	20.3	18.7	29.0
Widowed	22.3	25.0	20.7	
Never married	23.2	24.1	24.9	29.8

Source: GSS pooled 2000, 2002, 2004, 2006—percent "very happy." Eurobarometers for EU15 from 2000 to 2006—% "very satisfied" (Austria, Belgium, Denmark, Finland, France, Germany, Greece, Ireland, Italy, Luxembourg, the Netherlands, Portugal, Spain, Sweden, and United Kingdom). Krueger et al. (2007)—table 5.1 using Princeton Affect and Time Survey data. Latinobarometer 2005—% "very satisfied" (Argentina, Bolivia, Brazil, Colombia, Costa Rica, Chile, Dominican Republic, Ecuador, El Salvador, Guatemala, Honduras, Mexico, Nicaragua, Panama, Paraguay, Peru, Uruguay, and Venezuela). Education categories for the LB are "<9 years schooling," "10–12 years schooling," and ">12 years schooling."

Note: U-index is proportion of time that rating of "sad," "stressed," or "pain" exceeds "happy."

EB = Eurobarometer, LB = Latinobarometer.

U-shape in age in more detail next. The patterns across individuals are essentially the same then, for subjective well-being (SWB) and NTA in the United States, Latin America, and Europe. It turns out that the happiness derived from sex in both SWB studies and in U-index studies is especially high. Blanchflower and Oswald (2004b) found that sexual activity enters strongly positively into happiness equations.[5] Indeed, in Kahneman and Krueger (2006) and Kahneman et al. (2004b), "intimate relations" has the lowest rating (i.e., gives the most happiness), while "commuting" has the highest. Though somewhat surprisingly, in K2S3, "walking" gave more happiness than "making love" among U.S. women, although the reverse was the case among French women (table 1.22)!

In section 1.8 of their chapter, K2S3 do some international comparisons of SWB in two representative cities—one in France and the other in the United States—and ask whether the standard measure of life satisfaction and the NTA yield the same conclusion concerning relative well-being. Specifically, they designed a survey to compare overall life satisfaction, time use, and recalled affective experience during episodes of the day for random samples of women in Rennes, France, and Columbus, Ohio. The authors argued that these cities were selected because they represented "middle America" and "middle France." Krueger et al. also presented results using time allocation derived from national samples in the United States and France to extend their analysis beyond these two cities. The city sample consisted of 810 women in Columbus, Ohio, and 820 women in Rennes, France. Respondents were invited to participate based on random-digit dialing in the spring of 2005 and were paid approximately $75 for their participation. The age range spanned from eighteen years old to sixty-eight years old, and all participants spoke their country's dominant language at home. The Columbus sample was older (median age of forty-four years old versus thirty-nine years old), more likely to be employed (75 percent versus 67 percent), and better educated (average of 15.2 years of school versus fourteen years) than the Rennes sample, but the Rennes sample was more likely to currently be enrolled in school (16 percent versus 10 percent). The life satisfaction question was taken from the World Values Survey (WVS).

The distribution of reported life satisfaction in Columbus, Ohio, and Rennes, France, for women found by K2S3 is presented in the first two columns of part A of table 7.4 using the 4-step life satisfaction scale. Life satisfaction is based on the question, "Taking all things together, how satisfied are you with your life as a whole these days—not at all satisfied, not

---

5. Blanchflower and Oswald (2004b) found that higher income does not buy more sex or more sexual partners. Married people have more sex than those who are single, divorced, widowed, or separated. The happiness-maximizing number of sexual partners in the previous year is calculated to be one. Highly educated females tend to have fewer sexual partners. Homosexuality has no statistically significant effect on happiness.

Table 7.4   **Life satisfaction and country characteristics: France, Denmark, the United Kingdom, and the United States**

	K2S3, 2006 Women		Eurobarometer, 2000–2006 Women		
	U.S.	France	France	Denmark	U.K.
A. 4-step life satisfaction					
Not at all satisfied	1.6	1.1	4.5	0.6	2.2
Not very satisfied	21.4	16.1	15.1	2.7	8.4
Satisfied	51.0	70.0	64.5	31.7	56.6
Very satisfied	26.1	12.9	15.9	65.0	32.9
Score	3.00	2.94	2.92	3.62	3.21
N	810	816	7,074	6,700	9,457

	France	Denmark	U.K.	U.S.
B. 10-step life satisfaction for women: WVS				
1981–1984	6.75	8.27	7.55	7.73
1989–1993	6.82	8.07	7.65	7.65
1999–2004	6.97	8.23	7.68	7.65
C. 4-step life satisfaction for men and women combined: World Database of Happiness				
2001	2.90	3.59	3.17	3.35
2002	2.89	3.59	3.14	3.33
2003	2.86	3.56	3.16	3.41
2004	2.96	3.60	3.22	3.42
D. Macrodata				
GDP/capita (PPP U.S.$, 2004)	$29,300	$31,914	$30,821	$39,676
Gini coefficient	32.7	24.7	36.0	40.8
Unemployment rate	8.6%	3.3%	5.4%	4.7%
Long-term unemployment	44.8%	20.7%	27.5%	10.7%
Youth unemployment	23.9%	7.6%	13.9%	10.5%

Source: http://hdrstats.undp.org/indicators/.

Notes: Score is obtained by calculating a weighted average of responses, where 1 = "not at all satisfied," 2 = "not very satisfied," 3 = "satisfied," and 4 = "very satisfied." "Youth unemployment" and "long-term unemployment" are both for males. "Youth unemployment" is for ages 15 to 24. "PPP" means "purchasing power parity."

very satisfied, fairly satisfied, or very satisfied?" Krueger et al. found that American women reported higher levels of life satisfaction than the French, regardless of whether the proportion who said they were "very satisfied" or the overall score was used. Yet they also found that on average, the French spent their days in a more positive mood. Moreover, the national time-use data they used also indicated that the French spend relatively more time engaged in activities that tend to yield more pleasure than do Americans. Their results, they argue, "suggest that considerable caution is required in comparing standard life satisfaction data across populations with different cultures." In particular, the Americans seem to be more emphatic when

Table 7.5   Life satisfaction averages: 2000–2006 Eurobarometers

	Not at all satisfied (%)	Not very satisfied (%)	Fairly satisfied (%)	Very satisfied (%)	N
France	4	15	65	16	13,554
Denmark	1	3	33	63	13,718

reporting their well-being. The U-index, K2S3 suggests, "apparently over-comes this inclination."

Kahneman et al. (2004a, 430) have argued that differences in the SWB ratings of Denmark and France) in the Eurobarometers, for example, are implausibly large, and they "raise additional doubts about the validity of global reports of subjective well-being, which may be susceptible to cultural differences in the norms that govern self descriptions." For example, in the Eurobarometers from 2000 to 2006, the average distributions for life satisfaction for these two countries are as seen in table 7.5. Such differences are consistently repeated in multiple data sets, regardless of whether happiness or life satisfaction is used. It is clearly problematic to compare one country's happiness answers to those of another country. Nations have different languages and cultures, and in principle, that may cause biases—perhaps large ones—in happiness surveys. At this point in research on subjective well-being, the size of any bias is not known, and there is no accepted way to correct the data, although the literature has made some progress in exploring this issue (for instance, by looking inside a nation like Switzerland at subgroups with different languages). In the long run, research into ways to difference out country fixed effects will no doubt be done, and the work of K2S3 in this regard is obviously important. For example, the strong well-being performance in some happiness surveys of countries such as Mexico and Brazil in the 2002 ISSP (Blanchflower and Oswald 2005) may or may not ultimately be viewed as completely accurate. In Blanchflower and Oswald (2005), one check was done by comparing happiness in the English-speaking nations of Great Britain, Ireland, New Zealand, Northern Ireland, and the United States. The main attraction is that this automatically avoids translation problems. Moreover, this smaller group of nations has the advantage that they are likely to be more similar in culture and philosophical outlook, and that in turn may reduce other forms of bias in people's answers. However, it does appear that there is considerable stability in cross-country rankings of life satisfaction in English-speaking countries (Blanchflower and Oswald 2005, 2006; Leigh and Wolfers 2006).

7.3   Econometric Evidence on Life Satisfaction and Happiness

As I will show in more detail next, there is also a great deal of stability in the rankings of European countries across a number of surveys, including the Eurobarometers (1973 to 2006), the EQLS (2003), and the European Social Survey (2002). Further, it seems that there is evidence from the WVS and the ISSP (2002) supporting a happiness ranking where the United States is ranked above France, as implied in K2S3's life satisfaction data, rather than below it, as implied by their U-index. In fact, I am unable to find *any* data file where the ranking reverses, as occurs with the U-index. The evidence is essentially the same, both when we look at happiness, life satisfaction, health, or family life, and conversely, when we look at a variety of measures of *unhappiness* including high blood pressure, stress, lack of sleep, pain, and being "down and depressed."

Where feasible I present data comparing the United States and France, but there are only a few data files that include both countries, so we make use of data from a number of European data files that allow a direct comparison with Denmark—which will be included in K2S3's analysis shortly—plus the United Kingdom, which is of particular interest to this author. In almost all of what follows, the United Kingdom ranks above France: Denmark is mostly at the top of the happiness rankings in Europe, especially when life satisfaction is used. If we refer to figure 7.2, panels A and B, which are based on Eurobarometer data, Denmark ranks above the United Kingdom, which itself ranks above France, in every year of data we have available. Indeed, based simply on life satisfaction averages, France usually ranks below the large majority of the EU-15 (the European Union comprised of Austria, Belgium, Denmark, Finland, France, Germany, Greece, Ireland, Italy, Luxembourg, the Netherlands, Portugal, Spain, Sweden, and the United Kingdom). For example, in the raw data from the latest Eurobarometer available, number 65.2 for March through May 2006, France ranked fourteenth out of thirty countries.[6] Controlling for a variety of characteristics over a long run of thirty years, France ranked seventeenth out of thirty.[7]

Columns (3) through (5) of part A of table 7.4 report results using the most recent subset of the data from the Eurobarometers for 2000 to 2006, which shows that France ranks third behind Denmark and the United

6. Average life satisfaction scores were Denmark (3.61), Luxembourg (3.39), Sweden (3.39), the Netherlands (3.36), Ireland (3.28), Finland (3.23), Belgium (3.19), the United Kingdom (3.19), Cyprus (3.12), Slovenia (3.10), Austria (3.08), Spain (3.08), Turkish Cyprus (3.02), France (3.00), Malta (2.98), West Germany (2.95), Czech Republic (2.89), Italy (2.86), Turkey (2.85), Poland (2.79), Croatia (2.78), East Germany (2.72), Estonia (2.72), Greece (2.67), Slovakia (2.66), Lithuania (2.58), Latvia (2.56), Hungary (2.47), Portugal (2.44), Romania (2.31), and Bulgaria (1.97).

7. When an ordered logit is run using these Eurobarometer data from 1973 to 2006—pooled across all member countries, plus candidate countries Croatia, Norway, and Turkey, with a standard set of controls as in table 8, column (5)—the rankings are as follows, with rank in parentheses: Denmark (1), the Netherlands (2), Norway (3), Sweden (4), Luxembourg (5), Ireland (6), the United Kingdom (7), Finland (8), Belgium (9), Austria (10), Cyprus (11), Slovenia (12), Malta (13), Spain (14), Germany (15), Turkey (16), France (17), Czech Republic (18), Italy (19), Croatia (20), Poland (21), Portugal (22), Estonia (23), Greece (24), Slovakia (25), Latvia (26), Lithuania (27), Hungary (28), Romania (29), and Bulgaria (30).

Kingdom. Part B of table 7.4 presents data on women using the WVS on a 10-point life satisfaction scale and replicates that ranking. Part C of the table uses data for men and women combined from the *World Database of Happiness,* which includes all four countries. Once again France ranks at the bottom, with Denmark second, the United Kingdom third, and the United States at the top.

In the final part of table 7.4 I present some macroeconomic data on GDP per capita, the Gini coefficient, and the most recent unemployment rate (Office of National Statistics 2007). In comparison with France, the United States has (a) a lower unemployment rate, (b) a higher GDP per capita, and (c) a higher Gini coefficient. France has especially high rates of long-term unemployment and youth unemployment. Denmark has an especially low unemployment rate and low Gini coefficient. Despite the well-known difficulty of making suicide rates comparable across countries, it appears that the rates in France for both men and women are well above those for the United States. This is illustrated in table 7.6. This ranking is more consistent with SWB data rankings than it is with rankings based on NTA.

Table 7.6   Suicide rates (per 100,000)

	United States											
	1950	1955	1960	1965	1970	1975	1980	1985	1990	1995	2000	2002
Total	7.6	10.2	10.6	11.1	11.5	12.7	11.8	12.3	12.4	11.9	10.4	11.0
Male	17.7	15.9	16.4	16.7	16.7	18.9	18.6	19.9	20.4	19.8	17.1	17.9
Female	2.5	4.5	4.9	6.1	6.5	6.8	5.4	5.1	4.8	4.4	4.0	4.2

	France											
	1950	1955	1960	1965	1970	1975	1980	1985	1990	1995	2000	2003
Total	15.2	15.9	15.8	15.0	15.4	15.8	19.4	22.5	20.0	20.6	18.4	18.0
Male	23.7	24.6	23.9	23.0	22.8	22.9	28.0	33.1	29.6	30.4	27.9	27.5
Female	7.2	7.8	8.2	7.5	8.4	9.0	11.1	12.7	11.1	10.8	9.5	9.1

	Denmark											
	1950	1955	1960	1965	1970	1975	1980	1985	1990	1995	2000	2001
Total	23.3	23.3	20.3	19.3	21.5	24.1	31.6	27.9	23.9	17.7	13.6	13.6
Male	31.7	32.0	27.2	24.0	27.4	29.9	41.1	35.1	32.2	24.2	20.2	19.2
Female	15.0	14.8	13.6	14.7	15.7	18.4	22.3	20.6	16.3	11.2	7.2	8.1

	United Kingdom											
	1950	1955	1960	1965	1970	1975	1980	1985	1990	1995	1999	2004
Total	9.5	10.7	10.7	10.4	7.9	7.5	8.8	9.0	8.1	7.4	7.5	7.0
Male	12.7	13.6	13.3	12.2	9.4	9.0	11.0	12.4	12.6	11.7	11.8	10.8
Female	6.5	8.0	8.2	8.7	6.5	6.0	6.7	5.8	3.8	3.2	3.3	3.3

Source: http://www.who.int/mental_health/prevention/suicide/country_reports/en/index.html.

Happiness from a further source, the ISSP, which also contains data from the two countries, is supportive of the fact that happiness in the United States is *higher* than it is in France. Data on the two countries are available in the 1998, 2001, and 2002 sweeps. In the first two sweeps, happiness data is available on a 4-point scale in response to the question, "How happy are you with your life in general—not at all happy, not very happy, fairly happy, or very happy?" Responses are found in table 7.7. The overall score for the French increased between 1998 and 2001. In the 2002 ISSP, responses were provided on a 7-point scale, and the U.S. score was once again considerably higher than the French for both men and women. As can be seen in table 7.8, the average score across respondents in the United States was higher for both men and women; however, the proportion who were unhappy—completely, very, or fairly—was higher. For men in the United States, 4.3 percent in this category were unhappy, compared with 3.1 percent in France,

Table 7.7   **Happiness: 1998 and 2000 ISSP**

	Not at all (%)	Not very (%)	Fairly (%)	Very (%)	Score (%)	N
2001 U.S.	1	7	51	41	3.3	1,129
1998 U.S.	2	9	52	37	3.2	1,272
2001 France	1	9	62	27	3.2	1,330
1998 France	3	20	64	13	2.9	1,082

Table 7.8   **Happiness: 2002 ISSP**

	Female	Male	All
United States			
Completely unhappy	0.2	0.0	0.1
Very unhappy	1.5	1.2	1.4
Fairly unhappy	2.5	3.1	2.8
Neither	5.4	6.8	6.0
Fairly happy	31.9	36.3	33.7
Very happy	45.7	41.6	44.0
Completely happy	13.0	11.1	12.2
Score	5.56	5.47	5.52
N	672	488	1,160
France			
Completely unhappy	0.1	0.2	0.1
Very unhappy	0.3	0.5	0.3
Fairly unhappy	3.2	2.4	3.0
Neither	13.4	10.9	12.6
Fairly happy	48.8	49.1	48.9
Very happy	23.6	25.0	24.1
Completely happy	10.7	12.0	11.1
Score	5.24	5.31	5.26
N	1,216	617	1,833

while for women, the numbers were 4.2 percent and 3.6 percent, respectively. We now turn to the econometric evidence where we are able to hold constant a number of factors including labor market and marital status, age, gender, and schooling. The rankings remain essentially unchanged.

7.3.1   Econometric Evidence on the Microdeterminants of Happiness

Rank orderings of the United States and France are consistent, whether we examine happiness, life satisfaction, or other variables relating to the family, no matter what data file or year we examine. Tables 7.9 and 7.10 explore differences in happiness between the United States and France using the ISSP 1998, 2001, and 2002 data previously described.[8] In all three years of data, the United States ranks above France, although there is some variation in the rankings across other countries. For example, the United Kingdom is above the United States in 1998 and 2001, but below it in 2002; it is also above Denmark in all three years, while Denmark is below France in 2001. In most other data files we examine, Denmark ranks at the top in Europe, especially on life satisfaction. Columns (3) and (4) provide estimates of ordered logits estimating how satisfied an individual is with their family life. The idea here is to ensure the rankings are not driven by different interpretations of the word "happy," although they are still potentially impacted by the reticence of the French to be emphatic when reporting their well-being. Rankings are similar to those based on happiness, with Americans more satisfied than the French. It does seem, however, that people in the United States value time with their families very highly. Interestingly, when individuals in the ISSP are asked whether they wished they could spend more time with their families, more than half of respondents reported they would like to spend "much more time," compared with a third in France and the United Kingdom and a fifth in Denmark (table 7.11).

It is appropriate to explore further the ranking by country using the SWB measures from other data files to see if the rankings are consistent. This is what is done in tables 7.12 through 7.14, and it turns out they are. Table 7.12 uses data from eighty-two countries from the four sweeps of the WVS of 1981 to 2004 on both life satisfaction and happiness. Ordered logits are estimated in columns (1) and (2) with the dependent variable—life satisfaction—and responses are scored on a scale of one to ten, where one is least satisfied and ten is most satisfied. The sample size is just over one-quarter million observations—only three country dummies are included, with the remaining country dummies all excluded for simplicity. The first column only includes nineteen year dummies and country dummies for France, Denmark, the United Kingdom, and the United States, with all other countries

8. The exact question asked is Q.17: "If you were to consider your life in general, how happy or unhappy would you say you are, on the whole?"—1 = completely happy, 2 = very happy, 3 = fairly happy, 4 = neither happy nor unhappy, 5 = fairly unhappy, 6 = very unhappy, and 7 = completely unhappy.

Table 7.9   **Happiness equations: 1998 and 2001 ISSP**

	1998		2001	
	(1)	(2)	(3)	(4)
Denmark	.6415 (7.32)	.6554 (7.39)	.2451 (2.86)	.2664 (3.05)
France	−.2635 (3.00)	−.3977 (4.49)	.2699 (3.22)	.3043 (3.59)
U.K.	.8500 (10.55)	.8920 (10.97)	.5855 (7.64)	.7097 (9.16)
Australia	.6791 (8.06)	.6196 (7.17)	.2599 (3.12)	.2942 (3.41)
Austria	.3595 (4.02)	.3139 (3.48)	.3252 (3.63)	.4093 (4.52)
Brazil			1.2895 (16.34)	1.4270 (17.10)
Bulgaria	−1.4468 (16.31)	−1.4724 (16.39)		
Canada	.2404 (2.63)	.0987 (1.06)	.5587 (6.42)	.5751 (6.45)
Chile	−.5378 (6.32)	−.6176 (7.20)	.4707 (5.64)	.5407 (6.39)
Cyprus	−.2714 (2.95)	−.4533 (4.88)	−.9342 (10.26)	−1.0880 (11.83)
Czech Republic	−.3740 (4.41)	−.4048 (4.73)	−.5579 (6.47)	−.5132 (5.87)
East Germany	−.6886 (7.70)	−.5614 (6.25)	−.3648 (3.18)	−.2484 (2.16)
Finland			−.3058 (3.65)	−.3262 (3.79)
Hungary	−1.5248 (17.34)	−1.4973 (16.84)	−.7982 (9.71)	−.6713 (8.06)
Ireland	1.2023 (13.53)	1.2171 (13.51)		.0850 (1.02)
Israel	−.1655 (1.88)	−.3189 (3.59)	−.3637 (4.10)	−.4534 (5.06)
Italy	−.3475 (3.88)	−.4527 (5.03)	−.6034 (6.64)	−.8020 (8.56)
Japan	.0343 (0.41)	−.1062 (1.26)	.1487 (1.76)	.0985 (1.15)
Latvia	−1.4895 (17.63)	−1.5736 (18.41)	−1.4145 (15.85)	−1.3995 (15.50)
Netherlands	.7338 (9.48)	.7252 (9.30)		
New Zealand	.7760 (8.70)	.7544 (8.31)	.7155 (8.27)	.7782 (8.80)
Norway	.2935 (3.58)	.2269 (2.73)	.0872 (1.06)	.0850 (1.02)
Philippines	.2444 (2.79)	−.0038 (0.04)	.1119 (1.28)	.0772 (0.87)
Poland	−.0188 (0.21)	−.0332 (0.38)	−.5691 (6.61)	−.5061 (5.83)
Portugal	−.9207 (10.49)	−1.0417 (11.82)		
Russia	−1.3633 (16.72)	−1.4252 (17.16)	−2.5134 (32.28)	−2.5377 (32.23)
Slovakia	−.9608 (11.40)	−1.1135 (13.04)		
Slovenia	−.7625 (8.47)	−.9077 (9.99)	−.5625 (6.31)	−.6460 (7.17)
South Africa			−.1925 (2.46)	−.0077 (0.10)
Spain	.1531 (2.03)	.0883 (1.17)	−.2714 (3.20)	−.2837 (3.31)
Sweden	.2767 (3.18)	.1541 (1.75)		
Switzerland	.5572 (6.49)	.5453 (6.28)	.7205 (8.12)	.7698 (8.52)
U.S.	.8065 (9.49)	.8325 (9.72)	.7800 (8.98)	.9193 (10.45)
Age	−.0738 (17.72)			−.0630 (15.17)
Age^2	.0006 (14.76)			.0006 (13.29)
Male	−.0960 (4.23)			−.0180 (0.80)
Personal controls	No	Yes	No	Yes
Cut1	−3.6133	−5.4182	−3.5164	−4.9288
Cut2	−1.5153	−3.2445	−1.7275	−3.0885
Cut3	1.4123	−.2039	1.1509	−.1180
N	37,875	37,521	35,950	35,219
Pseudo R^2	.0607	.0857	.0765	.0964

Source: 1998 and 2001 ISSP.

Notes: Personal controls are marital status and labor market status dummies. Excluded country: West Germany. "If you were to consider your life in general, how happy would you say you are, on the whole— not at all happy, not very happy, fairly happy, or very happy?"

Table 7.10 **Happiness and role of the family: 2002 ISSP**

	Happiness		Family	
	(1)	(2)	(3)	(4)
Denmark		−.1159 (1.53)		.3825 (4.95)
France		−.3039 (4.40)		−.4605 (6.41)
U.K.		.3613 (5.65)		.3082 (4.65)
U.S.	.6701 (8.30)	.4169 (5.45)	.7448 (9.36)	.3612 (4.56)
Age	−.1084 (7.26)	−.0705 (19.55)	−.1032 (7.06)	−.0675 (18.53)
Age^2	.0011 (7.29)	.0006 (17.50)	.0010 (6.91)	.0006 (17.03)
Male	−.0261 (0.35)	.0507 (2.68)	−.0758 (1.02)	.1118 (5.87)
No formal education	.5095 (1.36)	.0208 (0.49)	−.1011 (0.28)	.0432 (1.05)
Above lowest formal	.2813 (2.02)	.1833 (4.32)	−.0020 (0.01)	.1848 (4.43)
Higher secondary	.5644 (3.97)	.2459 (5.81)	.0738 (0.21)	.2191 (5.28)
Above secondary	.5243 (3.75)	.2957 (6.52)	.0035 (0.01)	.2207 (4.93)
University degree	.8726 (6.44)	.4026 (8.92)	.1145 (0.33)	.2392 (5.37)
Married	.9005 (9.00)	.7009 (26.23)	1.1943 (11.93)	.8491 (31.05)
Widowed	.0561 (0.30)	−.2500 (5.54)	.4089 (2.24)	−.1107 (2.41)
Divorced	−.0866 (0.63)	−.2372 (5.46)	.0597 (0.44)	−.3134 (6.96)
Separated	−.4838 (2.16)	−.3636 (5.53)	−.3306 (1.53)	−.5151 (7.85)
Public sector	.0291 (0.29)	.0392 (1.41)	−.0114 (0.12)	.0050 (0.18)
Self-employed	.0980 (0.65)	.1061 (3.11)	.1601 (1.08)	.0911 (2.69)
Unpaid family worker	−.7075 (0.91)	.0398 (0.33)	.2213 (0.25)	−.0415 (0.35)
Unemployed	−.2388 (1.24)	−.5482 (12.92)	−.2223 (1.17)	−.3923 (9.24)
Student	.0559 (0.28)	.1459 (3.13)	.0872 (0.42)	.1028 (2.16)
Retired	−.0991 (0.67)	−.0496 (1.34)	−.0267 (0.18)	−.0625 (1.68)
Housewife	−.0016 (0.01)	.0363 (1.01)	−.0246 (0.18)	.0038 (0.11)
Disabled	−.5181 (1.04)	−.4661 (6.60)	−.5115 (1.11)	−.3052 (4.29)
Other labor market	−.3538 (1.35)	−.2712 (4.43)	−.5177 (1.94)	−.2909 (4.77)
Austria		.4277 (6.34)		.5102 (7.24)
Brazil		.4371 (6.13)		−.3380 (4.64)
Bulgaria		−1.6116 (20.47)		−1.3513 (16.66)
Chile		.4715 (6.41)		.5708 (7.70)
Cyprus		−.0927 (1.16)		−.1089 (1.38)
Czech Republic		−.7562 (10.08)		−.8577 (11.23)
East Germany		−.6619 (6.41)		−.1039 (0.98)
Estonia		−.2654 (4.06)		−.2251 (3.37)
Finland		−.3428 (4.44)		−.3863 (4.86)
Flanders		−.3712 (4.98)		−.2767 (3.62)
Hungary		−.5945 (7.41)		−.2962 (3.59)
Ireland		−.0298 (0.41)		.4107 (5.34)
Israel		−.2329 (3.00)		.1679 (2.13)
Japan		.2953 (3.70)		−.2731 (3.40)
Latvia		−1.1807 (14.87)		−1.1642 (14.13)
Mexico		.5591 (7.34)		.8134 (10.61)
Netherlands		−.2270 (3.06)		−.1761 (2.30)
New Zealand		.2682 (3.30)		.1114 (1.34)
Norway		−.1811 (2.48)		−.0272 (0.37)
Philippines		.1092 (1.37)		.0601 (0.74)
Poland		−.7878 (10.48)		−.3929 (5.11)
Portugal		−.3820 (4.82)		−.2205 (2.75)

Table 7.10   (continued)

	Happiness		Family	
	(1)	(2)	(3)	(4)
Russia		–1.0997 (15.45)		–1.0436 (14.00)
Slovakia		–.9487 (12.21)		–.8533 (10.61)
Slovenia		–.4791 (6.15)		–.1456 (1.81)
Sweden		–.2411 (3.06)		.0495 (0.60)
Switzerland		.3338 (4.28)		.2935 (3.68)
Taiwan		–.3847 (5.59)		–.4845 (6.95)
West Germany		–.4315 (5.36)		–.0499 (0.60)
Cut1	–8.1600	–7.5073	–6.3764	–6.4968
Cut2	–6.0305	–5.9530	–5.2860	–5.4063
Cut3	–4.5138	–4.5258	–3.9864	–4.1993
Cut4	–3.0443	–2.9599	–3.0898	–3.0322
Cut5	–.7444	–.8420	–1.3159	–1.1549
Cut6	1.1677	1.1391	.2919	.7428
Pseudo R^2	.0460	.0456	.0444	.0442
N	2,885	44,468	2,859	43,657

Notes: Excluded categories are: "lowest formal qualification," "private sector employee," and Australia. *T*-statistics are in parentheses. Columns (1) and (3) are U.S. and France only. Columns (1) are (2) are responses to the question, "If you were to consider your life in general, how happy or unhappy would you say you are, on the whole?" (Respondents answered on a 7-point scale.) Column (2) refers to the following question: "All things considered, how satisfied are you with your family life?" (Respondents answered on a 7-point scale.) Scale is "completely unhappy," "very unhappy," "fairly unhappy," "neither," "fairly happy," "very happy," and "completely happy."

set as the omitted category for simplicity. Column (2) adds controls for age, gender, marital status, and labor market status. Happiness is higher among the married (Zimmermann and Easterlin 2006) and the educated and is especially low among the unemployed (Blanchflower and Oswald 2004a, 2004b). In both columns the country ranking remains as follows: France, the United Kingdom, the United States, and Denmark. In columns (3) and (4) the dependent variable is a 4-step happiness variable and the rankings are a little different: France, the United States, the United Kingdom, and again Denmark at the top. These results are consistent with the findings of Veenhoven (2000), who examined the first three waves of the WVS and found that among the three possible ways of ranking countries—based on responses of individuals on how happy they are, how satisfied they are, and how they would rate their lives on a scale from the worst to the best possible life—the ranking stays roughly the same.

Table 7.13 uses data from another source, the 2003 EQLS ($n = 26,000$), which obviously excludes the United States and follows a similar form, but this time separate results are reported on a 10-step scale for life satisfaction and happiness. Data are also available on the individual's assessment of their overall health on a 5-point scale: poor, fair, good, very good, and excellent.

Table 7.11	**Wanting to spend time with the family—ranked by percentage in 2005**	
	1997 (%)	2005 (%)
United States	41.9	55.3
Dominican Republic		55.3
Mexico		43.5
Philippines	50.8	38.7
Canada	23.3	37.8
South Africa		36.7
France	34.3	33.7
Israel	35.6	33.5
New Zealand	23.9	28.6
Australia		28.5
Ireland		28.1
United Kingdom	31.6	27.7
East Germany	29.8	25.7
Sweden	27.9	25.7
Norway	25.5	24.8
Slovenia	26.3	23.3
West Germany	24.5	21.4
Denmark	21.0	21.2
Portugal	34.1	19.8
Russia	23.9	19.3
Hungary	19.1	18.7
Switzerland	22.8	17.1
Bulgaria	14.7	16.7
Czech Republic	25.2	15.1
Spain	7.8	15.0
Finland		14.4
South Korea		13.1
Japan	7.5	9.1
Taiwan		8.9
Cyprus	25.2	7.2
Bangladesh	5.1	
Italy	15.7	
Latvia	15.6	
Netherlands	14.6	
Poland	23.4	

Source: 1997 ISSP ($n = 32,783$) and 2005 ($n = 43,440$).

Notes: Question asked is, "Suppose you could change the way you spend your time, spending more time on some things and less time on others. Which of the things on the following list would you like to spend more time on, which would you like to spend less time on, and which would you like to spend the same amount of time on as now?" (1 = Much more time, 2 = A bit more time, 3 = Same time as now, 4 = A bit less time, and 5 = Much less time.) Tabulated are the proportions saying "much more time" with their family.

Table 7.12   Life satisfaction and happiness: 1981–2004 World Values Survey (ordered logits)

	Life satisfaction		Happiness	
Denmark	.9958 (31.91)	1.0033 (31.47)	.8450 (24.83)	.8625 (24.78)
France	−.1073 (3.88)	−.1470 (5.11)	.4227 (13.64)	.4426 (13.74)
U.K.	.5004 (22.79)	.2823 (11.91)	.8036 (30.05)	.6773 (23.67)
U.S.	.5197 (23.77)	.3480 (14.59)	.6959 (28.04)	.5800 (21.41)
Age		−.0377 (22.09)		−.0491 (26.11)
Age^2		.00046 (24.75)		.00050 (24.63)
Male		−.0765 (8.45)		−.0848 (8.38)
Married		.1907 (14.98)		.4063 (28.44)
Living together		.2133 (10.00)		.3131 (13.04)
Divorced		−.3442 (14.18)		−.3737 (13.82)
Separated		−.4235 (12.29)		−.4364 (11.36)
Widowed		−.4123 (18.33)		−.4927 (19.98)
Part-time employee		−.0252 (1.56)		−.0064 (0.36)
Self-employed		.0361 (2.32)		.0612 (3.50)
Retired		−.2202 (12.43)		−.2276 (11.73)
Home worker		.0607 (4.21)		.1494 (9.35)
Student		−.0158 (0.84)		.0824 (3.87)
Unemployed		−.6850 (40.79)		−.4884 (26.36)
Other		−.2326 (6.80)		−.0245 (0.64)
Cut1	−3.4057	−4.0057	−3.6190	−4.3648
Cut2	−2.8445	−3.4499	−1.4905	−2.2030
Cut3	−2.2542	−2.8627	1.0105	.4280
Cut4	−1.8110	−2.4062		
Cut5	−1.0434	−1.6032		
Cut6	−.5878	−1.1143		
Cut7	−.0103	−.4836		
Cut8	.8544	.4453		
Cut9	1.5985	1.2323		
Year dummies	19	19	19	19
Schooling dummies	0	10	0	10
N	263,097	188,529	257,881	185,629
Pseudo R^2	0.0112	.0191	.0131	.0336

Notes: Excluded category is "full-time employees." Excluded countries are: Albania, Algeria, Argentina, Armenia, Australia, Austria, Azerbaijan, Bangladesh, Belarus, Belgium, Bosnia and Herzegovina, Brazil, Bulgaria, Canada, Chile, China, Colombia, Croatia, Czech Republic, Dominican Republic, Egypt, El Salvador, Estonia, Finland, Georgia, Germany, Greece, Hungary, Iceland, India, Indonesia, Iran, Iraq, Ireland, Israel, Italy, Japan, Jordan, Korea, Kyrgyzstan, Latvia, Lithuania, Luxembourg, Macedonia, Malta, Mexico, Moldova, Morocco, the Netherlands, New Zealand, Nigeria, Norway, Pakistan, Peru, Philippines, Poland, Portugal, Puerto Rico, Romania, Russia, Saudi Arabia, Serbia and Montenegro, Singapore, Slovakia, Slovenia, South Africa, Spain, Sweden, Switzerland, Taiwan, Tanzania, Turkey, Uganda, Ukraine, Uruguay, Venezuela, Vietnam, and Zimbabwe.

Table 7.13   Happiness: 2003 European Quality of Life Survey (ordered logits)

	Life satisfaction			Happiness		
Austria	.4090 (5.10)	.4271 (5.27)	.4289 (4.49)	.1428 (1.79)	.1567 (1.93)	.2364 (2.47)
Belgium	.0382 (0.49)	.0601 (0.76)	.1178 (1.21)	-.1505 (1.94)	-.1305 (1.64)	.0248 (0.26)
Bulgaria	-2.5368 (31.15)	-2.4404 (29.46)	-1.5446 (14.49)	-1.9696 (23.99)	-1.7896 (21.30)	-1.0179 (9.45)
Cyprus	-.0981 (1.04)	-.5691 (5.95)	-.3993 (3.47)	-.0203 (0.22)	-.5992 (6.26)	-.5023 (4.35)
Czech Republic	-.8607 (10.67)	-.8486 (10.29)	-.4109 (3.99)	-.6880 (8.65)	-.5519 (6.77)	-.0797 (0.78)
Denmark	1.1301 (14.11)	.9682 (11.68)	.9946 (10.42)	.4876 (6.17)	.3591 (4.35)	.4889 (5.15)
Estonia	-1.4143 (15.42)	-1.1176 (11.94)	-.5002 (4.52)	-1.0424 (11.19)	-.5971 (6.27)	-.0060 (0.05)
Finland	.7337 (9.31)	.8776 (10.95)	.9307 (10.07)	.2892 (3.73)	.5505 (6.87)	.6638 (7.17)
France	-.5155 (6.67)	-.5407 (6.87)	-.5271 (5.60)	-.5903 (7.70)	-.6114 (7.77)	-.5381 (5.72)
Germany	-.0595 (0.75)	.0175 (0.22)	.1688 (1.77)	-.1787 (2.28)	-.0340 (0.43)	.1886 (1.98)
Greece	-.5031 (6.23)	-.7647 (9.29)	-.4913 (4.61)	-.2915 (3.64)	-.5331 (6.53)	-.1970 (1.86)
Hungary	-1.3205 (16.37)	-1.1253 (13.75)	-.6237 (6.28)	-.7612 (9.36)	-.4981 (6.02)	-.0120 (0.12)
Ireland	.3055 (3.83)	.1194 (1.48)	-.0726 (0.66)	.3099 (3.82)	.0534 (0.65)	-.0187 (0.17)
Italy	-.2241 (2.89)	-.3280 (4.15)	-.2784 (2.82)	-.3707 (4.79)	-.5112 (6.42)	-.3979 (3.99)
Latvia	-1.6794 (21.04)	-1.2665 (15.48)	-.5631 (5.52)	-1.4945 (18.57)	-.9902 (11.95)	-.3624 (3.52)
Lithuania	-1.8015 (22.55)	-1.4053 (17.23)	-.6031 (5.91)	-1.4176 (17.51)	-.9009 (10.83)	-.1988 (1.92)
Luxembourg	.3766 (4.04)	.3448 (3.61)	.2902 (2.38)	.1996 (2.19)	.1745 (1.84)	.2715 (2.24)
Malta	-.0742 (0.80)	-.1755 (1.84)	.0016 (0.01)	.0692 (0.75)	.0152 (0.16)	.1816 (1.49)
Netherlands	.0326 (0.43)	.1135 (1.46)	.1602 (1.70)	-.2649 (3.46)	-.2190 (2.76)	-.1452 (1.52)
Poland	-1.1107 (13.66)	-.7742 (9.34)	-.2635 (2.61)	-.9345 (11.47)	-.5367 (6.40)	-.0732 (0.72)
Portugal	-1.3621 (17.13)	-.9364 (11.45)	-.5650 (5.66)	-1.1363 (14.13)	-.6304 (7.62)	-.2909 (2.88)
Romania	-1.0805 (13.45)	-.8107 (9.93)	.1680 (1.59)	-.6932 (8.76)	-.3469 (4.29)	.4908 (4.66)
Slovakia	-1.5512 (19.34)	-1.5434 (18.76)	-1.1304 (11.09)	-1.3157 (16.74)	-1.2635 (15.61)	-.8267 (8.23)
Slovenia	-.3313 (3.61)	-.2557 (2.75)	.0524 (0.48)	-.4307 (4.72)	-.3449 (3.70)	-.0521 (0.48)
Spain	.0092 (0.12)	.0423 (0.52)	.2027 (2.02)	-.0578 (0.72)	-.0038 (0.05)	.1765 (1.74)
Sweden	.4545 (5.70)	.3178 (3.90)	.3886 (4.14)	.1275 (1.61)	.0330 (0.41)	.1446 (1.54)
Turkey	-1.5390 (18.43)	-1.4167 (16.39)	-.7061 (6.83)	-1.2119 (14.74)	-1.1451 (13.31)	-.5424 (5.24)
Age		-.0372 (8.56)	-.0435 (8.79)		-.0301 (6.89)	-.0352 (7.09)
Age^2		.0004 (11.16)	.0005 (11.11)		.0003 (7.70)	.00038 (7.72)
Male		-.1795 (7.43)	-.1942 (7.11)		-.1817 (7.44)	-.1801 (6.55)

16–19 years schooling	.1903 (5.72)		.1360 (3.60)		.1829 (5.44)		.1370 (3.59)
20+ years schooling	.3223 (8.75)		.1855 (4.41)		.2517 (6.75)		.1473 (3.47)
Still studying	.2112 (2.21)		.0567 (0.52)		.3352 (3.51)		.1643 (1.50)
No schooling	−.2564 (2.88)		−.2819 (2.80)		−.2349 (2.62)		−.2533 (2.51)
Self-employed	.1516 (1.43)		.1700 (1.39)		.0218 (0.20)		−.0419 (0.33)
Manager	.3012 (2.91)		.3177 (2.69)		.1377 (1.29)		.0787 (0.65)
Other white collar	.0928 (0.91)		.1125 (0.96)		−.0582 (0.55)		−.1233 (1.03)
Manual worker	−.0248 (0.25)		.0583 (0.52)		−.1044 (1.02)		−.1115 (0.95)
Home worker	.0303 (0.29)		.1658 (1.39)		−.0013 (0.01)		.0685 (0.56)
Unemployed	−.7898 (7.40)		−.5403 (4.46)		−.6951 (6.35)		−.5801 (4.66)
Retired	.1176 (1.15)		.2819 (2.43)		.0995 (0.95)		.1657 (1.39)
Student	.3706 (2.80)		.4919 (3.22)		.1355 (1.01)		.1877 (1.22)
Married/living together	.4165 (11.5)		.3121 (7.56)		.6819 (18.57)		.6410 (15.36)
Separated/divorced	−.2513 (5.05)		−.1561 (2.79)		−.2846 (5.66)		−.1613 (2.86)
Widowed	−.1051 (2.00)		−.0621 (1.06)		−.1905 (3.59)		−.1374 (2.32)
Excellent health	2.3432 (41.06)		2.2364 (34.51)		2.8968 (49.23)		2.7734 (41.60)
Very good health	1.9204 (38.47)		1.8470 (33.09)		2.2610 (44.35)		2.1651 (38.07)
Good health	1.4378 (32.19)		1.3678 (27.81)		1.6980 (37.22)		1.6213 (32.31)
Fair health	.8783 (20.27)		.8278 (17.52)		1.0135 (22.98)		.9574 (19.93)
Log household income (Euros)			.3854 (19.33)				.2980 (14.93)
Cut1	−4.2796		−.6592	−4.9381			−1.7221
Cut2	−3.7286		−.0796	−4.3122			−1.0977
Cut3	−3.1262		.5638	−3.6354			−.3606
Cut4	−2.6458		1.0899	−3.0620			.2562
Cut5	−1.5797		2.2845	−2.0282			1.4275
Cut6	−1.0325		2.8925	−1.4683			2.0587
Cut7	−.2024		3.8177	−.6348			3.0205
Cut8	1.0723		5.2106	.6150			4.4443
Cut9	1.9941		6.1853	1.5450			5.4696
N	25,991	25,603	20,047	25,283	25,654		19,818
Pseudo R²	.0535	.0885	.0973	.0297	.0825		.0867
Age minimum	47	46	39	50			46

Notes: Excluded categories: "single," "other labor market activity," ≦ 15 years of schooling, "poor health," and the U.K.

Four separate controls for health status are included in column (2) for life satisfaction and in column (5) for happiness, along with a standard set of controls. Household income in Euros is also available in the data file, which is added in natural logarithms, in columns (3) and (6). This is the first time in a cross-country data file on happiness that income has been available in one currency (Euros). In all cases the rankings for the three main countries of interest are France, then the United Kingdom, and finally highest-ranked Denmark. Eastern European countries have low levels of happiness (Blanchflower 2001; Sanfey and Teksoz 2007); life satisfaction and happiness is U-shaped in age, minimizing in the mid-forties for life satisfaction and in the fifties for happiness. Adding controls for income lowers the age minimum. Happiness rises with education and income, regardless of whether health is controlled for. Married people and those living together, as well as those in good health, are particularly happy. The unemployed are especially unhappy (Blanchflower and Oswald [2004a]; Carroll [2007] for Australia; Hinks and Gruen [2007] and Powdthavee [2007] for South Africa).

Money buys happiness. Interestingly, and perhaps surprisingly from an economist's point of view, the coefficients of the other variables in the well-being equations of table 7.13 hardly alter when income is controlled for. The amount of happiness bought by extra income is not as large as some would expect. To put this differently, the noneconomic variables in happiness equations enter with large coefficients, relative to those of income. Following Blanchflower and Oswald (2004a), table 7.13, or its OLS equivalent (see table 7A.1), can be used to do a form of happiness calculus. The relative size of any two coefficients provides information about how one variable would have to change to maintain constant well-being in the face of an alteration in the other variable. To compensate for a major life event, such as becoming a widow or a ending a marriage, it would be necessary to provide an individual with additional income. Viewing widowhood as an exogenous event, and so a kind of natural experiment, this number may be thought of as the value of marriage. A different interpretation of this type of correlation is that happy people are more likely to stay married. It is clear that this hypothesis cannot easily be dismissed if only cross-section data are available. However, panel data on well-being suggest that similarly large effects are found when looking longitudinally at changes (thus differencing out person-specific fixed effects). If higher income goes with more happiness and characteristics such as unemployment and being black go with less happiness, it is reasonable to wonder whether a monetary value could be put on some of the other things that are associated with disutility. Further calculation using the life satisfaction data in table 7A.1 suggests that compared with being a manual worker, to compensate for unemployment would take a rise in net income of approximately €3,900 per month, which is very large, given the mean in the data of €1,392. Compared to being single, to compensate for being married or cohabiting would take

Table 7.14   Happiness, life satisfaction: 2002 European Social Survey (ordered logits)

	Happiness		Life satisfaction	
France	−.0016 (0.03)	.0588 (1.24)	−.5082 (10.71)	−.4803 (10.03)
Denmark	.8828 (19.15)	.7462 (16.01)	1.1833 (25.38)	1.0605 (22.55)
U.K.	.2033 (5.01)	.1386 (3.39)	−.0617 (1.55)	−.1435 (3.57)
Married	.5126 (19.35)	.4891 (18.42)	.2702 (10.25)	.2339 (8.86)
Separated	−.4287 (5.73)	−.4585 (6.10)	−.4754 (6.39)	−.5149 (6.86)
Divorced	−.1309 (3.10)	−.1249 (2.96)	−.2130 (5.06)	−.2062 (4.89)
Widowed	−.4401 (10.00)	−.4067 (9.26)	−.4055 (9.26)	−.3704 (8.48)
Age	−.0789 (24.00)	−.0634 (19.24)	−.0725 (22.14)	−.0564 (17.17)
Age^2	.0007 (23.77)	.0007 (21.98)	.0007 (23.77)	.0007 (21.95)
Male	−.1421 (7.85)	−.1807 (9.95)	−.1550 (8.59)	−.1967 (10.86)
Schooling	.0403 (17.03)	.0224 (9.41)	.0486 (20.62)	.0302 (12.68)
Self-employed	−.0461 (1.45)	−.0811 (2.54)	−.0575 (1.81)	−.0879 (2.76)
Not employed	−.2922 (13.25)	−.1454 (6.53)	−.3163 (14.36)	−.1678 (7.55)
Good health		−.5999 (26.65)		−.5906 (26.25)
Fair health		−1.2547 (45.77)		−1.2830 (46.88)
Bad health		−2.1052 (47.99)		−2.1141 (48.80)
Very bad health		−2.9244 (34.24)		−3.0003 (36.15)
Cut1	−6.3055	−6.8664	−5.0623	−5.6024
Cut2	−5.6224	−6.1758	−4.5712	−5.0994
Cut3	−4.9425	−5.4806	−4.0161	−4.5278
Cut4	−4.2389	−4.7518	−3.3945	−3.8793
Cut5	−3.7357	−4.2258	−2.9508	−3.4121
Cut6	−2.7478	−3.1797	−2.1598	−2.5686
Cut7	−2.2507	−2.6484	−1.7411	−2.1194
Cut8	−1.4475	−1.7908	−1.0251	−1.3520
Cut9	−.2258	−.5009	.1222	−.1381
Cut10	.9345	.6989	1.1579	.9339
N	40,903	40,879	40,852	40,825
Pseudo R^2	.0149	.0382	.0138	.0369
Age minimum	56	45	52	40

Notes: Excluded categories are "very good health," "single," and "employee," plus: Austria, Belgium, Czech Republic, Finland, Germany, Greece, Hungary, Ireland, Israel, Italy, Luxembourg, the Netherlands, Norway, Poland, Portugal, Slovenia, Spain, Sweden, and Switzerland.

€1,770.[9] Blanchflower and Oswald (2004a) also found large effects for the United States using the GSS data. These effects seem large and inconsistent with the claims of Kahneman et al. (2004a) that the size of the effects of circumstances on well-being are "surprisingly small."

Table 7.14 examines data from the 2002 ESS across twenty E.U. countries, plus Israel and Switzerland. Data are provided in columns (1) through

9. This is done simply by dividing the coefficient of unemployment by the coefficient of household income (i.e., 0.6847/0.0001715 = 3,903 Euros). The size of these effects is even higher using the happiness data (i.e., 6,420 Euros for unemployment).

(3) on happiness and life satisfaction. The rankings are very similar to those reported in table 7.13—France, then the United Kingdom, then Denmark at the top. The patterns in the data are similar to those identified previously—happiness and life satisfaction is higher for the most educated, the married, the employed, and the healthy. Happiness and life satisfaction are U-shaped in age. Table 7.15 uses data from a single Eurobarometer, number 57.2, on life-satisfaction (5-step), also with and without health status dummies. There is a U-shape in age in every case. Once again, in all six cases, the rankings are France, then the United Kingdom, then highest-ranked Denmark.

Identical rankings to this are found in table 7.16, which uses over three-quarter million observations from a long time series of Eurobarometers on life satisfaction (4-step). The rank ordering is France, the United Kingdom, and Denmark for the period 1975 to 2006, as well as for *all* subperiods. The rankings were also the same when thirty separate equations were individually run with the same controls in every year (results not reported). It is also apparent from table 7A.2 that the structure of OLS life satisfaction equations is similar across the main European countries. Interestingly, the patterns of the life satisfaction appear to be very similar to those in the happiness data of the United States.

Blanchflower and Oswald (2008b) found that psychological well-being is U-shaped through life. A difficulty with research on this issue is that there are likely to be omitted cohort effects (earlier generations may have been born in, say, particularly good or bad times). First, using data on 500,000 randomly sampled Americans and West Europeans, the paper designs a test that can control for cohort effects. Holding other factors constant, we showed that a typical individual's happiness reaches its minimum—on both sides of the Atlantic and for both males and females—during middle age. Second, evidence was provided for the existence of a similar U-shape through the life course in Eastern European, Latin American, and Asian nations. Third, a U-shape in age is found in separate well-being regression equations in seventy-two developed and developing nations. Fourth, using measures that are closer to psychiatric scores, Blanchflower and Oswald (2008b) document a comparable well-being curve across the life cycle in two other data sets: (a) in the GHQ-N6 (General Health Questionnaire [six negative questions]) mental health levels among a sample of 16,000 Europeans, and (b) in reported depression and anxiety levels among one million U.K. citizens.[10] Evidence of a U-shape in age is found in *all* life satisfaction and happiness equations reported in this paper.[11]

Easterlin (2006) argues that happiness in the United States, as well as family satisfaction and job satisfaction in the United States, follow an *inverse*

10. Clark (2007) finds a similar result in the United Kingdom using data from the BHPS, even after controlling for cohort effects.
11. See tables 7.11 through 7.16 and tables 7.20 and 7.21.

Table 7.15   **Life satisfaction in Europe: 2002 Eurobarometer (ordered logits)**

Age	−.0686 (10.97)	−.0524 (8.26)
Age^2	.0006 (10.56)	.0005 (9.03)
Male	−.0956 (2.79)	−.1366 (3.94)
ALS 16–19	.2396 (5.51)	.1616 (3.67)
ALS ≥ 20	.3558 (6.95)	.2533 (4.89)
Still studying	.4607 (4.83)	.1785 (1.84)
Married	.3649 (6.24)	.3094 (5.23)
Remarried	.1566 (1.12)	.1712 (1.22)
Living as married	.0441 (0.65)	.0519 (0.76)
Lived together	−.4266 (5.12)	−.4029 (4.80)
Divorced	−.3551 (4.18)	−.3256 (3.80)
Separated	−.3424 (2.73)	−.2905 (2.30)
Widowed	−.2354 (2.75)	−.2528 (2.93)
Home worker	−.0752 (1.12)	−.2046 (3.03)
Unemployed	−.6153 (6.94)	−.7256 (8.15)
Austria	.3848 (4.33)	.3325 (3.70)
Denmark	1.3696 (15.04)	1.3512 (14.55)
East Germany	−.8624 (9.94)	−.7610 (8.70)
Finland	.4217 (4.79)	.5945 (6.67)
France	−.7296 (8.29)	−.6743 (7.60)
Greece	−1.6273 (18.30)	−1.6692 (18.48)
Ireland	.4194 (4.68)	.3555 (3.92)
Italy	−.3468 (3.93)	−.2360 (2.64)
Luxembourg	.8863 (8.56)	1.0032 (9.57)
Netherlands	.7914 (8.97)	.9653 (10.79)
Portugal	−1.6154 (18.32)	−1.2698 (14.17)
Spain	−.2256 (2.52)	−.1340 (1.48)
Sweden	.8549 (9.65)	.9918 (11.03)
U.K.	.4863 (5.85)	.5822 (6.93)
West Germany	−.2427 (2.75)	−.1162 (1.31)
Good health		−.6605 (16.25)
Fair health		−1.2178 (24.90)
Bad health		−1.8047 (25.42)
Very bad health		−2.4710 (19.85)
Cut1	−5.7366	−6.2917
Cut2	−3.9623	−4.4689
Cut3	−2.7567	−3.2146
Cut4	.1500	−.1654
N	16,032	15,992
Pseudo R^2	.0911	.1197
Age minimum	57	52

Source: Eurobarometer number 57.2: Health Issues, Cross-Border Purchases, and National Identities, April to June 2002.

Notes: Excluded categories are "ALS < 16," "retired," "excellent health," "single," and Belgium. Equations also include thirteen occupation dummies.

Table 7.16   Life satisfaction in Europe: 1975–2006 Eurobarometers (ordered logits)

	1975–1989	1990–1999	2000–2006	1975–2006	1975–2006
France	-1.5161 (88.25)	-1.4750 (68.29)	-1.3120 (52.90)	-1.4516 (23.07)	-1.4453 (123.72)
Denmark	.5820 (33.06)	.6031 (26.85)	.7707 (30.27)	.6346 (52.57)	.6311 (52.64)
U.K.	-.4656 (28.88)	-.5582 (27.77)	-.3871 (16.72)	-.4738 (42.96)	-.4685 (42.73)
Age	-.0389 (24.25)	-.0389 (20.22)	-.0365 (17.97)	-.0379 (36.35)	-.0439 (51.02)
Age^2	.00047 (27.08)	.00043 (21.14)	.00043 (19.86)	.00044 (39.84)	.00047 (51.96)
Male	-.1754 (18.19)	-.0995 (9.31)	-.0843 (7.04)	-.1275 (20.83)	-.0942 (18.76)
Married	.3341 (25.83)	.3063 (20.17)	.5527 (31.33)	.3630 (42.50)	.3511 (49.32)
Living together	.0490 (1.93)	.1442 (6.18)	.2338 (10.27)	.1268 (9.42)	.1562 (14.23)
Divorced	-.6085 (21.31)	-.4494 (16.53)	-.3219 (11.68)	-.4759 (30.20)	-.4055 (31.47)
Separated	-.7687 (18.55)	-.5679 (12.91)	-.4587 (10.78)	-.6017 (24.65)	-.5303 (25.42)
Widowed	-.3319 (16.10)	-.2200 (8.97)	-.1292 (4.59)	-.2566 (18.71)	-.2314 (20.58)
ALS 16–19	.2485 (24.71)	.1778 (13.86)	.1819 (11.16)	.2137 (30.26)	.2234 (37.68)
ALS ≥ 20	.4407 (33.33)	.3836 (25.62)	.4729 (25.82)	.4385 (51.61)	.4622 (66.14)
Still studying	.4254 (20.90)	.4591 (18.34)	.6357 (21.44)	.4998 (36.08)	.4997 (44.35)
Self-employed	.0801 (5.40)	.0167 (0.88)	.0628 (2.81)	.0514 (4.97)	.0358 (4.33)
Home worker	-.0332 (2.52)	-.0594 (3.50)	-.1582 (7.87)	-.0510 (5.60)	-.0412 (5.34)
Retired	-.0235 (1.37)	-.0950 (5.01)	-.1389 (6.75)	-.0863 (8.02)	-.1115 (12.76)
Unemployed	-1.0206 (54.66)	-1.0112 (49.64)	-1.1590 (46.81)	-1.0593 (88.25)	-.9557 (95.69)
Belgium	-.5811 (34.07)	-.7433 (34.84)	-.8530 (34.71)	-.6852 (58.64)	-.6809 (58.52)
Germany	-.8913 (52.16)	-1.2599 (66.97)	-1.3673 (62.25)	-1.1622 (07.17)	-1.1457 (106.75)
Ireland	-.4684 (26.80)	-.3616 (16.67)	-.3109 (12.60)	-.3968 (33.38)	-.3974 (33.62)
Italy	-1.7333 (99.51)	-1.3532 (62.52)	-1.4872 (58.95)	-1.5650 (31.22)	-1.5468 (131.58)
Luxembourg	-.2219 (8.95)	-.1188 (4.43)	-.1432 (5.02)	-.1594 (10.48)	-.1523 (10.04)
Austria					-.7195 (41.96)
Bulgaria					-3.4622 (108.59)
Croatia					-1.6853 (49.75)

Cyprus					−.7811 (22.28)
Czech Republic					−1.4738 (46.91)
Estonia					−1.9726 (61.17)
Finland					−.6119 (36.28)
Greece					−1.9742 (156.20)
Hungary					−2.3950 (74.57)
Latvia					−2.2816 (71.80)
Lithuania					−2.3225 (71.07)
Malta					−.8704 (18.67)
Norway					−.0103 (0.40)
Poland					−1.7470 (52.54)
Portugal					−1.8885 (142.58)
Romania					−2.8584 (87.56)
Slovakia					−2.2004 (70.75)
Slovenia					−.8661 (26.28)
Spain					−1.0737 (81.08)
Sweden					−.0893 (5.27)
Turkey					−1.2908 (34.25)
Year dummies	14	7	6	29	29
Cut1	−4.6814	−4.8268	−5.0042	−4.7075	−4.8679
Cut2	−3.0561	−2.9365	−3.1052	−2.9500	−3.0738
Cut3	−.2110	−.2103	.0150	−.0900	−.2416
N	234,939	164,693	130,077	529,709	768,993
Pseudo R^2	.0731	.0656	.0908	.0749	.0845
Age minimum	41	45	42	43	47

Source: Eurobarometers, 1975 to 2006. Excluded categories are "single," "employee," "ALS < 16," and the Netherlands. No data for 1996.

Table 7.17	Happiness ordered logit equations: 1972–2006 GSS	
Age	+.0152 (5.18)	–.0276 (8.92)
Age^2	–.00011 (3.76)	.00031 (10.21)
Time (1972 = 0)	–.0032 (3.52)	.0044 (4.79)
Married		.9872 (49.23)
Cut1	–1.6061	–1.9501
Cut2	1.1330	.9123
N	46,153	46,149
Pseudo R^2	.0011	.0299

U-shape in age.[12] His evidence was based on data from the General Social Surveys from 1973 to 1994. It is true that in the raw data, or in specifications that do not include income or marital status as controls, there is an *inverse* U-shape in the data of these three variables—but only in the United States.[13] However, once marital status alone is included, the U-shape flips and the sign of the time trend reverses, as can be seen in the two ordered logits with *t*-statistics in parentheses in table 7.17, estimated on the GSS data from 1972 to 2006.[14] Easterlin (2006) only includes controls for gender, education, and year of birth and its square, and I replicate his results with these variables using the longer time run of data from 1973 to 2006. I include controls for gender, schooling, race, region, birth decade, marital status, and labor market status in table 7.18.[15] In each case there is a U-shape in age after the inclusion of controls.[16]

I estimated fourteen separate OLS equations for the largest European countries using the 1972 to 2006 Eurobarometers; in each case the dependent variable was life satisfaction, scored from one to four, with only age and its square as controls. We report signs of the variables if significant at 1 percent on a two-tailed test. If insignificant, a zero is entered. In every country except Austria there is a significant U-shape in age. The coefficients, all of which were highly significant, can be found in table 7.19. When controls are included in table 7A.1—for education, gender, marital status, labor market status, and time—all of these countries had significant U-shapes in age. Table 7.20 uses 5-step happiness data for thirteen Asian countries for 2003

12. However, Easterlin (2006) did find a U-shape in health and satisfaction with their financial situation. Analogously, Mroczek and Spiro (2005) found that subjective well-being follows an inverted U-shape, peaking at around retirement age.

13. If an ordered logit is run with each of these five variables, along with only age and its square, there is an inverse U-shape for happiness, family satisfaction, and job satisfaction (workers only). There is a U-shape for the family's financial situation, while for the health variable, only the age square term is significant and negative.

14. Note in the data that the proportion married falls from 71.9 percent in 1972 to 48.1 percent in 2006.

15. I use a slightly different health variable than the one used by Easterlin (2006). I used "health," whereas Easterlin used "Sathealth," which was only available for a subset of years.

16. Health satisfaction declines with age in the raw data, which is consistent with the findings of Deaton (2008), who also found that health satisfaction declined with age.

Table 7.18   **Happiness in the U.S. (ordered logits)**

	Happiness 1973–2006	Financial situation 1973–2006	Family situation 1973–1994	Health 1972–2006
Age	−.0168 (4.11)	−.0209 (5.32)	−.0171 (2.55)	−.0615 (14.51)
Age²	.0002 (5.31)	.0004 (9.82)	.0002 (2.45)	.0004 (9.86)
Married	.7629 (26.65)	.1593 (5.87)	1.4303 (35.82)	.2514 (8.88)
Widowed	−.3187 (7.05)	−.2519 (5.87)	.4710 (7.89)	−.0094 (0.96)
Divorced	−.2303 (6.08)	−.5496 (15.13)	.1492 (2.78)	−.0629 (1.64)
Separated	−.4843 (8.56)	−.6057 (11.27)	−.1039 (1.42)	−.2047 (3.57)
Male	−.1769 (8.42)	.0107 (0.54)	−.3776 (13.06)	−.0520 (2.39)
Years schooling	.0570 (17.33)	.0787 (24.99)	.0271 (6.33)	.1420 (40.53)
Black	−.4233 (14.74)	−.5367 (19.62)	−.1456 (3.97)	−.3020 (10.45)
Other race	−.1588 (3.23)	−.1035 (2.24)	.0174 (0.20)	.3007 (6.11)
Part-time	−.1178 (3.61)	−.2360 (7.52)	−.1053 (2.39)	−.1988 (5.82)
Temp. worker	−.2791 (4.28)	−.1396 (2.22)	−.0703 (0.82)	−.4426 (6.44)
Unemployed	−.7613 (13.37)	−1.2248 (21.38)	−.0498 (0.71)	−.4486 (7.73)
Retired	−.0222 (0.55)	−.1763 (4.60)	−.0705 (1.33)	−.6291 (14.85)
Student	.1004 (1.75)	−.0141 (0.26)	.0233 (0.31)	−.2497 (4.19)
Home worker	−.1206 (3.99)	−.1416 (4.90)	−.1765 (4.60)	−.5754 (18.03)
Other	−.6738 (9.12)	−.8077 (11.36)	−.2245 (2.15)	−1.9501 (24.90)
Self-employed	.1363 (3.89)	.1390 (4.10)	.0257 (0.54)	.2398 (6.46)
Cut1	−1.4343	−.1456	−3.5776	−3.5952
Cut2	1.4994	1.9331	−2.7383	−1.6977
Cut3			−2.1230	.5157
Cut4			−1.2882	
Cut5			−.5270	
Cut6			1.0421	
N	46,034	46,168	23,911	38,256
Pseudo R²	.0451	.0507	.0403	.752
Age minimum	42	26	43	77

Source: 2006 GSS. All equations also include nine birth cohort decadal dummies and eight region dummies.

Notes: HAPPY: "Taken all together, how would you say things are these days—would you say that you are very happy, pretty happy, or not too happy?" (Coded 3, 2, 1, respectively.) SATFIN: "We are interested in how people are getting along financially these days. So far as you and your family are concerned, would you say that you are pretty well satisfied with your present financial situation, more or less satisfied, or not satisfied at all?" (Coded 3, 2, 1, respectively.) SATFAM: "For each area of life I am going to name, tell me the number that shows how much satisfaction you get from that area. Your family life: (1) A very great deal, (2) A great deal, (3) Quite a bit, (4) A fair amount, (5) Some, (6) A little, (7) None." (Reverse coded here.) HEALTH: "Would you say in general your health is excellent, good, fair, or poor?"

and 2004, drawn from the Asianbarometers.[17] The variables work in the same way as for other countries, and there are U-shapes in age with minima of forty-six from column (3) for the two years pooled. However, there is no

17. The 5-step happiness scale is "very unhappy," "not too unhappy," "neither," "pretty happy," and "very happy." The raw means by country were: Brunei (4.45), Cambodia (3.34), China (3.73), Indonesia (3.71), Japan (3.70), Korea (3.37), Laos (3.66), Malaysia (3.93), Myanmar (3.71), Philippines (3.82), Singapore (3.99), Thailand (3.88), and Vietnam (3.87).

Table 7.19   OLS life satisfaction equations: 1972–2006 Eurobarometers

	Age	Age^2	Minimum	N
Austria	–.0035	0	n.a.	19,309
Belgium	–.00692	.000055	63	61,840
Denmark	–.00331	.000028	60	61,023
Finland	–.01312	.000117	56	19,646
France	–.01943	.000208	47	63,253
Germany	–.00512	.000056	46	92,815
Greece	–.01741	.000127	68	49,863
Ireland	–.00766	.000105	36	59,983
Italy	–.00745	.000054	69	63,587
Netherlands	–.00918	.000084	55	61,699
Portugal	–.01572	.000096	82	41,286
Spain	–.01510	.000140	54	41,201
Sweden	–.00768	.000073	53	19,602
U.K.	–.00619	.000077	40	81,992

U-shape in the raw data, as was found in the United States. Analogously, simply adding marital status variables generates a significant U-shape. Well-being is U-shaped in age, whether measured by life satisfaction, happiness, or the U-index, once controls are included—even in the raw data in many countries. Cambodians and South Koreans are the least satisfied, while those from Brunei and Singapore are the most satisfied.

Table 7.21 uses data on 5-step life satisfaction for nine Asian and nine European countries from the Asia-Europe Survey (ASES) of 2001. Happiness is U-shaped in age and rises with education. The unemployed are especially unhappy in Europe but are also unhappy in Asia. In both Asia and Europe, native English speakers are especially happy—those with no understanding of English at all are less happy. The Swedish are especially happy and the Portuguese especially unhappy. There is a similar pattern to the Asian country dummies to those reported in table 7.20: Koreans are especially unhappy, and Malaysians and Singaporeans are notably happy.

7.4   Econometric Evidence on Hypertension, Unhappiness, and Pain

The question then is whether the pattern of results we have seen using happiness and life satisfaction are repeated when we make use of self-reported data on unhappiness, including high blood pressure, strain, inability to sleep, tiredness, stress, and pain. It turns out that the results mostly go through. A modern literature has claimed that countries like Denmark, Ireland, and the Netherlands are particularly happy, while nations such as Germany, Italy, and Portugal are less happy. Yet it is arguably implausible that words such as "happiness" or "satisfaction" can be communicated unambiguously and in exactly the same way across countries, so it is not easy to know

Table 7.20　　　　　**Happiness equations: Asia, 2003–2004**

	2003 (1)	2004 (2)	2003–1004 (3)
Age	−.0609 (3.64)	−.0530 (3.51)	−.0545 (4.89)
Age^2	.0006 (2.94)	.0006 (3.38)	.0005 (4.25)
Male	.1131 (2.34)	.0055 (0.12)	.0556 (1.96)
2004			.0974 (2.06)
Married	.5337 (8.21)	.3379 (5.56)	.4297 (9.72)
Divorced/separated	−.7679 (5.31)	−.4338 (3.11)	−.5873 (5.88)
Widowed	−.3372 (2.13)	−.3545 (2.46)	−.3298 (3.13)
Elementary school	−.2265 (1.53)	.1359 (1.14)	−.0271 (0.29)
High school	−.1977 (1.35)	.2888 (2.35)	.0487 (0.52)
Vocational school	.1407 (0.89)	.2014 (1.25)	.2784 (2.56)
Professional school	−.0057 (0.04)	.4041 (2.92)	.1959 (1.92)
University	−.0763 (0.50)	.4324 (3.22)	.1735 (1.74)
Business owner, mining	−.2329 (1.03)	.0195 (0.08)	−.0839 (0.57)
Business owner, retail	−.0436 (0.22)	.1060 (0.76)	.0880 (0.84)
Vendor/street trader	−.3903 (2.14)	−.0467 (0.38)	−.2284 (2.51)
Business owner > 30 workers	.0765 (0.27)	.1698 (0.52)	.2185 (1.08)
Self-employed professional	−.1191 (0.52)	−.0972 (0.47)	−.0453 (0.32)
Senior manager	.1003 (0.42)	.3179 (1.38)	.2387 (1.56)
Employed professional	−.3691 (1.90)	.1311 (1.03)	−.0526 (0.52)
Clerical worker	−.1217 (0.68)	.0468 (0.44)	−.0016 (0.02)
Sales worker	−.1244 (0.66)	−.0897 (0.82)	−.0678 (0.75)
Manual worker	−.4373 (2.54)	−.1523 (1.62)	−.2525 (3.18)
Driver	−.3220 (1.52)	−.1068 (0.73)	−.2073 (1.81)
Other worker	−.2107 (1.10)	.0259 (0.26)	−.0708 (0.81)
Homemaker	−.1748 (0.99)	.0829 (0.86)	.0332 (0.42)
Student	−.0042 (0.02)	−.0244 (0.18)	.0371 (0.36)
Retired	−.3681 (1.73)	.3568 (1.83)	−.0487 (0.38)
Unemployed	−.3312 (1.77)	−.3040 (2.53)	−.2613 (2.77)
Brunei	2.0931 (20.87)		1.8634 (22.63)
Cambodia	−1.1444 (11.56)		−1.2613 (16.21)
China		.1355 (1.75)	.1703 (2.27)
Indonesia	.7814 (7.88)		.4968 (6.32)
Korea	−.4566 (6.02)	−.5237 (5.49)	−.5538 (9.67)
Laos	.1558 (1.58)		−.0544 (0.69)
Malaysia	.4374 (5.53)	1.1094 (11.45)	.7029 (11.90)
Myanmar	.2563 (3.18)	.0389 (0.38)	.1005 (1.65)
Philippines	.8101 (8.06)		.6123 (7.39)
Singapore	.9663 (9.88)		.7894 (9.86)
Thailand	.1916 (2.35)	.8087 (8.00)	.4205 (6.89)
Vietnam	.3507 (4.34)	.8255 (8.04)	.5075 (8.22)
Cut1	−5.2402	−4.9904	−5.0458
Cut2	−3.2705	−2.7417	−2.9530
Cut3	−1.7456	−.9109	−1.2860
Cut4	.4602	1.4327	.9750
N	8,063	9,656	17,719
Pseudo R^2	.0187	.0754	.0459

Source: Asianbarometers, 2003 to 2004.

Notes: Excluded categories are Japan, "single," "self-employed in agriculture," and "no formal education."

Table 7.21 **5-step life satisfaction: Asia and Europe (ordered logits)**

	All	Asia	Europe
Age	−.0389 (6.05)	−.0202 (2.19)	−.0582 (6.45)
Age^2	.0004 (6.59)	.0003 (2.97)	.0006 (6.39)
Male	.0050 (0.14)	−.0602 (1.35)	.0446 (1.04)
Years of education	.0144 (3.96)	.0107 (1.71)	.0173 (3.90)
Part-time 15–34 hrs.	−.1321 (2.54)	−.0856 (1.20)	−.1748 (2.28)
Part-time < 15 hrs.	−.3989 (4.23)	−.3739 (3.07)	−.4217 (2.82)
Unemployed	−.8698 (12.25)	−.6509 (6.23)	−1.0340 (10.60)
Retired	.0185 (0.31)	.1725 (1.85)	−.0375 (0.45)
Student	.0665 (1.03)	.0246 (0.26)	.1135 (1.28)
Disabled	−.8076 (6.27)	−.2873 (1.17)	−.9950 (6.50)
Home worker	.0225 (0.47)	.1144 (1.80)	−.1279 (1.75)
China	−.6128 (5.80)	.0222 (0.24)	
Indonesia	−.9945 (9.50)	−.3335 (3.77)	
Japan	−1.0882 (10.58)	−.4530 (4.98)	
Malaysia	.5612 (5.60)	1.2387 (13.80)	
Philippines	−.6495 (6.09)		
Singapore	.4854 (5.32)	1.1575 (12.46)	
South Korea	−1.1532 (11.14)	−.4814 (5.43)	
Taiwan	−.8515 (8.25)	−.2023 (2.29)	
Thailand	.0830 (0.79)	.7481 (8.35)	
France	−.1068 (1.02)		−.0552 (0.46)
Germany	.2187 (2.13)		.2779 (2.33)
Greece	−.6369 (6.27)		−.5683 (4.90)
Ireland	−.0280 (0.34)		−.0226 (0.27)
Italy	−.1751 (1.67)		−.0999 (0.82)
Portugal	−.8867 (8.76)		−.8485 (7.24)
Spain	.1017 (0.97)		.1885 (1.56)
Sweden	.7458 (7.53)		.7707 (6.96)
Living with spouse	.2354 (6.00)	.0429 (0.78)	.4417 (7.72)
Living with children	.0440 (1.28)	.0685 (1.36)	.0325 (0.67)
Living alone	−.2406 (4.38)	−.1437 (1.44)	−.1417 (2.02)
No English	−.2741 (4.38)	−.2748 (5.18)	−.3007 (5.54)
English native speaker	.1855 (2.79)	.1615 (1.66)	.2377 (2.59)
Cut1	−4.0738	−3.1443	−4.3091
Cut2	−2.5235	−1.5143	−2.8690
Cut3	−.7316	.1917	−.9634
Cut4	1.2928	2.3497	.9668
N	18,148	9,126	9,022
Pseudo R^2	.0470	.0501	.0402

Source: Asia-Europe Survey (ASES): A multinational comparative study in eighteen countries, 2001 (ICPSR study number 22324).

Notes: Excluded categories are the: United Kingdom in columns (1) and (3) and the Philippines in column (2), and "full-time worker." *T*-statistics in parentheses.

whether such cross-national well-being patterns are believable. Evidence on blood pressure across nations suggests that such happiness findings are credible. This is illustrated in table 7.22, which uses data from two individual Eurobarometers—number 56.1 for 2001 in columns (1) through (5), and the more recent number 64.4 for December 2005 to January 2006. Column (1) of table 7.22 reports an ordered logit estimating whether an individual has high blood pressure from Blanchflower and Oswald (2008a), who showed that self-reported *high blood pressure* across individuals and countries is negatively correlated with self-reported happiness. Denmark ranks lowest on blood pressure and France ranks highest. More recently, Mojon-Azzi and Sousa-Poza (2007) show that even with more objective measures of hypertension, a negative relationship between high blood pressure problems and life satisfaction can be observed. They examined life satisfaction (scored in the normal way from one to four) and self-reported blood pressure, including whether the respondent took blood pressure medication, for a sample of people age fifty and older from the Survey on Health, Ageing and Retirement in Europe. Their main results can be found in table 7.23. Note that the correlation with life satisfaction was higher with taking medication (correlation = -0.79) than with self-reported high blood pressure (correlation = -0.66). Happy countries seem to have fewer blood pressure problems. This has two implications. First, it suggests that there may be a case to take seriously the subjective happiness measurements made across the world: they follow a pattern like the (inverse of) high blood pressure estimates. Second, in constructing new kinds of economic and social policies in the future, where well-being rather than real income is likely to be a prime concern, there are grounds for economists to study people's blood pressure. The results on blood pressure validate the differences in happiness across nations, in part because people can report high blood pressure in a more objective way than they report levels of happiness.

The second column of table 7.22, which is taken from Blanchflower and Oswald (2008a, column [4], table 5), estimates an OLS where the dependent variable is a measure of psychological distress constructed (in the spirit of the well-known GHQ score) by amalgamating answers to the following questions.

Have you recently:
1. Lost much sleep over worry?
2. Felt constantly under strain?
3. Felt you could not overcome your difficulties?
4. Been feeling unhappy and depressed?
5. Been losing confidence in yourself?
6. Been thinking of yourself as a worthless person?

To the answers to each of these six, we assigned the integers 0, 1, 2, 3—depending on whether each was answered "not at all," "no more than usual,"

Table 7.22   Unhappiness equations: 2001–2006 (ordered logits)

	Blood pressure OLOGIT (1)	GHQ-N6 OLS (2)	Unhappy OLOGIT (3)	Strain OLOGIT (4)	Lost sleep OLOGIT (5)	Down and depressed OLOGIT (6)	Pain OLOGIT (7)
France	-.1628 (1.60)	.6379 (4.12)	.2477 (2.85)	.2797 (3.19)	.2477 (2.85)	-.1010 (1.17)	-.0942 (0.99)
Denmark	-.5664 (5.18)	-.6924 (4.38)	-.3992 (4.43)	-.2454 (2.69)	-.3992 (4.43)	-.2508 (2.87)	-.2196 (2.37)
U.K.	-.5073 (5.13)	-.0158 (0.11)	.1519 (1.86)	-.0539 (0.64)	.1519 (1.86)	-.2050 (2.51)	-.2730 (3.10)
Austria	.1772 (1.80)	-.0985 (0.63)	.0516 (0.60)	-.0816 (0.92)	.0516 (0.60)	-.2598 (2.99)	.2702 (3.04)
East Germany	.6290 (6.70)	.8156 (5.21)	.2159 (2.52)	.5190 (5.99)	.2159 (2.52)	-.2564 (2.99)	.1323 (1.47)
Finland	.1967 (1.99)	.5969 (3.81)	.2817 (3.22)	.3776 (4.27)	.2817 (3.22)	.0235 (0.28)	.3676 (4.17)
Greece	-.1284 (1.26)	.6818 (4.33)	.7509 (8.61)	.6417 (7.21)	.7509 (8.61)	.6611 (7.88)	-.0768 (0.82)
Ireland	-.2044 (1.96)	-.0254 (0.16)	.0787 (0.90)	-.0859 (0.96)	.0787 (0.90)	-.0239 (0.28)	-.4457 (4.59)
Italy	.1764 (1.76)	2.2381 (14.26)	1.1709 (13.58)	1.0001 (11.35)	1.1709 (13.58)	.9197 (11.08)	.2801 (3.12)
Luxembourg	-.2635 (2.14)	-.1069 (0.57)	-.0350 (0.33)	-.1633 (1.53)	-.0350 (0.33)	-.2997 (2.74)	-.1870 (1.61)
Netherlands	-.4413 (4.19)	-.2764 (1.77)	.1471 (1.70)	-.1331 (1.49)	.1471 (1.70)	-.3231 (3.81)	-.1954 (2.16)
Portugal	.6478 (6.60)	.4654 (2.87)	.3101 (3.50)	.1795 (1.98)	.3101 (3.50)	.3919 (4.47)	.2049 (2.21)
Spain	-.0715 (0.70)	.0852 (0.55)	.4111 (4.77)	-.1156 (1.29)	.4111 (4.77)	.1460 (1.68)	-.2219 (2.33)
Sweden	-.7688 (6.98)	-.1259 (0.81)	-.0285 (0.32)	.1365 (1.54)	-.0285 (0.32)	-.2545 (2.92)	.4133 (4.53)
West Germany	.3636 (3.77)	.0516 (0.33)	-.3562 (4.00)	.1174 (1.34)	-.3562 (4.00)	-.3861 (3.63)	.1269 (1.17)
Bulgaria						.1444 (1.68)	.3881 (4.27)
Croatia						.5969 (7.09)	.4603 (5.06)
Cyprus						.3463 (3.33)	.0174 (0.15)
Czech Republic						-.0178 (0.21)	.5497 (6.40)
Estonia						.0173 (0.20)	.3809 (4.30)
Hungary						-.2502 (2.85)	.3138 (3.54)
Latvia						.6850 (8.29)	.5832 (6.68)
Lithuania						1.0796 (12.96)	.5414 (6.11)
Malta						.5618 (5.47)	.1774 (1.64)
Poland						.7116 (8.42)	.8483 (9.64)
Romania						.4892 (5.69)	.5797 (6.46)

	(1)	(2)	(3)	(4)	(5)	(6)	(7)
Slovakia						.2033 (2.43)	.8426 (9.76)
Slovenia						.2586 (3.11)	.5024 (5.67)
Turkey						1.2514 (14.21)	.2272 (2.31)
Turkish Cyprus						.9654 (9.13)	.2866 (2.50)
Age	.0675 (9.18)	.0958 (8.73)	.0580 (9.42)	.0551 (8.66)	.0580 (9.42)	.0426 (9.62)	.0432 (9.22)
Age^2	-.00035 (4.89)	-.0010 (9.22)	-.0006 (9.17)	-.0006 (9.75)	-.0005 (9.17)	-.00037 (8.28)	-.00014 (2.96)
Male	.0222 (0.55)	-.4727 (7.73)	-.3122 (9.20)	-.1338 (3.91)	-.3122 (9.20)	-.3316 (13.33)	-.3302 (12.44)
Age left schooling	-.0173 (3.53)	-.0211 (2.77)	-.0022 (0.53)	-.0044 (1.03)	-.0022 (0.53)	-.0241 (7.82)	-.0388 (11.88)
Constant/cut 1	2.6653	1.4913	.6249	.8070	.6249	.1346	1.0880
Cut 2	4.2449	2.5083	2.6542	2.5083	1.0063	1.5043	2.1977
Cut 3	5.8586	4.1751	4.4382	4.1751	2.6996	3.1742	3.1486
Cut 4	4.4722					4.9244	4.63040
Pseudo/adjusted R^2	.0847	.1349	.0487	.0449	.0487	.0439	.0826
N	15,396	15,379	15,658	15,633	15,658	28,185	28,151
Age maximum	96	48	48	46	58	58	160

Source: Columns (1) through (5): Eurobarometer number 56.1: Social Exclusion and Modernization of Pension Systems, September to October 2001 (ICPSR study number 3475), and Blanchflower and Oswald (2008a). Column (6): Eurobarometer number 64.4: Mental Well-Being, Telecommunications, Harmful Internet Content, and Farm Animal Welfare, December 2005 to January 2006 (ICPSR study number 4667).

Notes: The dependent variable in column (1) is a measure of reported problems of high blood pressure. The question that forms the dependent variable is, "Would you say that you have not at all, no more than usual, rather more than usual, much more than usual . . . had problems of high blood pressure?" (1 = not at all, 2 = no more than usual, 3 = rather more than usual, and 4 = much more than usual.) The dependent variable in column (2) is a psychological distress score measured on a scale from zero to eighteen. A GHQ-N6 score amalgamates answers to six questions. Have you recently: lost much sleep over worry? Felt constantly under strain? Felt you could not overcome your difficulties? Been feeling unhappy and depressed? Been losing confidence in yourself? Been thinking of yourself as a worthless person? Its mean in the sample is 3.6 (standard deviation = 3.7). The question that forms the dependent variable (in columns [3] through [5]) is, "Would you say that you have not at all, no more than usual, rather more than usual, much more than usual . . .": (a) column (3) = been feeling unhappy and depressed; (b) column (4) = been feeling constantly under strain; (c) column (5) = lost much sleep over worry. Personal controls included in columns (1) through (5) are ten dummy variables relating to the individual's experiences before the age of 18, sixteen labor-force status dummies, and eight marital-status dummies. Belgium is the excluded nation. The dependent variable in column (6) models the following question: "These questions are about how you feel and how things have been with you during the past four weeks. For each question, please give the one answer that comes closest to the way you have been feeling. How much of the time during the past four weeks have you felt downhearted and depressed?" (All the time, most of the time, sometimes, rarely, or never.) In column (7) the question is, "During the past four weeks, how much, if at all, has pain interfered with your activities?" (Extremely, quite a lot, moderately, a little, or not at all.) In empirical estimation we reversed the ordering. Personal controls included in columns (6) and (7) are sixteen labor-force status dummies and eight marital-status dummies. Belgium is the excluded nation. T-statistics are in parentheses. OLOGITS = ordered logits.

Table 7.23   Hypertension measures: Mojon-Azzi and Sousa-Poza (2007)

	Satisfaction score	High blood pressure (%)	Taking blood pressure medication (%)
Austria	3.25	30.9	31.3
Belgium	3.33	30.5	26.1
Denmark	3.65	28.6	26.4
France	3.02	27.9	30.8
Germany	3.19	35.4	34.9
Greece	3.23	33.0	32.6
Israel	3.04	41.4	41.8
Italy	3.00	36.1	35.9
Netherlands	3.56	24.8	24.2
Spain	3.30	34.3	32.4
Sweden	3.33	28.8	27.9
Switzerland	3.43	25.6	27.9

"rather more than usual," or "much more than usual." The numerical answers were summed, and we term the result a GHQ-N6 measure, where N stands for "negative." The mental distress score denoted in the GHQ-N6 must therefore lie between zero and eighteen for a person. Across Europe, the mean of the variable is 3.6 (standard deviation 3.7). These six are the six negative questions from the fuller GHQ-12 measure of psychological distress. The data set does not provide data on the other six positive questions. Thus our focus is upon negative affect. The rank ordering is the same once again—France as the most depressed, then the United Kingdom, and then Denmark as the least depressed. Column (3) then estimates an ordered logit with the dependent variable of whether an individual reports that they feel "unhappy or depressed." Column (4) models whether they "had been feeling constantly under strain," and column (5) refers to whether they had "lost much sleep over worry." The rankings once again, in all cases, showed France as the most depressed and Denmark as the least depressed. Column (6) of table 7.22 uses a different question from another Eurobarometer, number 64.4 for 2005 and 2006, in which the respondent was asked whether, during the preceding four weeks, they had felt "downhearted and depressed." Rankings were the same—France, then the United Kingdom, and then Denmark.

Atlas and Skinner (2007) examined the prevalence of pain in the U.S. population using the 2004 Health and Retirement Study (HRS) for approximately 18,000 people aged fifty and older. Among fifty to fifty-nine-year-olds, rates of pain ranged from 19 percent for male college graduates to 55 percent among female respondents who did not finish high school. A variety of covariates in the HRS such as occupation, industry, and marital status attenuated, but did not erase, these gradients. Atlas and Skinner found differences across educational groups, with rates of people aged fifty

Table 7.24   **Pain: 2006 Eurobarometer no. 64.4**

	Men	Women
ALS < = 15 years	17	24
ALS 16–19 years	9	12
ALS > = 20 years	7	9

to fifty-nine troubled by pain ranging from 20 percent for men with a college education to 55 percent of women who did not finish high school. Data from the Eurobarometer, number 64.4 for 2006, allows us to examine this issue across thirty-one European countries ($n = 28,000$). Respondents were asked, "During the past four weeks, how much, if at all, has pain interfered with your activities? Extremely, quite a lot, moderately, a little, or not at all?" The weighted percentage for the EU29 average reporting "quite a bit" or "extremely" by gender can be found in table 7.24. The data here are consistent with those reported by Atlas and Skinner for the United States—pain declines with education. I find that pain *rises* with age in Europe for all levels of education, whereas Skinner and Atlas found some evidence of the same for the more educated but found the reverse, surprisingly, for the least educated: pain fell with age from age fifty and older. Column (7) of table 7.22 estimates an ordered logit and confirms that, ceteris paribus, pain declines with level of education, rises with age, and is lower for men. Countries with the highest amount of pain are all from Eastern Europe (Poland, Slovakia, Latvia, Romania, Czech Republic, Lithuania, Slovenia, Croatia, Bulgaria, and Estonia) and all have low rankings on happiness and life satisfaction equations (tables 7.13 and 7.16).[18] Countries with the least pain, in order, are Ireland and the United Kingdom. The French report higher levels of pain than either the British or the Danish. Alongside the evidence on hypertension, the evidence from the incidence of pain does seem to further validate the findings from the SWB data rather than the U-index. It is difficult to believe that data on pain and blood pressure are as susceptible to the K2S3 criticisms that the French are less emphatic when reporting their well-being.[19]

There seems to be very clear evidence, then, that the patterns in both

18. I ran a happiness equation (how much of the time have you felt happy over the past four weeks—never, rarely, sometimes, most of the time, or all the time?) with the same data set. The rankings of these countries out of thirty-one was Poland (17), Slovakia (20), Latvia (30), Romania (24), Czech Republic (14), Lithuania (27), Slovenia (13), Croatia (23), Bulgaria (31), and Estonia (29). The overall correlation between the country coefficients from the pain and happiness equations was –0.61.

19. In ongoing work, Andrew Oswald and I have also found that pulse rates are also highly correlated with (un)happiness scores. Indeed, the structure of a pulse equation is very similar to that of a GHQ score in terms of its determinants. This work is being conducted using data from the English National Health Surveys of 1998 to 2007.

happiness and unhappiness equations are remarkably stable across data sets, countries, and question formats. They also appear to be broadly consistent in other attitudinal questions relating to the state of the economy, the government, and even law and order. The evidence does seem to suggest dramatic stability in the cross-country rankings. Table 7.25 examines happiness and life satisfaction data as well as data on unhappiness from a recently available sweep of the ESS of 2006 and 2007. The broad structure of both the happiness and life satisfaction equations are as before—U-shaped in age and higher for women, the more educated, the married, the healthy, and the employed. We also estimate an equation relating to the respondent's standard of living. The structure of the unhappiness equations—here relating to depression, loneliness, and anxiety—have the inverse structure. The country rankings can be seen in table 7.26—in all cases, Denmark was highest (lowest) and France was lowest (highest) for happiness and unhappiness, respectively. I explored responses to a number of other attitudinal variables relating to the respondent's well-being over the preceding week, whereas the other questions, as Krueger and Schkade (2007, 5) suggest, "elicit a global evaluation of one's life."[20] Ordered logits were again estimated with the same controls as in table 7.25: once again they had a similar structure, as shown before. For example, in all cases, happiness was U-shaped in age and unhappiness followed an inverted U-shape. In four of the five "happiness" questions, Denmark ranked higher than France, while in four of the six "unhappiness" questions, Denmark ranked lower than France. Countries in table 7.27 are ranked by coefficient size, from positive to negative. The rankings of countries when the questions relate to relatively short time periods, such as a week, are somewhat different from those obtained when questions covering the respondent's life more globally are examined. This seems more consistent with findings of the U-index that relate to even shorter time periods.

7.5   The Macroeconomics of Well-Being

I have increasingly become interested in the well-being data in the role of a macro policymaker. In the raw data, happiness (and life satisfaction) is negatively correlated with unemployment (figure 7.3) and inflation (figure 7.4). It also appears that happiness is positively correlated with GDP growth (figure 7.5—taken from Leigh and Wolfers [2006]). When a nation is poor, it appears that extra riches raise happiness. However, income growth in richer countries is not correlated with growth in happiness. This is the Easterlin hypothesis (Easterlin 1974) and is illustrated in figure 7.6, which uses data

20. The question asked was as follows: "Using this card, please tell me how much of the time during the past week. (a) None or almost none of the time, (b) Some of the time. (c) Most of the time. (d) All or almost all of the time?"

Table 7.25   Happiness and unhappiness equations: 2006–2007 European Social Survey (ordered logits)

	Life satisfaction (1)	Happiness (2)	Standard of living (3)	Depressed (4)	Lonely (5)	Anxious (6)
Age	-.0653 (17.43)	-.0757 (19.98)	-.0681 (18.05)	.0144 (3.33)	.0127 (2.88)	.0168 (3.93)
Age²	.0006 (17.77)	.0007 (18.86)	.0007 (19.79)	-.0001 (4.40)	-.0001 (2.91)	-.0002 (5.98)
Male	-.0900 (4.51)	-.1396 (6.94)	.0133 (0.67)	-.3881 (16.32)	-.1367 (5.49)	-.3476 (14.87)
Bulgaria	-1.8246 (26.25)	-1.8829 (26.66)	-2.7447 (38.91)	.2715 (3.39)	.5862 (7.00)	.1460 (1.95)
Denmark	1.2081 (18.03)	.8112 (12.22)	.9930 (14.62)	-.8543 (9.84)	-.7340 (7.68)	-2.1782 (25.00)
Estonia	-.5613 (8.41)	-.5132 (7.66)	-1.2267 (18.23)	.1649 (2.16)	.1317 (1.59)	-.3774 (5.18)
Finland	.7498 (12.06)	.5886 (9.46)	.1653 (2.63)	-1.1273 (13.82)	-.5382 (6.34)	-1.4849 (20.38)
France	-.6308 (10.07)	-.2637 (4.28)	-.6065 (9.78)	-.1376 (1.88)	.2460 (3.16)	-.3743 (5.48)
Germany	-.3417 (5.80)	-.3654 (6.22)	-.4580 (7.70)	-.0690 (1.00)	-.1783 (2.35)	-2.3118 (31.74)
Great Britain	-.0972 (1.61)	.0187 (0.31)	-.0795 (1.30)	-.2742 (3.78)	-.0736 (0.95)	-.8920 (13.19)
Hungary	-1.1962 (17.76)	-.7658 (11.09)	-1.2413 (18.31)	1.1965 (15.90)	.3155 (3.84)	-.0889 (1.21)
Norway	.3543 (5.57)	.3362 (5.27)	.2900 (4.52)	-.7612 (9.36)	-.4393 (5.08)	-2.2072 (26.72)
Poland	-.3125 (4.72)	-.4102 (6.22)	-1.0352 (15.76)	.3509 (4.68)	.0381 (0.46)	-.8912 (12.15)
Portugal	-1.1116 (17.94)	-.7288 (11.76)	-.9754 (15.79)	.1535 (2.15)	.5163 (6.79)	-.3686 (5.38)
Romania	-.4946 (7.40)	-.6367 (9.52)	-.9658 (14.52)	-.7713 (9.95)	.2046 (2.56)	-.3411 (4.74)
Russia	-1.3802 (22.47)	-1.2003 (19.42)	-2.3763 (37.78)	.3083 (4.36)	.7754 (10.44)	.1851 (2.77)
Slovakia	-.9316 (14.15)	-.9521 (14.41)	-1.0570 (15.98)	.3217 (4.23)	.7914 (9.94)	-.5862 (8.05)
Slovenia	-.0498 (0.74)	-.0513 (0.76)	-.5968 (8.86)	-.4390 (5.51)	.0248 (0.30)	-1.3731 (17.94)
Spain	.3175 (5.02)	.2956 (4.65)	-.1610 (2.54)	-.2762 (3.69)	-.1086 (1.34)	-1.6832 (22.57)
Sweden	.5252 (8.35)	.3757 (5.99)	.3889 (6.10)	-.6693 (8.52)	-.2806 (3.39)	-1.1832 (16.49)
Switzerland	.6907 (10.77)	.5006 (7.87)	.4709 (7.28)	-.0641 (0.85)	-.3779 (4.42)	-.2113 (3.01)
Primary	.2376 (3.89)	.3142 (5.06)	.2698 (4.39)	-.2885 (4.27)	-.2050 (2.99)	-.1396 (2.03)
Lower secondary	.3300 (5.37)	.3879 (6.21)	.4361 (7.06)	-.4830 (7.04)	-.4047 (5.81)	-.2502 (3.60)

(continued)

Table 7.25 (continued)

	Life satisfaction (1)	Happiness (2)	Standard of living (3)	Depressed (4)	Lonely (5)	Anxious (6)
Upper secondary	.4452 (7.20)	.4967 (7.91)	.5728 (9.21)	−.6224 (8.97)	−.5085 (7.21)	−.3773 (5.38)
Nontertiary	.5597 (8.16)	.5880 (8.47)	.6731 (9.77)	−.6502 (8.38)	−.4655 (5.88)	−.3994 (5.13)
1st stage tertiary	.5781 (9.13)	.5610 (8.73)	.8667 (13.59)	−.6736 (9.42)	−.5457 (7.46)	−.3842 (5.33)
2nd stage tertiary	.7583 (8.33)	.8046 (8.73)	1.1244 (12.36)	−.8300 (7.67)	−.8173 (7.02)	−.3794 (3.64)
Married	.4380 (14.44)	.6749 (22.00)	.4855 (15.92)	−.2097 (5.79)	−.9238 (24.54)	−.0283 (0.79)
Civil partner	.1576 (2.32)	.2969 (4.34)	.1816 (2.68)	−.1814 (2.22)	−.4824 (5.70)	.0722 (0.92)
Separated	−.4863 (5.42)	−.3335 (3.75)	−.5256 (5.96)	.4741 (4.88)	.5793 (6.02)	.5072 (5.23)
Separated (civil)	−.4096 (1.75)	−.5080 (2.04)	−.5818 (2.46)	.0237 (0.09)	.0299 (0.11)	−.3953 (1.37)
Divorced	−.0341 (0.78)	.0680 (1.54)	−.1768 (4.01)	.0591 (1.15)	.1415 (2.78)	.1090 (2.14)
Widowed	−.1442 (3.09)	−.2350 (4.98)	−.1357 (2.90)	.2502 (4.68)	.6951 (12.91)	.3614 (6.78)
Dissolved (civil)	−.3086 (2.31)	−.2289 (1.66)	−.6762 (4.90)	.4097 (2.60)	.4304 (2.86)	.6273 (4.02)
Student	.1985 (4.45)	.1130 (2.53)	.2913 (6.40)	−.0716 (1.33)	−.1473 (2.72)	.0039 (0.08)
Unemployed	−.9607 (16.42)	−.6475 (11.10)	1.0584 (18.32)	.5804 (9.17)	.4485 (6.96)	.4314 (6.70)
Unemployed (not looking)	−.7776 (9.97)	−.5443 (6.88)	−.8716 (11.03)	.4712 (5.41)	.5392 (6.19)	.4546 (5.20)
Disabled	−.5285 (8.08)	−.4053 (5.96)	−.5751 (8.56)	.8379 (11.64)	.5534 (7.53)	.6312 (8.67)
Retired	.0896 (2.44)	.0587 (1.59)	−.1088 (2.97)	.0927 (2.19)	.0915 (2.05)	.1516 (3.60)
Military service	−.2866 (0.96)	−.5011 (1.53)	−.6952 (2.16)	.5182 (1.39)	.1838 (0.45)	.8609 (2.29)
Home worker	−.0085 (0.22)	.0031 (0.08)	−.0797 (2.09)	.1112 (2.57)	.2229 (4.80)	.0792 (1.83)
Other lf	−.0747 (0.76)	.0461 (0.47)	−.0302 (0.31)	.4364 (4.07)	.3025 (2.76)	.2826 (2.63)
Bad health	.4034 (5.36)	.4580 (5.92)	.3564 (4.74)	−.5158 (6.54)	−.2409 (3.09)	−.2997 (3.75)
Fair health	.8716 (12.01)	.9745 (13.05)	.8008 (11.06)	−1.0676 (14.02)	−.6548 (8.72)	−.7573 (9.85)
Good health	1.4213 (19.28)	1.5147 (20.00)	1.2440 (16.95)	−1.6578 (21.35)	−.9363 (12.25)	−1.2391 (15.85)
Very good health	1.9183 (24.98)	2.0326 (25.82)	1.6860 (22.05)	−2.1002 (25.47)	−1.2024 (14.76)	−1.5664 (19.04)

Cut1	-4.2391	-5.2394	-4.4362	-1.7911	-.6224	-2.1631
Cut2	-3.6320	-4.5536	-3.8224	.5269	1.2865	.2997
Cut3	-3.0043	-3.7943	-3.1211	2.0986	2.5759	1.9788
Cut4	-2.3563	-3.0901	-2.4627			
Cut5	-1.8710	-2.5543	-1.9433			
Cut6	-.9569	-1.4430	-1.0441			
Cut7	-.4357	-.8456	-.4025			
Cut8	.4154	.1110	-.5434			
Cut9	1.7241	1.4642	1.9403			
Cut10	2.8699	2.6767	3.1896			
Pseudo R^2	.0767	.0711	.0885	.0961	.0941	.1160
N	34,786	34,638	34,780	34,592	34,674	34,643
Age min./max.	49	53	46	39	50	33

Source: European Social Survey, 2006 to 2007.

Notes: Excluded categories: Belgium, "single," "very bad health," "paid work," and "no formal education." (a) All things considered, how satisfied are you with your life as a whole nowadays? (b) And how satisfied are you with your present standard of living? Please answer using this card, where zero means "extremely dissatisfied" and ten means "extremely satisfied." Taking all things together, how happy would you say you are? (Extremely unhappy = 0 to extremely happy = 10.) Using this card, please tell me how much of the time during the past week (a) you felt depressed; (b) you felt lonely; and (c) you felt anxious. (None or almost none of the time, some of the time, most of the time, or all or almost all of the time.)

Table 7.26   **Well-being rankings: 2006–2007 European Social Surveys**

	Denmark	France	Great Britain
1) Life satisfaction	1	14	9
2) Happiness	1	10	7
3) Standard of living	1	11	7
4) Depressed	18	11	12
5) Lonely	19	6	12
6) Anxious	17	8	12

Table 7.27   **Happiness and unhappiness rankings: 2006–2007 European Social Surveys**

	Denmark	France	Great Britain
Happiness ranks			
You were happy?	10	4	5
You enjoyed life?	4	2	5
You had a lot of energy?	11	7	17
You felt calm and peaceful?	1	16	18
You felt really rested when you woke up in the morning?	12	15	19
Unhappiness ranks			
You felt that everything you did was an effort?	7	13	10
Your sleep was restless?	9	7	2
You felt sad?	17	13	12
You could not get going?	11	19	6
You felt tired?	8	6	3
You felt bored?	17	13	5

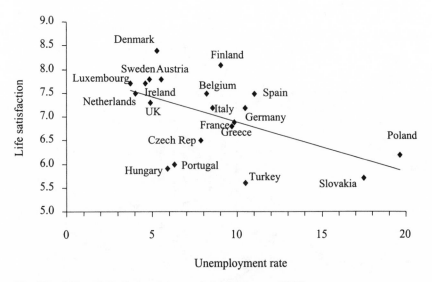

Fig. 7.3   Life satisfaction and the unemployment rate (2003)

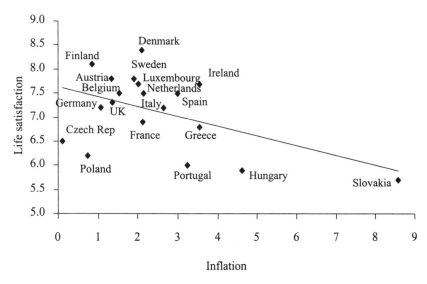

Fig. 7.4   Life satisfaction and inflation (2003 HICP)

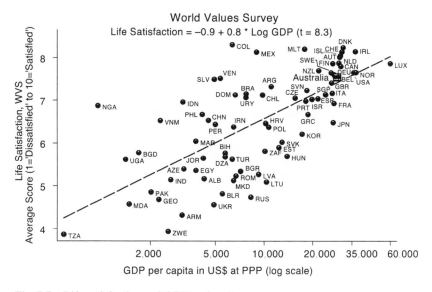

Fig. 7.5   Life satisfaction and GDP per capita

from the 1995 through 2000 WVS; the slope of the function for Western countries is approximately horizontal.

There is a small body of literature that uses SWB data across countries and through time to estimate a "misery index." Di Tella, McCulloch, and Oswald (2001, 2003) and Di Tella and MacCulloch (2007) use life satisfaction data to show that people are happier when both inflation and unemploy-

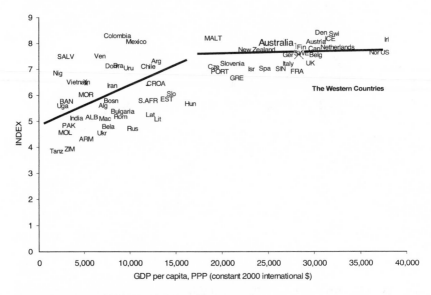

Fig. 7.6   1995 to 2000 World Values Survey result

ment are low. They all find that unemployment depresses well-being more than does inflation. Di Tella and MacCulloch (2007) suggest that left-wing individuals care more about unemployment relative to inflation than do right-wingers. Wolfers (2003) has also shown that greater macro volatility undermines well-being.

Table 7.28 uses aggregate life satisfaction data from the country*year cell of the World Database of Happiness, with the dependent variable as the score on a 4-step scale. Results are reported without a lagged dependent variable in columns (1) and (3) and with one added in columns (2) and (4), but this has little effect on the results. In columns (3) and (4), GDP per capita is added in U.S. dollars but is always insignificant once controls for unemployment and inflation are included. The rank ordering of countries once again is lowest-ranked France, then the United Kingdom, followed by the United States, and then highest-ranked Denmark. Both unemployment and inflation lower happiness. A 1 percentage point increase in unemployment has a larger impact than a 1 percentage point increase in inflation in all four columns. If GDP per capita is included without controls for inflation or unemployment but with country and year dummies, it enters positively and significantly. If an additional term is included, where GDP is interacted with a poor country dummy, the results were as seen in table 7.29, with *t*-statistics in parentheses.[21] Both terms are significant and positive, but the slope for

21. "Poor" is defined here as having 2004 GDP per capita of less than $20,000, which includes the Czech Republic ($6,263), Hungary ($5,626), Italy ($19,506), Mexico ($6,006), Poland ($5,032), Portugal ($11,090), Slovakia ($4,483), and Spain ($15,403)—GDP per capita in U.S. dollars in parentheses.

Table 7.28   Macrolife satisfaction: 1973–2006 (ordered logits)

	(1)	(2)	(3)	(4)
Life satisfaction$_{t-1}$		.5713 (13.83)		.5689 (13.64)
Inflation$_t$	−.0056 (3.87)	−.0029 (2.32)	−.0061 (4.11)	−.0031 (2.37)
Unemployment$_t$	−.0126 (6.26)	−.0046 (2.77)	−.0119 (5.69)	−.0046 (2.63)
GDP$_t$			.000002 (1.46)	.00001 (0.51)
Austria	−.0819 (3.20)	−.0458 (2.24)	−.0783 (3.04)	−.0452 (2.19)
Belgium	−.0266 (1.46)	−.0181 (1.26)	−.0250 (1.36)	−.0178 (1.22)
Czech Republic	−.3133 (9.38)	−.1284 (4.18)	−.2737 (5.59)	−.1175 (2.81)
Denmark	.3816 (20.73)	.1710 (7.94)	.3707 (18.67)	.1688 (7.64)
Finland	.0484 (1.86)	.0248 (1.21)	.0493 (1.90)	.0252 (1.22)
France	−.2940 (16.01)	−.1253 (6.64)	−.2920 (15.85)	−.1253 (6.61)
Germany	−.1334 (7.17)	−.0563 (3.65)	−.1333 (7.16)	−.0566 (3.66)
Greece	−.4725 (21.48)	−.1937 (7.31)	−.4474 (16.05)	−.1876 (6.41)
Hungary	−.6310 (18.77)	−.2768 (7.30)	−.5785 (11.73)	−.2640 (5.73)
Ireland	.0764 (3.88)	.0329 (2.10)	.0847 (4.11)	.0360 (2.17)
Italy	−.3445 (18.72)	−.1375 (6.77)	−.3346 (17.06)	−.1354 (6.50)
Japan	−.5266 (23.77)	−.2317 (8.27)	−.5519 (19.79)	−.2403 (7.45)
Luxembourg	.0779 (3.55)	.0475 (2.71)	.0497 (1.71)	.0395 (1.71)
Mexico	−.2705 (6.53)	−.2517 (4.32)	−.2167 (3.89)	−.2371 (3.63)
Netherlands	.1835 (9.50)	.0792 (4.68)	.1844 (9.53)	.0799 (4.60)
Poland	−.2952 (6.80)	−.1135 (2.97)	−.2511 (4.76)	−.1014 (2.27)
Portugal	−.5259 (24.67)	−.2211 (8.11)	−.4917 (15.47)	−.2130 (6.64)
Slovakia	−.4588 (10.64)	−.1769 (4.34)	−.4112 (7.63)	−.1641 (3.45)
Spain	−.1276 (5.30)	−.0528 (2.69)	−.1075 (3.89)	−.0472 (2.10)
Sweden	.1590 (6.03)	.0736 (3.36)	.1544 (5.81)	.0726 (3.29)
U.S.	.1674 (5.64)	.1137 (4.02)	.1465 (4.46)	.1081 (3.56)
Constant	3.1310	1.4209	3.2277	1.4230
Adjusted R^2	.9375	.9631	.9376	.9630
N	457	423	455	421

Source: World Database of Happiness and OECD, 1973 to 2006.
Notes: The U.K. is excluded category. *T*-statistics in parentheses. Equations also include thirty-one year dummies. GDP is per capita in U.S. dollars. Data on GDP unavailable in 2006 for Czech Republic and Ireland.

the richer countries is less steep than found for the poorer countries—there is diminishing marginal utility of income. This is the Easterlin effect, and it does suggest that rising GDP per capita raises happiness less for developed than for developing countries, which is consistent with the findings of Deaton (2008), who argues that "it is *not true* that there is some critical level of GDP per capita above which income has no further effect on happiness" (2008, 16–17). It is also consistent with the findings of Helliwell (2003), who uses data from the first three sweeps of the WVS and finds that in a life satisfaction equation across countries, "national average income also has diminishing returns, since the logarithm of average per capita income takes a positive coefficient, while the square takes a negative coefficient" (345). This result is different from the findings of Easterlin (1974, 1995) that happiness does not increase for long time spans, despite large increases

Table 7.29   Life satisfaction equations: 1972–2006 Eurobarometers

	Without a lagged dependent variable	With a lagged dependent variable
GDP$_t$	.000016 (11.84)	.00000247 (2.12)
GDP poor country$_t$	.0000287 (6.46)	.00000746 (2.14)

in income. Consistent with this result is the fact that happiness levels for a number of E.U. countries have increased over time. Indeed, in the pooled microdata files of the Eurobarometers from 1973 to 2006, if we simply regress life satisfaction in an OLS on a time trend only, there is a significant upward trend in life satisfaction for ten countries—Denmark, the United Kingdom, France, Finland, Ireland, Luxembourg, the Netherlands, Spain, Sweden, and Italy. There is a negative trend for Portugal, Germany, and Belgium and no significant trend for Austria and Greece.[22]

Table 7.30 uses microdata on over 700,000 individuals from fifteen countries for which I have long-time series-of-inflation data dating back to the 1950s (Austria, Belgium, Denmark, Finland, France, Germany, Greece, Ireland, Italy, the Netherlands, Norway, Portugal, Spain, Sweden, and the United Kingdom), drawn from the Eurobarometers from 1973 to 2006 and reported in Blanchflower (2007). As in table 7.28, which uses macrodata, controls are included for the unemployment rates and the inflation rate, but here, standard errors are clustered at the country*year cell. Once again both macrovariables enter negatively, and the ranking is Denmark, then the United Kingdom, and finally lowest-ranked France. Column (2) adds the variable reflecting the *average* annual inflation experience of each individual in our sample, given their age, their country, and the year the life satisfaction survey was conducted; this term is insignificant. Column (3) substitutes the average annual experience term for the *highest* annual inflation rate experienced by each individual over their adult life. This term is negatively signed and significant, and its inclusion has essentially no effect on either the coefficients of inflation or unemployment. An individual who has experienced high inflation in the past has lower happiness today, even holding constant today's inflation and unemployment rates. Unemployment appears to be more costly than inflation in terms of its impact on well-being. In Blanchflower (2007), I used these data to estimate a misery-index, which measures the relative effect of a 1 percentage point increase in unemployment compared with a 1 percentage point increase in inflation. The estimates imply individuals weight the loss from unemployment 1.6 times more than

22. Data are available for 1973 to 2006 for Belgium, France, Denmark, Germany, Ireland, Italy, Luxembourg, Netherlands, and the United Kingdom; for 1981 to 2006 for Greece; for 1985 to 2006 for Portugal and Spain; and from 1995 to 2006 for Austria, Finland, and Sweden.

Table 7.30 Microlife satisfaction: Europe, 1973–2006 (ordered logits)

	(1)	(2)	(3)	Age < 40 (4)	Age ≥ 40 (5)
Inflation$_t$	-.0094 (5.16)	-.0095 (5.18)	-.0096 (5.25)	-.0102 (4.83)	-.0128 (5.89)
Unemployment rate$_t$	-.0114 (5.82)	-.0115 (5.88)	-.0119 (6.05)	-.0109 (5.71)	-.0081 (4.20)
Average inflation experience			-.0010 (1.02)		
Highest inflation experience			-.0001 (3.44)	-.0002 (2.62)	-.00003 (2.85)
Age	-.0133 (16.42)	-.0133 (16.38)	-.0134 (16.74)	-.0067 (1.87)	-.0048 (3.83)
Age^2	.0001 (18.68)	.0001 (18.58)	.0001 (19.11)	-.0000 (0.01)	.00007 (7.41)
Male	-.0327 (10.48)	-.0328 (10.43)	-.0329 (10.51)	-.0424 (11.94)	-.0230 (5.69)
16–19 yrs. schooling	.0873 (17.72)	.0873 (17.73)	.0871 (17.80)	.0723 (10.70)	.0931 (18.85)
20+ yrs. schooling	.1664 (26.12)	.1665 (26.13)	.1664 (26.23)	.1530 (21.10)	.1666 (21.92)
Still studying	.1178 (7.88)	.1174 (7.84)	.1174 (7.82)	.1127 (9.02)	-.0080 (0.11)
Married	.1186 (19.86)	.1185 (19.84)	.1189 (19.92)	.1325 (20.30)	.1275 (17.81)
Living as married	.0481 (7.38)	.0483 (7.38)	.0496 (7.61)	.0569 (8.20)	.0406 (3.65)
Divorced	-.1621 (20.04)	-.1623 (20.05)	-.1622 (20.05)	-.1693 (15.76)	-.1415 (14.86)
Separated	-.2065 (19.13)	-.2065 (19.12)	-.2061 (19.12)	-.2085 (13.83)	-.1839 (12.83)
Widowed	-.0866 (13.17)	-.0864 (13.09)	-.0852 (12.95)	-.0938 (3.35)	-.0723 (9.77)
Self-employed	.0057 (1.22)	.0057 (1.20)	.0056 (1.19)	.0295 (4.69)	-.0097 (1.71)
Home worker	-.0243 (4.80)	-.0244 (4.80)	-.0244 (4.81)	-.0293 (4.50)	-.0205 (3.43)
Student	.0710 (4.90)	.0713 (4.92)	.0715 (4.93)	.0589 (4.94)	.0487 (0.73)
Retired	-.0395 (6.88)	-.0394 (6.84)	-.0395 (6.89)	-.1463 (6.23)	-.0348 (5.96)
Unemployed	-.3657 (29.77)	-.3658 (29.74)	-.3660 (29.71)	-.3574 (30.25)	-.3909 (24.68)
Austria	-.0956 (4.17)	-.0969 (3.45)	-.0904 (3.96)	-.0720 (2.65)	-.1142 (4.90)
Belgium	-.0807 (0.23)	-.0955 (4.17)	-.0807 (4.39)	-.0432 (2.11)	-.1164 (5.99)
Denmark	.3220 (21.96)	.3212 (21.82)	.3206 (21.78)	.3515 (21.58)	.2969 (19.72)
Finland	-.0001 (0.00)	.0014 (0.07)	.0032 (0.16)	.0397 (1.60)	-.0283 (1.49)
France	-.3271 (23.35)	-.3254 (23.29)	-.3254 (22.99)	-.3044 (17.94)	-.3440 (25.36)

Table 7.30 (continued)

	(1)	(2)	(3)	Age < 40 (4)	Age ≥ 40 (5)
Germany	-.2286 (19.35)	-.2297 (19.18)	-.2229 (18.85)	-.2255 (17.82)	-.2289 (17.34)
Greece	-.4596 (20.71)	-.4512 (18.89)	-.4485 (20.32)	-.3443 (15.86)	-.5500 (20.14)
Ireland	.0524 (3.50)	.0540 (3.61)	.0549 (3.68)	.0471 (2.83)	.0651 (4.01)
Italy	-.3434 (17.47)	-.3374 (15.85)	-.3306 (16.34)	-.2789 (12.53)	-.3850 (20.09)
Netherlands	.1199 (10.55)	.1179 (10.12)	.1181 (10.33)	.1549 (11.70)	.0869 (7.23)
Norway	.1072 (3.47)	.1064 (3.44)	.1057 (3.42)	.1423 (4.65)	.0757 (2.30)
Portugal	-.4979 (21.41)	-.4939 (21.13)	-.4973 (21.47)	-.3746 (15.68)	-.6047 (25.23)
Spain	-.1240 (7.41)	-.1206 (7.10)	-.1200 (7.14)	-.0794 (3.98)	-.1632 (9.79)
Sweden	.1057 (8.12)	.1054 (8.07)	.1054 (8.04)	.1386 (7.04)	.0821 (6.27)
Constant	3.5198	3.5262	3.5264	3.4315	3.2963
N	703,172	703,172	703,172	332,202	370,970
R²	.1549	.1549	.1550	.1481	.1639

Source: Eurobarometers, 1973 to 2006, and Blanchflower (2007).

Notes: Excluded categories are the U.K., "employee," "no children," "left school before age 15," and "single." All equations include twenty year dummies. Standard errors are clustered by country and year. "Average inflation experience" refers to the average annual inflation rate experienced by an individual over their life to the survey date. "Highest inflation experienced" refers to the highest annual inflation rate experienced by an individual over their life to the survey date.

the loss in well-being from inflation.[23] Columns (4) and (5) of the table provide separate estimates for those younger than forty years old and for those age forty and older. Interestingly, for the younger group, the misery-index is close to 1.4, whereas for the older group, it is approximately 2.1, while the size of the loss of happiness for the unemployed is similar.[24] Interestingly, the highest inflation term, which is negative and significant in both cases, is much larger in size in the former case, although its mean is much lower (20.2 and 116.2, respectively).

In table 7.31 I explore the impact of the macroeconomy on individual happiness and life satisfaction using self-reported views on unemployment, inflation, and inequality from three recent Eurobarometers from 2006 and 2007. The results are very similar to those based on using the macrodata; we also have evidence that inequality lowers happiness. In the first column the results from estimating a series of ordered logits are reported, with 4-step happiness as the dependent variable. In addition to the standard controls of labor market and marital status, schooling, gender, age, and country dummies, plus a number of additional controls not available in other data files were used. First, if the respondent is a member of a minority group, as well as if they are not part of the majority but do not associate themselves with a particular group, they enter significantly and negative with the effect three times larger. Second, controls are included to distinguish whether they owned their house outright or with a mortgage, both which enter significantly positive. Third, I include a control identifying whether the respondent belonged to a religious organization, which is also significant and positive. Fourth, following Di Tella and MacCulloch (2005) and Alesina, Di Tella, and MacCulloch (2004), I include controls for an individual's political views on a scale from one (left wing) to ten (right wing) and show that right-wingers are happiest. Finally, I include three variables based on an individual's response to a question asking what topics "worry you the most?" I include responses relating to unemployment, inequality, and the cost of living (inflation); multiple responses are possible. Unemployment and inflation lowers happiness, as does inequality, following Alesina, Di Tella, and MacCulloch (2004) and Blanchflower and Oswald (2004a). Column (2) uses data from Eurobarometer number 66.1,

---

23. The misery-index is calculated in Blanchflower (2007) as the coefficient of the unemployment rate plus the loss for the unemployed themselves, divided by the coefficient on the inflation rate. The loss to the individual from being unemployed can be calculated from the coefficient of being "unemployed" in a life-satisfaction microregression like the one reported in column (1) of table 7.18: estimated with OLS to keep the units consistent, we get −0.3657. The entire well-being cost of a 1 percentage point increase in the unemployment rate is therefore given by the sum of two components. Combining the two, we have $0.0114 + 0.0036 = 0.0147$ as society's overall well-being cost for a 1 percentage point rise in the unemployment rate divided by 0.0094. The implication is that the well-being cost of a 1 percentage point increase in the unemployment rate equals the loss brought about by an extra 1.56 percentage points of inflation.

24. Calculated as $(0.0102 + 0.0036)/0.0109 = 1.27$ and $(0.0128 + 0.0039)/0.0081 = 2.06$, respectively.

Table 7.31 **Happiness, life satisfaction, and views on the macroeconomy, 2006–2007 (ordered logits)**

	Happiness	Life satisfaction	
Inequality (current)	−.1976 (5.77)		
Unemployment (current)	−.0787 (2.71)	−.0745 (2.79)	
Inflation (current)	−.2313 (8.40)	−.1468 (4.83)	
Inflation (equal)			−.0409 (0.97)
Inflation (higher)			−.0671 (1.83)
Unemployment (equal)			−.1895 (4.80)
Unemployment (higher)			−.2402 (6.56)
Age	−.0973 (19.20)	−.0785 (16.84)	−.0871 (14.48)
Age^2	.0008 (16.43)	.0007 (15.99)	.0008 (13.65)
Male	−.1655 (6.00)	−.1187 (4.60)	−.0566 (1.83)
ALS < 16	−.0958 (0.66)	.3097 (2.84)	−.3417 (0.82)
ALS 16–19	.1883 (1.30)	.6316 (5.72)	−.2154 (0.52)
ALS ≥ 20	.3747 (2.55)	.8830 (7.87)	.0368 (0.09)
Unemployed	−.7356 (10.43)	−.6970 (11.01)	−.8683 (10.77)
Retired	−.1756 (3.11)	.0142 (0.27)	−.1487 (2.19)
Married	.8203 (16.61)	.3283 (7.18)	.3544 (6.48)
Remarried	.6441 (6.42)	.2989 (3.16)	.3703 (3.28)
Living as married	.4075 (6.88)	.1736 (3.10)	.1033 (1.55)
Previously lived together	−.2089 (2.69)	−.2262 (3.21)	−.4206 (5.10)
Divorced	−.1563 (2.35)	−.2834 (4.50)	−.4249 (5.64)
Separated	−.5704 (5.15)	−.3983 (3.71)	−.4337 (3.49)
Widowed	−.4460 (6.80)	−.2379 (3.89)	−.3670 (4.85)
Austria	−.9599 (10.46)	.0404 (0.55)	−.0304 (0.35)
Bulgaria	−3.1762 (33.98)	−2.2106 (30.93)	−2.2350 (23.42)
Cyprus	−1.0438 (9.06)	.3658 (3.74)	.3694 (2.77)
Czech Republic	−1.2175 (13.65)	−.3675 (5.08)	−.3712 (4.40)
Denmark	.4515 (4.90)	1.9123 (23.45)	1.7403 (18.61)
East Germany	−1.2621 (11.05)	−.5185 (5.31)	−.4315 (3.97)
Estonia	−1.6008 (17.00)	−.6161 (8.28)	−.7205 (7.96)
Finland	−.4786 (5.31)	.7295 (9.88)	.4965 (5.88)
France	−.2727 (3.00)	−.0309 (0.42)	−.2405 (2.65)
Greece	−1.2132 (12.85)	−.6965 (9.42)	−1.0286 (12.59)
Hungary	−1.6718 (17.61)	−1.5970 (22.32)	−1.5296 (17.90)
Ireland	.2515 (2.73)	.8377 (11.11)	.7815 (8.75)
Italy	−1.1559 (12.49)	−.3288 (4.48)	−.6513 (7.02)
Latvia	−1.7255 (18.56)	−.9410 (12.72)	−1.1391 (13.10)
Lithuania	−1.8129 (19.28)	−1.0639 (14.30)	−1.0678 (11.90)
Luxembourg	−.0565 (0.51)	1.1205 (11.56)	1.2979 (10.77)
Malta	−.5982 (5.19)	.2136 (2.13)	.3762 (2.96)
Netherlands	.0978 (1.07)	1.2924 (16.78)	1.1640 (13.24)
Poland	−1.0093 (10.85)	−.5752 (7.84)	−.5261 (5.64)
Portugal	−.9639 (10.32)	−1.0027 (13.87)	−1.0446 (10.94)
Romania	−2.4141 (25.56)	−1.7300 (24.31)	−1.5874 (15.49)
Slovakia	−1.8201 (19.67)	−.8210 (11.21)	−.8749 (10.59)
Slovenia	−.6665 (7.25)	.2936 (4.04)	.1955 (2.26)
Spain	−.6784 (7.34)	.4474 (6.07)	.0516 (0.51)
Sweden	−.1260 (1.38)	1.2562 (16.46)	1.1273 (12.91)
U.K.	.1592 (1.84)	.7696 (11.20)	.8118 (9.32)

Table 7.31   (continued)

	Happiness	Life satisfaction	
West Germany	−.8584 (9.22)	.2374 (3.21)	.3455 (3.99)
Member religious org.	.2927 (5.20)	.0455 (1.17)	
Minority group	−.2695 (5.78)		
No group	−.1113 (3.52)		
Own house (outright)	.2112 (6.11)	.3899 (12.65)	.2414 (6.23)
Own house (mortgage)	.1099 (2.85)	.3356 (9.33)	.3188 (7.36)
Left wing (1–2)	.0478 (0.75)	.0123 (0.21)	.1210 (1.67)
Left (3–4)	.0028 (0.05)	.1584 (3.17)	.2116 (3.36)
Center (5–6)	.0843 (1.74)	.2392 (5.35)	.2259 (3.88)
Right (7–8)	.1413 (2.60)	.3746 (7.49)	.3792 (5.98)
Right wing (9–10)	.3454 (5.20)	.4856 (8.31)	.5561 (7.58)
Cut1	−7.1023	−4.1532	−5.6338
Cut2	−4.8577	−2.2430	−3.6509
Cut3	−1.4631	.8395	−.4712
N	26,526	29,017	20,472
Pseudo R^2	.1319	.1294	.1297

Source: Column (1) = Eurobarometer number 66.3: European Social Reality, November to December 2006 (ICPSR study number 4528). Column (2) = Eurobarometer number 66.1: European Values and Societal Issues, Mobile Phone Use, and Farm Animal Welfare, September to October 2006 (ICPSR study number 21281). Column (3) = Eurobarometer number 67.2: European Union Enlargement, Personal Data Privacy, National Economy and Scientific Research, April to May 2007 (ICPSR study number 21160).

Notes: Excluded categories: Belgium; "responsible for ordinary shopping and housework," "unmarried, having previously lived with a partner," "no formal education," "refused to answer left/right scale," and "majority group." All equations also include fifteen occupation dummies. *T*-statistics in parentheses. Survey questions: Q1. On the whole, are you very satisfied, fairly satisfied, not very satisfied, or not at all satisfied with the life you lead? Q2. Do you think that in (OUR COUNTRY), the inflation rate in 2006 was higher, lower, or equal to the one in 2005? Q3. Do you think that in (OUR COUNTRY), the unemployment rate in 2006 was higher, lower, or equal to the one in 2005? Q4. Taking all things together, would you say you are very happy, quite happy, not very happy, or not at all happy? Q5. Which topics worry you the most?: (a) unemployment, (b) the cost of living (inflation), (c) the gap between the rich and the poor (inequality). Q6. In political matters people talk of "the left" and "the right." How would you place your views on this scale? (1 [left] to 10 [right].)

which uses a 4-step life satisfaction dependent variable and confirms that both unemployment and inflation lowers pay—information on inequality is available in that survey.[25]

Column (3) also uses 4-step data on life satisfaction from a 2007 Eurobarometer, number 67.2, with slightly different attitudinal questions. Once again, the unemployed have lower life satisfaction; happiness is U-shaped in age and higher for the married and for those who own their own house. It is especially high in Denmark and low in Bulgaria. The main difference in

25. Similar results are also found using Eurobarometer number 64.1, which does not contain details of home ownership.

column (3) is that now, the macro controls relate to whether the respondent believes that inflation is lower than, equal to, or higher than it was a year earlier. Once again, happiness is lower when the respondent reports that inflation or unemployment is higher. Unemployment, inflation, and inequality all appear to lower happiness and life satisfaction.

7.6   Predictions and Expectations

I recall John Abowd saying to me at a very early seminar given at the National Bureau of Economic Research that the crucial test for happiness data is whether or not it has any predictive power. Little work has so far been done on this question, but in some recent work I found that life satisfaction levels in Eastern European countries is a good *predictor* of migration flows to the United Kingdom. On May 1, 2004, the so-called A8 accession countries (the Czech Republic, Estonia, Hungary, Latvia, Lithuania, Poland, Slovakia, and Slovenia) joined the European Union.[26] Citizens from the A8 nations obtained free movement and the right to work in the United Kingdom, Ireland, and Sweden as of May 1, 2004.[27] Gilpin et al. (2006) examined data for the United Kingdom drawn from the Worker Registration Scheme (WRS), which registers the A8 workers, and computed the number of WRS registrations as a percentage of the home country population, which showed it is correlated with GDP and unemployment. Gilpin et al. found that countries with the lowest GDP per head, such as Lithuania (€2,500), are more likely to be registered on the U.K. WRS than those from countries with a higher GDP, such as Slovenia (€11,400).[28] The propensity to migrate is even more highly correlated with life satisfaction than it is with GDP per capita (Blanchflower and Shadforth 2009).

Of interest is whether life satisfaction or happiness is correlated with people's *expectations* of the economic situation. It turns out that they are. Respondents in thirteen separate Eurobarometers for the period of 1995 to 2006 were asked the following questions.

> What are your expectations for the next twelve months: will the next twelve months be better, worse, or the same when it comes to a) your life in general, b) the economic situation in (our country), c) the financial situation of your household, d) the employment situation in (our country), and e) your personal job situation?

Data are available on fifteen countries for all twelve years (Austria, Belgium, Denmark, Finland, France, Germany, Greece, Ireland, Italy, Luxembourg,

---

26. In addition, Malta and (South) Cyprus also joined the European Union at that date. Bulgaria and Romania joined the European Union on January 1, 2007.

27. Finland, Greece, Portugal, and Spain opened their labor markets to these workers on May 1, 2006, while Italy followed in late July 2006. Five other countries (Belgium, Denmark, France, the Netherlands, and Luxembourg) alleviated restrictions in 2006 (Zaiceva 2006).

28. Expressed as Euros per inhabitant at 1995 exchange rates and prices.

the Netherlands, Portugal, Spain, Sweden, and the United Kingdom). Data for the fifteen accession and candidate countries (Republic of Cyprus, Czech Republic, Estonia, Hungary, Latvia, Lithuania, Malta, Poland, Slovakia, Slovenia, Bulgaria, Romania, Turkey, Croatia, and Cyprus [Turkish Cypriot Community]) are present for only 2004 to 2006. In eight separate surveys, respondents were also asked about their expectations for themselves ten years hence—"In the course of the next five years, do you expect your personal situation to improve, to stay about the same, or to get worse?" Life satisfaction is further reported in a subset of these surveys. We examine three of these responses here.

Table 7.32 reports the results of estimating ordered logits for parts b, d, and d of the question, as well as for life five years ahead. The dependent variable is coded as one if the response was "worse," two if it was "the same," and three if it was "better," so positive coefficients should be interpreted once again as suggesting that the variable raises the probability of life improving. Column (1) and (2) of table 7.32 relates to the individual's views on the economic situation, columns (3) and (4) to the employment situation, columns (5) and (6) to their life over the following twelve months, and columns (7) and (8) for life over the following five years. In each case, separate results are provided with and without three life satisfaction controls derived from the standard 4-category life satisfaction variable. Happiness enters significantly and positively in each of these equations. This is similar to findings by Guven (2007), who found by using data from the Netherlands and Germany that happiness increases savings and decreases expenditures, and that the marginal propensity to consume is lower for the happy people. Happy people, Guven also found, (a) are more risk averse in financial decisions, (b) expect to live longer, (c) are more concerned about the future than the present, (d) expect lower prices in the future, (e) are less likely to smoke, and (f) do not desire to move within a country.[29]

There is a common pattern in the control variables across all eight specifications. Optimism (a) rises with educational attainment, (b) is U-shaped in age, (c) is lower for the married, the widowed, and the unemployed, and (d) is higher when the level of current happiness is greater. The country ranking in relation to people's views on the economic and employment situations is once again France, then the United Kingdom, and then Denmark. The British, though, are especially optimistic that their life will improve, and the Danish are now less optimistic than the French. Happier people, it turns out,

---

29. Guven (2007) examined data on prices only for the Netherlands using data from the Dutch National Bank Household Survey, which is a panel of about 4,500 individuals from 1993 to 2006. Data on price expectations are of particular interest to macropolicy makers. Guven found that happier people expect lower prices than unhappy people for the next year and also in five years' time. Questions asked were (a) "Do you expect prices in general to rise, to remain the same, or to go down in the next 12 months? 1 = go down, 2 = remain the same, 3 = rise," and (b) "By what percentage do you expect prices in total to have risen after 5 years?"

Table 7.32   Economic, employment, and life expectations in Europe: 1995–2006 Eurobarometers (ordered logits)

	Economic situation		Employment situation		Life one year ahead		Life five years ahead	
	(1)	(2)	(3)	(4)	(5)	(6)	(7)	(8)
France	-.1992 (8.00)	-.1645 (5.65)	.2112 (8.41)	.2532 (8.65)	.5166 (20.17)	.6714 (22.18)	.2419 (7.76)	.3045 (8.99)
Denmark	.2793 (11.31)	.1640 (5.68)	.6710 (26.70)	.4432 (15.09)	.4741 (18.48)	.2439 (8.01)	.5509 (17.42)	.3427 (9.88)
U.K.	.1664 (7.23)	.0751 (2.80)	.5437 (23.41)	.4223 (15.64)	.8461 (35.52)	.7944 (28.28)	.8284 (28.01)	.7599 (23.68)
Not very satisfied		.5787 (22.91)		.5318 (21.01)		.9013 (34.32)		.8380 (28.38)
Fairly satisfied		1.0971 (44.84)		.9678 (39.53)		1.8423 (72.14)		1.7548 (61.65)
Very satisfied		1.3750 (52.90)		1.2523 (48.21)		2.3265 (85.19)		2.1457 (69.87)
Age	-.0247 (16.31)	-.0177 (10.33)	-.0260 (17.03)	-.0187 (10.89)	-.0454 (29.01)	-.0338 (18.99)	-.0717 (36.07)	-.0623 (29.09)
Age^2	.0002 (12.98)	.0001 (7.84)	.0002 (13.53)	.0001 (8.30)	.0002 (14.87)	.0001 (6.75)	.0004 (19.36)	.0002 (13.11)
Male	.1379 (15.73)	.1347 (13.62)	.0694 (7.86)	.0791 (7.96)	-.0424 (4.68)	-.0443 (4.30)	-.0015 (0.14)	.0119 (1.01)
ALS 16–19	.1058 (9.35)	.0659 (5.13)	.1005 (8.78)	.0713 (5.50)	.2280 (19.58)	.1650 (12.42)	.1279 (9.13)	.0714 (4.77)
ALS 20+	.2684 (20.75)	.1946 (13.26)	.2560 (19.61)	.1970 (13.31)	.4439 (33.20)	.3216 (21.07)	.3521 (21.82)	.2552 (14.80)
Still studying	-.1670 (2.25)	-.1396 (1.85)	-.0469 (0.63)	-.0399 (0.53)	.0261 (0.34)	.0510 (0.66)	-.1002 (1.20)	-.0596 (0.71)
Homemaker	-.0354 (1.93)	.0066 (0.32)	-.0279 (1.51)	.0150 (0.72)	-.1102 (5.83)	-.0677 (3.14)	-.1406 (6.12)	-.1088 (4.44)
Student	.4141 (5.51)	.3224 (4.20)	.2681 (3.53)	.2118 (2.75)	.2025 (2.62)	.0340 (0.43)	.2356 (2.75)	.0247 (0.29)
Unemployed	-.1722 (8.46)	-.0428 (1.85)	-.1666 (8.14)	-.0600 (2.58)	-.0674 (3.15)	.1738 (7.08)	-.3499 (13.55)	-.1498 (5.39)
Retired	-.0892 (5.14)	-.0679 (3.47)	-.0604 (3.43)	-.0479 (2.43)	-.2201 (12.24)	-.2062 (10.16)	-.2226 (10.02)	-.1828 (7.69)
Farmer	-.2591 (7.36)	-.2083 (5.22)	-.1874 (5.37)	-.1856 (4.68)	-.4208 (11.53)	-.3427 (8.32)	-.4239 (9.59)	-.3726 (7.98)
Fisherman	-.0987 (0.50)	-.1320 (0.60)	.2000 (1.02)	.1952 (0.90)	-.0221 (0.11)	-.0260 (0.11)	-.5545 (2.20)	-.5713 (2.13)
Professional	.1447 (4.13)	.1020 (2.58)	.0805 (2.30)	.0583 (1.47)	.3413 (9.34)	.2896 (6.94)	.2365 (5.29)	.2137 (4.50)
Shopkeeper	-.0329 (1.32)	-.0171 (0.60)	-.0257 (1.04)	-.0108 (0.38)	.0779 (3.02)	.0862 (2.90)	.0178 (0.56)	-.0094 (0.28)
Business proprietor	.0375 (1.13)	.0121 (0.32)	.0143 (0.43)	-.0043 (0.12)	.3133 (9.04)	.2671 (6.78)	.2642 (6.18)	.2180 (4.77)
Empd. professional	.1083 (3.66)	.0569 (1.75)	.1120 (3.78)	.0803 (2.47)	.2223 (7.12)	.1355 (3.92)	.2264 (5.85)	.1480 (3.64)
General mgmt.	.1640 (4.31)	.1272 (2.92)	.1348 (3.51)	.0950 (2.17)	.2302 (5.85)	.1340 (2.95)	.3875 (7.83)	.3203 (6.07)
Desk employee	.0631 (3.40)	.0663 (3.15)	.0472 (2.54)	.0503 (2.39)	.0721 (3.74)	.0536 (2.44)	.0458 (1.94)	.0284 (1.13)

Traveling worker	.0258 (0.96)	.0252 (0.83)	-.0047 (0.18)	-.0063 (0.21)	.1356 (4.84)	.1436 (4.50)	.0370 (1.07)	.0235 (0.64)
Service worker	-.0422 (2.18)	-.0454 (2.07)	-.0335 (1.72)	-.0383 (1.74)	.0488 (2.42)	.0534 (2.32)	.0243 (0.98)	.0095 (0.36)
Supervisor	-.1080 (2.59)	-.0957 (1.98)	-.0244 (0.59)	.0026 (0.06)	-.0648 (1.50)	-.0641 (1.28)	.0066 (0.13)	-.0130 (0.23)
Skilled manual worker	-.0704 (3.86)	-.0574 (2.78)	-.0369 (2.02)	-.0160 (0.78)	-.0719 (3.79)	-.0351 (1.63)	-.1154 (4.98)	-.0992 (4.01)
Married	-.0438 (3.42)	-.1087 (7.41)	-.0465 (3.62)	-.1111 (7.57)	-.2285 (17.11)	-.3427 (22.26)	.0059 (0.36)	-.0794 (4.41)
Living as married	-.0218 (1.30)	-.0485 (2.56)	.0154 (0.92)	-.0127 (0.67)	.0913 (5.17)	.0524 (2.61)	.2435 (10.99)	.2207 (9.25)
Divorced	-.1214 (5.98)	-.0807 (3.53)	-.0892 (4.37)	-.0520 (2.27)	-.0604 (2.86)	.0105 (0.44)	-.0211 (0.82)	.0410 (1.48)
Separated	-.0785 (2.26)	-.0024 (0.06)	-.0433 (1.24)	.0001 (0.00)	.0380 (1.04)	.1202 (2.91)	.0253 (0.57)	.0852 (1.80)
Widowed	-.0348 (1.77)	-.0266 (1.20)	-.0451 (2.26)	-.0462 (2.06)	-.2552 (12.59)	-.2605 (11.35)	-.0426 (1.74)	-.0044 (0.17)
Belgium	-.3270 (13.12)	-.3317 (11.44)	-.1187 (4.68)	-.1595 (5.43)	-.2593 (10.15)	.2989 (9.93)	.1800 (5.80)	.1593 (4.74)
Bulgaria	.2122 (5.88)	.6864 (17.75)	.6647 (18.04)	1.0273 (26.01)	-.3157 (8.37)	.5173 (12.75)	-.4646 (10.36)	.4203 (8.82)
Croatia	-.1509 (4.19)	-.0566 (1.49)	.1982 (5.45)	.2246 (5.88)	.0765 (2.02)	.3013 (7.54)	.1426 (3.22)	.4676 (10.13)
Cyprus	-.8493 (16.54)	-.9129 (17.29)	-.3879 (7.66)	-.5087 (9.77)	.2896 (5.70)	.2481 (4.72)	1.0663 (16.89)	1.3438 (20.56)
Czech Republic	.1033 (3.02)	.1450 (4.03)	.3946 (11.57)	.3714 (10.34)	-.0144 (0.40)	.0914 (2.41)	.1454 (3.49)	.0384 (0.89)
East Germany	-.5925 (22.24)	-.5337 (16.83)	-.6807 (24.45)	-.6763 (20.46)	-.2950 (11.00)	-.1412 (4.39)	-.4160 (12.80)	-.2058 (5.79)
Estonia	1.1382 (31.82)	1.2831 (34.11)	1.2997 (35.81)	1.3702 (35.92)	.6421 (17.21)	.9339 (23.53)	.8317 (18.25)	1.2139 (25.58)
Finland	.4106 (16.93)	.2582 (9.17)	.6297 (25.52)	.4264 (14.87)	.6797 (26.72)	.5604 (18.76)	.4954 (15.92)	.4136 (12.26)
Greece	-.5529 (21.75)	-.5137 (17.23)	-.3399 (13.19)	-.3586 (11.89)	.0693 (2.64)	.3453 (11.20)	.0956 (2.97)	.2697 (7.71)
Hungary	.1444 (4.07)	.3748 (10.02)	.3728 (10.49)	.5062 (13.51)	.0314 (0.84)	.4611 (11.65)	.1077 (2.49)	.6243 (13.78)
Ireland	.6633 (26.36)	.5098 (17.30)	.9641 (38.02)	.7708 (26.02)	.8581 (33.18)	.7793 (25.53)	1.0534 (32.12)	.9904 (27.92)
Italy	-.0966 (3.85)	-.0024 (0.09)	.2124 (8.36)	.2693 (9.13)	.7019 (27.05)	.7908 (25.84)	.4969 (15.59)	.6210 (17.96)
Latvia	.3341 (9.48)	.5381 (14.48)	.9425 (26.76)	1.0672 (28.71)	.4124 (11.13)	.8205 (20.80)	.4771 (10.86)	.9836 (21.31)
Lithuania	.7039 (19.56)	.9195 (24.23)	1.4142 (38.46)	1.5498 (39.97)	.3486 (9.22)	.7629 (18.98)	.3308 (7.40)	.8426 (17.98)
Luxembourg	-.0392 (1.33)	-.1869 (5.36)	-.1065 (3.50)	-.2719 (7.57)	.3717 (12.26)	.2367 (6.50)	.4776 (13.07)	.3217 (8.07)
Malta	-.2176 (4.20)	-.2520 (4.74)	.1570 (3.04)	.0601 (1.14)	.3609 (6.87)	.3433 (6.35)	.5864 (9.66)	.6571 (10.61)
Netherlands	-.1666 (6.71)	-.3647 (12.52)	.2334 (9.30)	-.0006 (0.02)	.2141 (8.43)	.0308 (1.03)	.3388 (10.93)	.2403 (7.13)
Poland	.2184 (6.00)	.3241 (8.47)	.5216 (14.56)	.5540 (14.68)	.2721 (7.16)	.5026 (12.47)	-.1493 (3.37)	.1291 (2.80)
Portugal	-.4662 (18.09)	-.4349 (14.29)	-.3092 (11.79)	-.2527 (8.23)	-.2748 (10.36)	-.0419 (1.34)	.5516 (17.01)	.8370 (23.60)
Romania	.5398 (14.11)	.8658 (21.55)	.4709 (12.23)	.6939 (17.12)	.4295 (10.78)	1.0253 (24.31)	.6149 (13.07)	1.2583 (25.48)

(continued)

Table 7.32 (continued)

	Economic situation		Employment situation		Life one year ahead		Life five years ahead	
	(1)	(2)	(3)	(4)	(5)	(6)	(7)	(8)
Slovakia	-.1874 (5.36)	-.0076 (0.21)	.4146 (11.92)	.5137 (13.99)	-.1950 (5.36)	.1520 (3.95)	.0773 (1.32)	.1372 (2.29)
Slovenia	.0386 (1.08)	-.0115 (0.31)	.0443 (1.23)	-.0643 (1.71)	.1894 (5.15)	.1585 (4.08)	-.2430 (5.85)	.1741 (4.01)
Spain	.4554 (18.19)	.3578 (12.21)	.6354 (25.07)	.4992 (16.82)	.7092 (27.37)	.7410 (24.22)	.1905 (4.46)	.2488 (5.63)
Sweden	.3511 (14.17)	.2350 (8.14)	.5797 (23.18)	.4554 (15.64)	.9136 (35.52)	.7816 (25.80)	.8418 (26.37)	.8604 (24.84)
Turkey	.8676 (21.72)	.9566 (23.01)	.8859 (22.43)	.9024 (21.91)	.6698 (15.84)	.8543 (19.30)	.7608 (23.91)	.6430 (18.59)
Turkish Cyprus	1.2484 (24.82)	1.3015 (25.14)	1.3926 (27.75)	1.3765 (26.64)	1.0391 (19.32)	1.1983 (21.32)	.2221 (4.66)	.5001 (10.12)
West Germany	-.2751 (11.14)	-.2565 (8.93)	-.1166 (4.62)	-.1199 (4.09)	-.1441 (5.72)	-.0879 (2.97)	-.3021 (9.94)	-.2264 (6.88)
Cut1	-.4833	.5491	-.1550	.7494	-2.3905	-.6778	-3.7664	-2.0448
Cut2	1.3971	2.4703	1.5584	2.4985	.4734	2.3522	-1.4665	.35400
N	225,315	179,205	224,578	178,295	232,551	184,890	155,518	139,559
Pseudo R^2	.0535	.0489	.0440	.0537	.0711	.1059	.0958	.1225

Notes: Excluded categories: "middle manager," "single," and "ALS < 16." *T*-statistics in parentheses. Ordered logits. Equations also include year dummies. Source for columns (1) through (6): Eurobarometer number 65.2 (2006), number 64.2 (2005), number 63.4 (2005), number 62.0 (2004), number 61.0 (2004),[a] number 60.1 (2003), number 58.1 (2002), number 56.2 (2001), number 54.1 (2000), number 52.0 (1999), number 50.0 (1998), number 48.0 (1997), number 46.0 (1996),[a] and number 44.1 (1995).[a] For columns (7) and (8): Eurobarometer number 65.2 (2006), number 63.4 (2005), number 62.0 (2004), number 61.0 (2004),[a] number 57.1 (2002), number 55.1 (2001), number 53.0 (2000), and number 47.1 (1997).

[a] = does not include life satisfaction data in the survey.

are less pessimistic about the state of the economy, as well as, unsurprisingly, about how their life will proceed. These country rankings are consistent with the evidence from the 2002 ESS previously reported in table 7.14, where the respondents report on their current views on the economy, the government, and democracy.

Interestingly, respondents seem more optimistic about their own lives than they are about the economy or the employment situation in their country. For example, in the United Kingdom, respondents are twice as likely to report that they think their own situation will improve than to report that they think either the economic situation or the employment situation of the country will improve. Moreover, the trend in the former is up, while the trend in the latter is down. The proportion of U.K. respondents saying that the situation will be "better" for the economic and employment situations and their life in general over the next twelve months is set out in table 7.33. Annual percentage point changes in the unemployment and inflation rates are also shown. There is some evidence that respondents' expectations about the wider economic and employment situation in the Eurobarometers are well correlated with actual $(t + 1)$ macro-outturns, as can be seen in table 7.34.

Figure 7.7, panel A plots the proportion of respondents in the Eurobarometers who say they expect the economic situation in the next twelve months in the United Kingdom to "improve" (inverted) against the changes in both the unemployment rate and the inflation rate. The responses to how the economic situation is expected to develop is also highly correlated with

Table 7.33   **Expectations twelve months ahead: U.K.**

	Your life in general	Economic situation	Employment situation	Annual pp changes in		Economic situation	
				Unemployment	Inflation	GfK	MORI
1995	38	25	21	−1.0	0.6	−6.9	−17.5
1996	42	25	27	−0.5	−0.1	−3.6	−6.9
1997	39	29	33	−1.1	−0.7	8.3	7.3
1998	39	21	23	−0.9	−0.2	−6.9	−17.0
1999	36	25	31	−0.2	−0.3	−4.4	−5.3
2000	41	24	28	−0.5	−0.5	−10.8	−9.2
2001	46	21	23	−0.7	0.4	−14.8	−22.2
2002	46	16	19	0.3	0.1	−8.1	−22.8
2003	49	17	20	−0.2	0.1	−18.4	−28.3
2004	44	18	20	−0.2	−0.1	−12.9	−21.8
2005	44	18	20	−0.1	0.8	−11.8	−20.6
2006	43	21	21	0.7	0.2	−17.9	−28.3

Source: Columns (1) to (3): as in table 18. Columns (4) and (5): Office of National Statistics. Columns (6) and (7): MORI General Economic Optimism Index (www.IPSOS-MORI.com—economic optimism over the next twelve months), Gfk NOP Consumer Confidence Survey. (Q4. How do you think the general economic situation in this country will develop over the next twelve months?)

Note: "pp" means "percentage point."

Table 7.34   Correlation matrix

	Correlation matrix: unemployment rate	Annual pp changes at time $t + 1$ in inflation
Economic situation	−0.70	−0.48
Employment situation	−0.65	−0.45

Note: "pp" means "percentage point."

other surveys of economic confidence, such as the Growth from Knowledge Group (GfK) and Market and Opinion Research International Inc. (MORI) measures of general economic confidence for the coming twelve months, which use the same questions. The correlations are 0.73 and 0.85, respectively, as shown in figure 7.7, panel B. Macroeconomic variables appear to impact individual's expectations about their own lives and what they expect to happen to the economy as a whole, as do their current levels of happiness.

7.7   Conclusions

There are broadly consistent patterns in the SWB microdata, no matter what data file is used and no matter which country—perhaps excluding the poorest countries with low life expectancy. Results using data on well-being seem very similar to the results obtained from NTA—and potentially more stable, as sample sizes are often large. *Happiness* appears to be (a) U-shaped in age, (b) higher for the most educated, (c) higher for the better paid, (d) higher for nonminorities, (e) higher for the employed, and (f) higher for married people. Analogous results are found using self-reported unhappiness data. However, when such questions are asked in relation to the week prior to interview, the country rankings are quite different and seem more consistent with findings with the U-index that relate to fifteen-minute intervals.

Responses on blood pressure and pain appear to validate the happiness and life satisfaction data, as they are likely less subject to any cultural and language differences that might arise—for example, if the French are less emphatic when reporting their well-being. Happy people and happy countries seem to have fewer blood pressure and pain problems.

There are long consistent time runs of data available for macroeconomic analysis dating back to the early 1970s. Well-being across *nations* is correlated with the unemployment rate, the current inflation rate, and the highest inflation rate in a person's adult life, as well as with GDP growth rates, especially in poorer countries. Happiness and life satisfaction data help to forecast economic patterns, including migration flows. Happy people are particularly optimistic about the prospects for the economy.

There are a number of SWB measures that can and already are being used as an NHI in one form or another. These seem to correlate strongly with other macro measures including the unemployment rate, the inflation

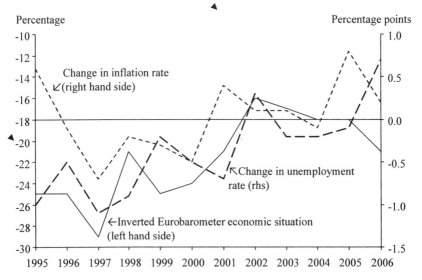

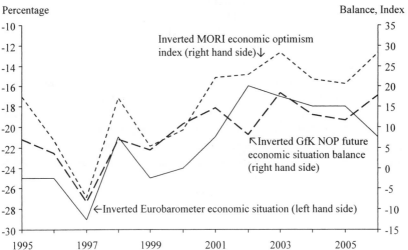

Fig. 7.7 Proportion of U.K. Eurobarometer respondents saying the economic situation in twelve months will improve (inverted): *A,* The change in unemployment and inflation rates will improve; *B,* Compared with other measures of economic confidence.

Source: Eurobarometers 1995 to 2006, MORI General Economic Optimism Index (www.IPSOS-MORI.com—economic optimism over the next twelve months), and the Gfk NOP Consumer Confidence Survey (Q4. How do you think the general economic situation in this country will develop over the next twelve months?).

rate, and even the suicide rate. The simplest and most widely available SWB measure is apparently the 4-step life satisfaction index, which is already available in similar form through ongoing annual surveys for all EU countries collected by the E.U. Commission, as well as in most Latin American countries. The fact that so much harmonized cross-country data are already available of this type is the singular attraction for this one measure. The one country where suitable data are unavailable is the United States, although 3-step happiness data have been available for many years in the GSS, which is quite small in size and now only collected biannually.[30] I recommend that a 4-step life satisfaction plus a 3-step happiness question are included as soon as possible at regular intervals in one or more large national surveys in the United States, such as the Current Population Survey (CPS). The CPS is an obvious place to include these questions, as they could be asked on more than one occasion to the same individual—perhaps in the first and last rotation groups, which would permit panel data analysis to be done over time for the same individuals. Such work has been possible in the United Kingdom using the BHPS and in Germany using the GSOEP, but to my knowledge, it has not been possible in the United States. This needs to change.

Research on NTA appears to be an important complement to this work, but the 4-step life satisfaction NHI, in my view, should be its starting point. Obviously nations have different languages and cultures, and in principle, this may cause biases in happiness surveys. Krueger et al. have identified that there appears to be a bias when comparing results from France with those from the United States. They found that on average, the French spent their days in a more positive mood and spent more of their time engaged in activities that tend to yield more pleasure than did Americans. The Americans seem to be more emphatic when reporting their well-being. Despite this, there are considerable similarities between the findings from the U-index and those from happiness and life satisfaction data. We are all trying to get utility proxy data for the u in the conventional utility function $u(y)$, and in principle, this is complementary to normal economics, not a rival to it. Happiness data no doubt have weaknesses, but it seems unlikely that they contain no useful information. A standard equation structure has now been replicated hundreds of times in a large number of nations, so we need to get to the bottom of it. Plus, income comes in positive and concave, inflation and unemployment hurt, and so on; all this seems to make sense to economists. Thus there are interesting regularities in well-being data. Whatever they mean, and whatever criticisms one might have of such data, it seems worth the time of economists and others attempting to understand why these patterns exist. It is good scientifically if rather different subjective well-being measures give similar equation structures. They seem to.

30. The World Database of Happiness does report data on 4-step life satisfaction (see table 7.2) for the United States, drawn from a number of small Gallup polls for the years 1991, 1997, and 2002 to 2004.

A big question going forward is how to incorporate the findings from national time use with those from the subjective well-being literature. Of interest will be whether there are differences, for example, between countries who speak the same language, such as the United Kingdom, Australia, Canada, and New Zealand. Are there significant differences between the results obtained from NTA and SWB in other countries besides the United States and France? If happiness is U-shaped in age, to what extent is the time use of the young different from that of the old? What is it that makes people unhappy during middle-age? Nations have different languages and cultures, and in principle, that may cause biases—perhaps large ones— in happiness surveys. At this point in research on subjective well-being, the size of any bias is not known, and there is no accepted way to correct the data, but progress is being made. National Time Accounting and SWB appear to be complements rather than substitutes. There is still much work to be done.

Appendix

Table 7A.1   OLS happiness equations: 2003 EQLS

	Life satisfaction	Happiness
Household income (Euros)	.0001754 (11.72)	.0000915 (6.60)
Age	−.0475 (9.31)	−.0346 (7.33)
Age^2	.0005 (11.50)	.0003 (8.08)
Male	−.1844 (6.41)	−.1525 (5.72)
16–19 years schooling	.1797 (4.61)	.1972 (5.46)
20+ years schooling	.2712 (6.21)	.2491 (6.15)
Still studying	.1016 (0.89)	.2236 (2.13)
No schooling	.2341 (1.31)	.0604 (0.36)
Self-employed	.2506 (1.98)	.0820 (0.70)
Manager	.4361 (3.55)	.2269 (2.00)
Other white collar	.2251 (1.86)	.0405 (0.36)
Manual worker	.1189 (1.01)	.0050 (0.05)
Home worker	.1785 (1.45)	.1114 (0.98)
Unemployed	−.6847 (5.49)	−.5874 (5.08)
Retired	.2864 (2.39)	.1786 (1.61)
Student	.5249 (3.33)	.2678 (1.84)
Very good health	−.3109 (6.05)	−.4164 (8.74)
Good health	−.7433 (14.94)	−.8651 (18.76)
Fair health	−1.3280 (24.70)	−1.5188 (30.50)
Poor health	−2.2910 (35.29)	−2.5683 (42.67)
Married/living together	.3389 (7.78)	.6240 (15.46)
Separated/divorced	−.2355 (3.99)	−.2292 (4.19)
Widowed	−.1400 (2.27)	−.1989 (3.48)
Constant	8.0087 (41.49)	8.7142 (48.12)

Notes: Equations also include twenty-seven country dummies. *T*-statistics are in parentheses.

Table 7A.2   OLS coefficients by country from life satisfaction and happiness equations

	Male	Age min.	ALS 16–19	ALS ≥ 20	Time	Married	Widowed	Self-employed	Student	Retired	Unemployed	N
Belgium	-.03	48	.03	.12	-.004	.15	-.12	-.05	.14	-.05	-.31	57,637
Denmark	-.06	44	.03	.10	.003	.14	-.04	-.03	.05	-.13	-.27	56,882
France	-.02	46	.10	.24	.005	.12	-.08	a	.33	.13	-.24	58,335
Germany	a	42	.02	.10	-.004	.11	-.04	.05	.12	-.05	-.52	85,631
Greece	-.01	56	.16	.28	a	.12	-.12	a	.29	a	-.21	47,801
Ireland	-.09	37	.14	.27	a	.12	-.07	.04	.22	-.04	-.55	55,839
Italy	a	56	.09	.12	.011	.15	-.07	.03	.13	a	-.39	59,032
Luxembourg	-.04	41	.06	.11	.003	.15	-.08	a	.12	a	-.41	23,297
Netherlands	-.08	46	.07	.12	.001	.16	-.16	a	.10	-.04	-.37	56,710
Portugal	.04	62	.08	.15	-.003	.05	-.12	.08	.16	-.04	-.29	38,354
Spain	-.02	51	.04	.11	.006	.11	-.11	.03	.11	a	-.27	38,969
Sweden	-.02	49	.06	.08	.019	.17	a	.01	a	-.09	-.25	18,427
U.K.	-.06	38	.10	.19	.002	.14	-.08	a	.18	-.07	-.40	76,346
Europe	-.03	46	.08	.16	.001	.11	-.10	.01	.17	-.05	-.37	768,993
U.S.	-.04	41	.09	.19	a	.28	a	.05	.17	a	-.23	46,035

Source: Eurobarometers and GSS 2006. OLS, dependent variable is 4-step life satisfaction and 3-step happiness in the United States. Excluded categories are "single," and "ALS ≤ = 15 years." Also includes dummies for home workers and those who are divorced. Data for the United States are from 1972 to 2006 (excluding 1979, 1981, 1992, 1995, 1997, 1999, 2001, 2003, and 2005), and data for Europe are from the Eurobarometers from 1973 to 2006 (excluding 1974 and 1996). Data for Greece are from 1981 to 2006; for Spain and Portugal are from 1985 to 2006; and for Sweden and Finland are from 1995 to 2006 (all excluding 1996). Age minimum calculated from the always highly significant age and age squared coefficients. Europe also includes Austria (1995 to 2006), Czech Republic, Hungary, Poland, Slovakia, Slovenia, Bulgaria, Romania, Croatia, Turkey, and Estonia (all 2004 to 2006), plus Norway (1990 to 1995), and includes country dummies for each.

[a]Means *t*-statistic < 2.

References

Alesina, A., R. Di Tella, and R. J. MacCulloch. 2004. Inequality and happiness: Are Europeans and Americans different? *Journal of Public Economics* 88 (9/10): 2009–42.

Atlas, S., and J. Skinner. 2007. Education and the prevalence of pain. Paper presented at the Conference on Aging, NBER. December, Carefree, AZ.

Blanchflower, D. G. 2001. Unemployment, well-being and wage curves in Eastern and Central Europe. *Journal of Japanese and International Economies* 15 (4): 364–402.

———. 2007. Is unemployment more costly than inflation? NBER Working Paper no. 13505. Cambridge, MA: National Bureau of Economic Research, October.

Blanchflower, D. G., and A. J. Oswald. 2000. The rising well-being of the young. In *Youth employment and joblessness in advanced countries,* ed. D. G. Blanchflower and R. B. Freeman, 289–328. Chicago: University of Chicago Press.

———. 2004a. Money, sex and happiness. *Scandinavian Journal of Economics* 106 (3): 393–415.

———. 2004b. Well-being over time in Britain and the USA. *Journal of Public Economics* 88 (7/8): 1359–86.

———. 2005. Happiness and the Human Development Index: The paradox of Australia. *The Australian Economic Review* 38 (3): 307–18.

———. 2006. On Leigh-Wolfers and well-being in Australia. *The Australian Economic Review,* 39 (2): 185–86.

———. 2008a. Hypertension and happiness across nations. *Journal of Health Economics* 27 (2): 218–33.

———. 2008b. Is well-being U-shaped over the life cycle? *Social Science and Medicine,* 66 (6): 1733–49.

Blanchflower, D. G., and C. Shadforth. 2009. Fear, unemployment and migration. *Economic Journal.* 119 (535): F136–F182.

Carroll, N. 2007. Unemployment and psychological well-being. *The Economic Record* 83 (262): 287–302.

Clark, A. E. 2005. Your money or your life: Changing job quality in OECD countries. *British Journal of Industrial Relations* 43 (3): 377–400.

———. 2007. Born to be mild? Cohort effects don't (fully) explain why well-being is U-shaped in age. IZA Discussion Paper no. 3170. Bonn, Germany: Institute for the Study of Labor, November.

Clark, A. E., P. Frijters, and M. Shields. 2007. Relative income, happiness, and utility: An explanation for the Easterlin paradox and other puzzles. *Journal of Economic Literature* 46 (1): 95–144.

Clark, A. E., and A. J. Oswald. 1994. Unhappiness and unemployment. *Economic Journal* 104 (2): 648–59.

Deaton, A. 2008. Income, health, and well-being around the world: Evidence from the Gallup World Poll. *Journal of Economic Perspectives* 22 (2): 53–72.

Di Tella, R., and R. J. MacCulloch. 2005. Partisan social happiness. *Review of Economic Studies* 72 (2): 367–93.

———. 2006. Some uses of happiness data in economics. *Journal of Economic Perspectives* 20 (1): 25–46.

———. 2007. Happiness, contentment and other emotions for central banks. NBER Working Paper no. 13622. Cambridge, MA: National Bureau of Economic Research, November.

Di Tella, R., R. J. MacCulloch, and J. P. Haisken-DeNew. 2005. Happiness adaptation to income and to status in an individual panel. Harvard Business School, Working Paper.

Di Tella, R., R. J. MacCulloch, and A. J. Oswald. 2001. Preferences over inflation and unemployment: Evidence from surveys of happiness. *American Economic Review* 91 (1): 335–41.

———. 2003. The macroeconomics of happiness. *Review of Economics and Statistics* 85 (4): 809–27.

Easterlin, R. A. 1974. Does economic growth improve the human lot? Some empirical evidence. In *Nations and households in economic growth: Essays in honor of Moses Abramowitz,* ed. P. A. David and M. W. Reder, 89–125. New York: Academic Press.

———. Will raising the incomes of all increase the happiness of all? *Journal of Economic Behavior and Organization* 27 (1): 35–47.

———. 2006. Life cycle happiness and its sources: Intersections of psychology, economics, and demography. *Journal of Economic Psychology* 27 (4): 463–82.

Easterlin, R. A., and A. C. Zimmermann. 2008. Life satisfaction and economic conditions in East and West Germany pre- and post-unification. *Journal of Economic Behavior and Organization* 68 (3/4): 433–44.

Ekman, P., R. Davidson, and W. Friesen. 1990. The Duchenne smile: Emotional expression and brain physiology II. *Journal of Personality and Social Psychology* 58 (2): 342–53.

Ekman, P., W. Friesen, and M. O'Sullivan. 1988. Smiles when lying. *Journal of Personality and Social Psychology* 54 (3): 414–20.

Ferrer-i-Carbonell, A. 2005. Income and well-being: An empirical analysis of the comparison income effect. *Journal of Public Economics* 89 (5/6): 997–1019.

Frey, B. S., and A. Stutzer. 2002a. *Happiness and economics.* Princeton, NJ: Princeton University Press.

———. 2002b. What can economists learn from happiness research? *Journal of Economic Literature* 40 (2): 402–35.

———. 2005. Happiness research: State and prospects. *Review of Social Economy* 63 (2): 207–28.

Frijters, P., J. Haisken-DeNew, and M. Shields. 2004. Money does matter! Evidence from increasing real incomes and life satisfaction in East Germany following reunification. *American Economic Review* 94 (3): 730–40.

Gerdtham, U., and M. Johannesson. 2001. The relationship between happiness, health, and socio-economic factors: Results based on Swedish microdata. *Journal of Socio-Economics* 30 (6): 553–57.

Gilpin, N., M. Henty, S. Lemos, J. Portes, and C. Bullen. 2006. The impact of free movement of workers from Central and Eastern Europe on the UK labour market. Department for Work and Pensions, Working Paper no. 29.

Graham, C. 2005. Insights on development from the economics of happiness. *World Bank Research Observer* 20 (2): 201–31.

Guven, C. 2007. Reversing the question: Does happiness affect individual economic behavior? Evidence from surveys from Netherlands and Germany. PhD thesis, University of Houston.

Helliwell, J. 2003. How's life? Combining individual and national variables to explain subjective well-being. *Economic Modelling* 20 (2): 331–60.

Hinks, T., and C. Gruen. 2007. What is the structure of South African happiness equations? Evidence from quality of life surveys. *Social Indicators Research* 82 (2): 311–36.

Kahneman, D., and A. B. Krueger. 2006. Developments in the measurement of subjective well-being. *Journal of Economic Perspectives* 20 (1): 3–24.

Kahneman, D., A. B. Krueger, D. Schkade, N. Schwarz, and A. Stone. 2004a. Toward national well-being accounts. *American Economic Review Papers and Proceedings* 94 (2): 429–34.

———. 2004b. A survey method for characterizing daily life experience: The Day Reconstruction Method (DRM). *Science* 306 (5702): 1776–80.

Kimball, M., H. Levy, F. Ohtake, and Y. Tsutsui. 2006. Unhappiness after Hurricane Katrina. NBER Working Paper no. 12062. Cambridge, MA: National Bureau of Economic Research, March.

Kingdon, G. G., and J. Knight. 2007. Community, comparisons and subjective well-being in a divided society. *Journal of Economic Behavior and Organization* 64 (1): 69–90.

Koivumaa-Honkanen, H., R. Honkanen, H. Viinamäki, K. Heikkilä, J. Kaprio, and M. Koskenvuo. 2001. Life satisfaction and suicide: A 20-year follow-up study. *American Journal of Psychiatry* 158 (3): 433–39.

Krueger, A. B., and D. A. Schkade. 2007. The reliability of subjective well-being measures. Princeton University, Department of Economics, Industrial Relations Section. Working Paper no. 516, January.

Leigh, A., and J. Wolfers. 2006. Happiness and the Human Development Index: Australia is not a paradox. *Australian Economic Review* 39 (2): 176–84.

Lelkes, O. (2007). Happiness over the life-cycle: Exploring age-specific preferences. In *Mainstreaming ageing: Indicators to monitor sustainable policies*, ed. B. Marin and A. Zaidi, 359–91. Vienna: European Centre, Ashgate.

Luttmer, E. 2005. Neighbors as negatives: Relative earnings and well-being. *Quarterly Journal of Economics* 120 (3): 963–1002.

Mojon-Azzi, S., and A. Sousa-Poza. 2007. Hypertension and life satisfaction: An analysis using data from the Survey of Health, Ageing and Retirement in Europe (SHARE). University of Hohenheim, Working Paper, Stuttgart, Germany.

Mroczek, D. K., and A. Spiro. 2005. Change in life satisfaction during adulthood: Findings from the Veterans Affairs Normative Aging Study. *Journal of Personality and Social Psychology* 88 (1): 189–202.

Office of National Statistics. 2007. First release: Labour market statistics, November. Available at http://www.statistics.gov.uk/pdfdir/lmsuk1107.pdf.

Oswald, A. J. 1997. Happiness and economic performance. *Economic Journal* 107 (445): 1815–31.

Powdthavee, N. 2005. Unhappiness and crime: Evidence from South Africa. *Economica* 72 (3): 531–47.

———. 2007. Are there geographical variations in the psychological cost of unemployment in South Africa? *Social Indicators Research* 80 (3): 629–52.

Propper, C., K. Jones, A. Bolster, S. Burgess, R. Johnston, and R. Sarker. 2005. Local neighbourhood and mental health: Evidence from the UK. *Social Science and Medicine* 61 (10): 2065–83.

Sanfey, P., and U. Teksoz. 2007. Does transition make you happy? *Economics of Transition* 15 (4): 707–31.

Senik, C. 2004. When information dominates comparison: Learning from Russian subjective panel data. *Journal of Public Economics* 88 (9/10): 2099–2123.

Shields, M. A., and S. Wheatley Price. 2005. Exploring the economic and social determinants of psychological well-being and perceived social support in England. Series A, *Journal of the Royal Statistical Society* 168 (3): 513–37.

Stevenson, B., and J. Wolfers. 2007. The paradox of declining female happiness. University of Pennsylvania, Wharton Business School. Working Paper.

Theodossiou, I. 1998. The effects of low-pay and unemployment on psychological well-being: A logistic regression approach. *Journal of Health Economics* 17 (1): 85–104.

Uppal, S. 2006. Impact of the timing, type and severity of disability on the subjective well-being of individuals with disabilities. *Social Science and Medicine* 63 (2): 525–39.

Van Praag, B., and A. Ferrer-i-Carbonell. 2004. *Happiness quantified.* Oxford: Oxford University Press.

Veenhoven, R. 2000. Freedom and happiness: A comparative study in 44 nations in the early 1990s. In *Culture and subjective well-being,* ed. E. Diener and E. Suh, 257–88. Cambridge, MA: MIT Press.

Winkelmann, L., and R. Winkelmann. 1998. Why are the unemployed so unhappy? Evidence from panel data. *Economica* 65 (257): 1–15.

Wolfers, J. 2003. Is business cycle volatility costly? Evidence from surveys of subjective well-being. *International Finance* 6 (1): 1–26.

Zaiceva, A. 2006. Reconciling the estimates of potential migration into the enlarged European Union. IZA Discussion Paper no. 2519. Bonn, Germany: Institute for the Study of Labor, December.

Zimmermann, A. C., and R. A. Easterlin. 2006. Happily ever after? Cohabitation, marriage, divorce, and happiness in Germany. *Population and Development Review* 32 (3): 511–28.

Thoughts on "National Time Accounting: The Currency of Life"

Erik Hurst

8.1 Introduction

In their article "National Time Accounting: The Currency of Life," Krueger et al. (see chapter 1 of this volume) propose an alternate way of computing individual well-being. The foundation of the new measure of well-being is the construction of a U-index (where the "U" stands for "unpleasantness"). The U-index is formed by surveying households about their enjoyment of the activities in which they participated during the prior day. For example, suppose last night the survey respondent had dinner with their spouse. Today, the respondent would be asked to assess the feelings they were experiencing during the previous night's dinner. The measurement of feelings occurs along a variety of dimensions (happiness, sadness, pain, stress levels, etc.). The measure of intensity of the feeling occurs along a 6-point scale (with six being the most intense feeling along the respective dimension). For an individual, an activity is deemed unpleasant if the negative feelings (sadness, pain, stress, etc.) experienced while engaging in the activity are more intense than the positive feelings (happiness) experienced while engaging in the activity. That is, for each individual-specific activity, the U-index is either one (negative emotions dominate) or zero (negative emotions do not dominate). The overall U-index for an activity in the population is simply the average U-index across all people performing the activity in the survey. That is, the average U-index for an activity globally takes on values between 0 and 100 percent. A global activity level U-index of one hundred means that 100 percent of the people engaging in that activity had a U-index of one.

Erik Hurst is the V. Duane Rath Professor of Economics and Neubauer Family Faculty Fellow at the Booth School of Business, University of Chicago, and a research associate of the National Bureau of Economic Research.

The goal of the U-index method is to compute activity level U-indices. With these U-indices in hand, researchers can use existing time diaries (such as the American Time Use Survey [ATUS] conducted by the Bureau of Labor Statistics [BLS]) to compute a measure of the average quality of an individual's day. In essence, they propose computing a measure that converts time units (like minutes for a given activity during a day) into unpleasantness units (using the U-index). The fraction of time people spend in relatively unpleasant activities could then be used as an alternate measure of well-being for individuals. This measure can be tracked over time (at the national level or group-specific levels) to ask whether individuals within a country are spending more time in pleasant activities today than they did at some time in the past. Likewise, the measure can be used to assess whether the well-being of one group (i.e., the lower educated) is converging or diverging from the well-being of another group (i.e., the higher educated).

Overall, I think this research design has merit. I think it would be good to create a time series of the U-index and see whether it adds any additional information in terms of computing trends in well-being aside from our existing traditional sources (wages, time allocation, overall GDP and inflation statistics, other happiness measures, etc.). I think the goal should be to assess whether changes in the U-index provide additional information about well-being above and beyond changes in other readily available series. The only way to know the answer to that question is to develop the U-index and monitor its properties over time. I applaud the authors for starting that process.

My comments will be structured around three points. My first set of comments (in section 8.2) expands upon the themes outlined in the previous paragraph. In that section, I ask what is it that we hope to capture about changing well-being using the U-index that would not already be captured by the changes in existing well-being measures. Also in that section, I talk about other conceptual issues pertaining to the measurement of well-being. In section 8.3, I take a more philosophical turn and ask how the U-index is designed to measure activities where extreme negative emotions are desired (such as many forms of art). In particular, I will ask how to interpret the U-index if people seek out (and are willing to pay) for stress or sadness (such as movies or television shows that market themselves as thrillers or dramas). In section 8.4, I offer a series of comments pertaining to the implementation of the U-index. In doing so, I address many potential selection issues inherent in the construction of the U-index. Some of these can be addressed empirically. All of them, however, need to be thought about before implementing the U-index for larger purposes (such as measuring changing aggregate well-being). The final section concludes.

8.2   Some Thoughts on Motivation

Before getting into specific comments with respect to how the U-index is constructed, I wanted to comment on some bigger issues. First, I want to think about what it is that the U-index is trying to measure. Second, I want to comment on what the U-index is intending to measure that is not measured by more general "happiness" surveys.

8.2.1   Why is the U-Index Necessary?

In Nordhaus' comment on the Krueger et al. chapter (see chapter 5 of this volume), he laid out a model of individual optimization that shows how, under certain assumptions, individual well-being evolves over time. One conclusion from his work is that if individuals have utility over consumption commodities (defined in a Beckerian sense) and also receive some process flow from spending time in a given activity, individual utility evolves at exactly the same rate as market wages, assuming that the productivity used to augment the production of each commodity (including market labor) grows at the same rate. This is seen in Nordhaus's equation 16.

In other words, according to the Nordhaus model, if market productivity and each component of nonmarket productivity grow at the same rate, the *change* in well-being for an individual over time is perfectly measured by the change in their return to working. The return to working is just the wage less any disutility from work. This is exactly analogous to using full income to measure individual well-being (where full income is just the wage multiplied by the time endowment). In these full-income models, there is no disutility to working. As a result, given a constant per period time endowment, the growth in full income is just the growth in the wage. The reason that the growth in the wage is the relevant measure for the change in well-being in these models is that consumers equate the marginal return across different activities. If individuals always have the opportunity to work, the marginal return to any activity should be set equal to the marginal return to working.

Therefore, the relevant question at hand is, when is the growth in the wage rate not the appropriate measure of well-being? The Nordhaus model shows a few instances. First, if there is changing disutility to work, changing well-being will not be appropriately measured by changes in the wage. Likewise, if there are different growth rates in productivity between market and nonmarket sectors, the growth in the wage rate will not perfectly capture the growth in well-being (see Nordhaus equation [16]). Lastly, if individuals are not on their labor supply curve, the wage may not truly represent their marginal value of time. This is not in the Nordhaus model but will fall out of any model of labor supply in which there are frictions in the labor market that cause labor supply to be "lumpy" (i.e., we can only work forty hours per week, twenty hours per week, or nothing).

Moreover, as emphasized in the Krueger et al. chapter, there are other things that individuals care about that are not embedded in models similar to the one put forth by Nordhaus. For example, we may care about national security (safety) or environmental quality. These extranalities are out of an individual's control, yet they enter into their utility function. So, changes in these extranalities will also affect the growth rate of individual well-being.

So, if that is the case, the goal of the U-index is very specific. The U-index (or any other subjective measure of well-being) hopes to capture either (a) changes in nonmarket technologies over time, (b) the changing ability of the wage to measure the marginal valuation of an individual's time (either due to changing disutility of work or because of changing constraints in the labor market), or (c) the changing nature of extranalities over time. These are fine goals to have for developing alternate measures of well-being. It would be valuable to understand how important these omissions are in terms of their effect on changes in well-being relative to changes in the wage. I share Nordhaus' belief that as this project moves forward, it would be useful to highlight what the U-index is intended to capture beyond our standard methods of measuring well-being (such as the full-income method). The authors currently do some of that. I just think it is important for them to continue doing so forcefully.

8.2.2   The U-Index versus Traditional Happiness Measures

This brings me to a related point. Not only do the authors have to convince people that there is value added in measuring changing well-being by a broader measure than just changes in the wage; they also have to convince people that their proposed U-index actually has the potential to add value relative to other existing broader measures of well-being. As noted in the Blanchflower comment on chapter 1 (see chapter 7 of this volume), there are many existing happiness or life satisfaction surveys collected within the United States and many other countries. Most of these surveys ask people some variant of the question, "On a whole, how satisfied are you with the life you lead?" As shown in the Blanchflower comment, the cross-sectional patterns of these existing happiness surveys are very similar in most instances to the cross-sectional patterns of the U-index.

One natural question to ask is, what is the gain of developing the U-index, given that we already have well-developed existing questions on happiness or life satisfaction? The U-index is an innovation on existing well-being measures in two directions. First, it measures life satisfaction at the individual activity level. Second, the U-index measures life satisfaction for a particular day (yesterday), where the short-term emotional memories of that activity are still fresh in respondents' minds.

In terms of measuring the components of an individual's changing well-being not captured by changes in the wage, how valuable is the activity level data? It depends on the component of well-being that is not being measured. Take, for example, large societal externalities like pollution, fear of terrorism, economic uncertainty, or the quality of our children's play (all of which were emphasized in the Krueger et al. piece as a rationalization for the U-index). The effects of these large societal externalities on well-being are likely not to be activity specific. For example, if I am more uncertain about terrorism, it is not likely to manifest itself only when I fly. I will sometimes be thinking about it when I am eating dinner, working at my job, or watching television. Similar stories can be told about the externalities from clean air or happy children. These types of externalities likely affect an individual's general emotional experience as opposed to activity-specific emotional experiences. If we think that the primary mismeasurement of changing well-being as proxied by the changing wage is that it does not account for large unmeasured societal externalities, it is not certain that activity-based measures of affect are better than general affect measures (like the existing measures of life satisfaction).

The activity-specific measures are likely to be very informative, however, if there are changing technological advances in the production of the experience by activity. For example, if we are truly happier now watching television because the quality of television sets has increased so dramatically (holding price constant), the U-index will likely be able to isolate this activity-specific trend.

In summary, the true innovation of the activity-specific U-indices, in terms of measuring previously unmeasured well-being, is that it can capture activity-specific advances in technology. The externalities can be measured by more general (nonactivity-specific) affect measures. A discussion by the authors of how the U-index could improve upon the unmeasured components of well-being with respect to existing measures of life satisfaction would be very useful. I think that such reasons do exist, so it should be easy for the authors to do.[1]

8.2.3   Relative Preferences and Adaptation

The last comment I wish to address in this section is how we would expect the U-index to evolve over time if people have relative (or adaptive) preferences. There is ample evidence (many by these authors) that convince me that relative well-being enters directly into utility functions. Such preferences explain in part why happiness measures tend not to trend upward over time,

---

1. One question that I have is whether there is any new information in how the U-index evolves over time relative to traditional happiness measures, but a time series on the U-index will allow us to answer this question. Again, as Blanchflower's comment has already indicated (see chapter 7 of this volume), the cross-sectional patterns in the U-index, for the most part, are very similar to the cross-sectional patterns in traditional happiness surveys. But in terms of changing well-being, we care about the changes in the U-index relative to the changes in traditional happiness surveys.

despite the huge increases in real incomes within an economy. I am not sure whether such preferences matter at all for the construction and measurement of the U-index. However, the existence of such preferences is certainly important for the interpretation of trends in the U-index. I would have liked a little more discussion about what the authors think with respect to the implementation (and the value of the implementation) of the U-index in a world where individuals care about relatives rather than absolutes. In such a world, would the U-index even measure changes in well-being resulting from changes in extranalities like pollution or terrorism? If everyone eventually gets used to the pollution and terrorism, would the negative effects on well-being actually show up in the U-index? I am not sure of the answers; I just thought that it should be addressed somewhere (especially given the previous work of some of the authors).

8.3   The Importance of Television Watching

One important output of the National Time Accounting system developed in chapter 1 was to measure changing well-being for men and women since 1965. In figures 1.9 through 1.11, Krueger et al. use their activity level U-index to show that over the last forty years, women experienced a smaller decline in unhappiness than did men. In this subsection, I discuss the importance of the U-index for television watching for making these conclusions.

In my 2007 *Quarterly Journal of Economics* paper with Mark Aguiar (hence referred to as AH2007), we documented the major trends in time use for men and women within the United States between 1965 and 2003.[2] To do this, we harmonized the five major nationally representative time-use studies conducted in the United States during this time period. The major trends can be summarized as follows. First, for men, total time spent in total market work declined substantially (by over ten hours per week). This number also includes ancillary work activities like commuting to work and taking breaks while at work. Men also increased the time they allocated to nonmarket work (by roughly five hours per week). Leisure time for men (time spent with friends, watching television, exercising, going to the movies, etc.) increased by roughly five hours per week during this time.

For women, there was a slightly smaller increase in leisure time (by about three hours per week). The increase in leisure was facilitated by women dramatically decreasing the time they allocated to nonmarket production (by about ten hours per week), while simultaneously increasing the time they spent in market work. The majority of the decline in nonmarket production was due to a decrease in food preparation and cleanup. Like us, Krueger

---

2. The paper is referenced in Krueger et al. (see chapter 1 of this volume).

et al. find that the increase in leisure (or decline in unhappiness) was greater for men. Also like us, they find that most of the increase took place prior to 1985.

The relevant question that the U-index can shed light upon is, "How much happier did men and women become over the last forty years?" To interpret the Krueger et al. results, we should note that AH2007 shows that almost the entire increase in leisure can be explained by an increase in television watching. This is similar to the Krueger et al. findings (which should not be surprising, given that they are using the same underlying data as AH2007). Over the last forty years, women have substituted housework, such as food prep, essentially for television watching. According to the U-index results (table 1.8), food prep and television watching are roughly similar in terms of unpleasantness (19.0 versus 18.1). Men, on the other hand, substituted market work for television watching. According to the U-index, this was a huge gain in well-being, given that market work is reported as being much more unpleasant compared to television watching (26.9 versus 18.0).

Reading the results of Krueger et al., I was struck by how individuals report feeling while they are watching television. Television is reported as being one of the more unpleasant leisure activities. In table 8.1, I summarize the time individuals spend on various leisure activities (from the 2003 to 2005 American Time Use Surveys) and the corresponding U-index for that activity as reported in Krueger et al.[3]

As seen in this table, individuals find many other leisure activities to be more enjoyable than watching television. For example, some of the most enjoyable activities, according to the U-index, are listening to music, engaging in sports or exercise, participating in religious activities, and relaxing or general leisure activities. However, households allocate very little time to these activities. Yet, individuals spend an abundance of time watching television, which is on par with washing dishes and cooking in terms of reported U-index.

Does this fact violate individual-revealed preference? It does if we take the U-index seriously. Take, as an example, watching television versus listening to music. In terms of cognitive resources needed to engage in the activity, both are similar. For example, one can just as easily passively watch television as they can passively listen to the radio. Additionally, the necessary start-up costs are probably lower for listening to music. A nice music system is equally as expensive (if not less expensive) than a nice television system. If people like music so much more than watching television (which they do according to the U-index), why are they watching so much television? Why

---

3. The sample used is similar to the sample used in Aguiar and Hurst (2007). Basically, the sample consists of twenty-one- to sixty-five-year-olds who were nonretired and nonstudents. The only difference is that Aguair and Hurst (2007) only looked at data from the 2003 ATUS, as opposed to aggregating together the ATUS from 2003 to 2005.

Table 8.1   **Hours per week spent in activity versus U-index: By leisure activity**

Leisure activity	Hours per week (2003)	U-index
Television watching	16.4	18.1
Hobbies	0.2	13.4
Socializing	7.0	13.5
Sports and exercise	2.2	7.4
Religion	2.0	6.4
Listening to music	0.2	0.0

Notes: This table shows the hours per week spent in the activity according to the ATUS from 2003 to 2005. The sample for the ATUS is the same used in Aguiar and Hurst 2007, which is basically all individuals between the ages of twenty-one and sixty-five who were nonstudents and who were nonretired. The U-index numbers came from the Krueger et al. chapter.

do people not shut off the television and turn on the radio? The failure of people to do so implies one of two things: either individuals are persistently irrational (and keep watching television despite their relatively low enjoyment as compared to listening to music), or the U-index is not capturing what it intends to capture.

Before addressing that latter question, I want to address one other question first. Particularly, does it matter how we view television watching for understanding changing well-being over time? Because of the fact that increased television watching has been one of the most dominant trends in how we allocate our time over the last forty years, we would expect the classification of how we view television watching to be critical to assessing changing well-being over time. Table 8.2 confirms this fact. In table 8.2, I first restate the change in the U-index for men and women between 1965 and 2003 as in Krueger et al. (figure 1.9). These are found in row 1 of panels A (men) and B (women). In row 2 of each panel, I assign television watching the same U-index as listening to music.[4] This latter assumption is extreme, but it serves an illustrative purpose. It says that if people choose to watch television, they must like television watching more than listening to music (at least on average). If we implicitly assume that the listening-to-music U-index is correct, the U-index for television watching has got to be at least as low as the U-index for listening to music. The results in row 2 of Table 8.2 show that the decline in the U-index over the last forty years is much greater for both men and women if we change the evaluation of television watching in a way that would be consistent with revealed preference. In other words, a simple change in the U-index to make the measure consistent with revealed preference only for television watching would dra-

---

4. I am indebted to Alan Krueger for running these hypotheticals using the actual data that underlies figure 1.9. I did nothing more than ask about the hypothetical; all the work was done by Alan.

Table 8.2   **Sensitivity of Krueger et al. change in U-index over time to the treatment of television watching**

	U-index (1965)	U-index (2003)	Difference (%)
Panel A: men			
Men (original)	20.9	19.6	−6.2
Men (adjusted)	18.8	16.6	−11.7
Panel B: women			
Women (original)	19.4	19.2	−1.0
Women (adjusted)	17.9	16.7	−6.2

Notes: This table explores the sensitivity of the change in the U-index over time for men and women to the U-index attributed to television watching. Row 1 of panels A and B show the original time trend in the U-index reported in Krueger et al., figure 1.9. Row 2 of panels A and B show the recomputed U-index in both years, assigning television watching the same U-index as listening to music. Given that listening to music is reported as being much more pleasant than watching television, and given the fact that television watching increased dramatically over this time period, the adjusted series shows much greater declines in the U-index than the original series.

matically change the conclusions about changing well-being over the last forty years.[5]

Such a discussion brings me to the more substantive (and philosophic) question of why people watch television and how the U-index would respond to those reasons. The premise of the U-index is to measure the intensity of positive and negative emotions during an experience. If the negative emotions were more pronounced than the positive emotions, the U-index takes a value of one for the individual during the activity (zero otherwise). The average U-index for an activity is the average of individual U-indices for individuals participating in the activity. The positive and negative emotions measured when computing the U-index include whether the individual felt happy, sad, pain, and stressed.

Often the goal of participating in various forms of art (such as movies, television, or music) is to experience extreme human emotions (positive or negative). Think of recent Oscar winning movies. Upon leaving *Million Dollar Baby* or *Schindler's List,* I felt really, really sad. If you asked me how I felt when watching *Million Dollar Baby,* I would have provided an extreme report on the sad scale. Was I happy during the movie? Absolutely not. Did I expect this going in to the movie? Without a doubt. (I am an avid reader of movie and television reviews before I view them.) The reason I went is to experience the human emotion, knowing that it would be extreme (and in the process, I may learn something about myself or human nature more

5. Again, this is done for illustrative purposes. It is also likely that television watching is measured correctly and that listening to music is measured incorrectly. In that situation, the results in row 1 of panels A and B of table 8.1 are measured correctly (given that listening to music is such a small portion of individual time).

generally). Much of television is also like this. I am an avid Miami Dolphins football fan. If you ask me how I felt (retrospectively) while I was watching a game, my answer would definitely depend on whether they won. I still watch the games every week, but I am honestly more sad than happy when I am watching the Dolphins, depending on how they are playing. This is verifiable within my family—I have been much sadder watching games this year, given the Dolphin's 1-15 win/loss record. This is common for most sports fans when following their team. They know one of the teams is going to lose while they are watching the game, yet they still knowingly watch.

More generally, there is a large industry within television that caters to extreme emotions. Movies on the Lifetime channel are often very depressing (yet garner sizeable ratings). A large fraction of Oprah's episodes are based on topics designed to illicit extreme negative emotions (elderly depression, violence against women, racism). Yet millions of people tune in daily. I never feel happy when I am watching television shows like *24, The Sopranos, Oz,* or *The Wire* (for example), but I am often very stressed or sad when watching them (less so with *The Sopranos,* more so with *Oz*). That is by design—*24* bills itself as a thriller, and that is exactly what I am seeking out when I watch the show. Often, dramas and thrillers are designed to deliver extreme negative emotions like sadness and stress.

The question that I think the authors need to think much harder about is, how does the U-index deal with such art forms where the design of the experience is to seek out negative emotions? This could be one reason that television watching has such a high U-index relative to other leisure activities. If part of the experience of watching television programs (or participating in art forms more generally) is to experience the full range of human emotions (both good and bad), am I really worse off when I watch shows that induce me to experience negative emotions? This seems very unlikely to me. People seek out such negative emotions (and advertisers regularly market those negative emotions). As previously seen, how we interpret an individual's well-being from watching television is critical to understanding the trends in well-being over time (given the large increase in television watching). Regardless, the chapter needs to at least acknowledge the U-indices' problem with television watching (or dealing with art forms more generally). The results, as currently presented, appear to be a strong violation of revealed preference. If people do not like television (especially compared to similar leisure activities), why do they watch so much of it?

8.4   The Potential Importance of Selection

As noted in the prior section, one of the drawbacks of the U-index seems to be its handling of experiences that are designed to elicit extreme negative emotions (like movies, music, or television). In this section, I set out three other issues pertaining to the U-index that the authors need to think about more explicitly in their framing of the U-index. My sense is that these issues can be dealt with empirically. They just need to be acknowledged. Additionally, these issues will only be relevant when we try to predict an activity's enjoyment out of sample. If the goal is to measure individual well-being, eliciting affect measures for each activity for a given individual will not be subject to the selection issues I describe next.

8.4.1   Selection Issue One: More on Revealed Preference

Suppose, for simplicity, that the sample for our survey is only comprised of three people. Suppose further that persons 1, 2, and 3 are exactly the same in all observable dimensions (income, family size, similar distance to job, etc.) except for that the three individuals allocate their time differently to the categories found in table 8.3, panel A. We will assume that for all other time-use categories, the individuals allocate identical amounts of time. However, for food prep, walking, and watching television, the three individuals spend different amounts of time in these activities. For example, person

Table 8.3   **Hypothetical example of the importance of selection when computing the U-index**

	Person		
	1	2	3
A Time allocation for three hypothetical individuals (in hrs./week)			
Time spent on food prep/cleanup	2	0	0
Time spent walking	0	2	0
Time spent watching TV	2	2	4
B Assumed "true" U-index for the three individuals			
Time spent on food prep/cleanup	8	17	14
Time spent walking	18	8	16
Time spent watching TV	9	10	8
C Assumed "measured" U-index for the three individuals			
Time spent on food prep/cleanup	8	—	—
Time spent walking	—	8	—
Time spent watching TV	9	10	8

Notes: This table provides a simple example to show the importance of revealed preference and selection when computing the U-index. In the first panel, I provide the allocation of time for three hypothetical individuals in three activities: food preparation and clean up, walking, and watching television. In my hypothetical example, person 1 does not do any waking, person 2 does not do any food prep, and person 3 does neither walking nor food prep. In the second panel, I make up a corresponding U-index that could be consistent with the data in panel A. For example, the reason that person 1 does not walk is that for them, walking is a very unpleasant activity. In the third panel, I show the U-index that would be measured using the methodology used by Krueger et al. Notice, given that Krueger et al. only measure the U-index for activities that an individual performs, they would not measure the U-index for walking for persons 1 and 3, nor would they measure the U-index for food preparation for persons 2 and 3. In panel C, a dash indicates the unmeasured U-index for activities that were not performed during the week.

2 spends two hours per week on food prep, zero hours per week walking, and two hours per week watching television. Given this information, what could we conclude? Given the patterns of time use, we may conclude that person 1 does not like walking relative to preparing meals or watching television. Likewise, person 3 may like watching television more than walking and preparing meals.

Suppose we further survey these households to construct a U-index (in a manner similar to Krueger et al.). Suppose the following would be the *true* (as opposed to the measured) unpleasantness that each household feels while performing each activity. Again, these numbers are just for illustrative purposes. I made my fictional U-index on a zero to one hundred scale for each individual for illustrative purposes (with zero being least unpleasant and one hundred being most unpleasant). This makes it easier to make my point. Table 8.3, panel B shows the true U-index for each activity for each individual. For example, person 1 gets eight units of unpleasantness from food prep, eighteen units of unpleasantness from walking, and nine units of unpleasantness from watching television. Given these affect measures for each activity, it is not surprising that person 1 does not engage in any walking.

What would be the average U-index for each activity if we averaged the U-indices across our three people? According to these figures, the average U-index would be thirteen, fourteen, and nine for meal preparation, walking, and watching television, respectively. In this fictional world, time spent watching television is the most enjoyable activity on average. As a result, it is not surprising that all three individuals allocated positive amounts of time to television watching.

However, given that the U-index as measured by Krueger et al. only records the affect for activities that individuals actually engage in, the actual data that I would have at my disposable to compute my fictional U-index would be as shown in table 8.3, panel C. The measured U-index only includes the U-index for activities in which the person chose to participate. This is exactly analogous to the data available to Krueger et al., who only observe an individual's affect for activities where the individuals allocate positive amounts of time. In my example, given the way we measure the data, the measured U-indices will differ dramatically than the actual U-indices. Specifically, the measured U-indices found that food prep, walking, and watching television have measured U-indices of eight, eight, and nine, respectively. This is a direct violation of the underlying uncensored data shown in the previous table. The reason for this is that the only people observed walking and preparing meals are the individuals who really enjoy those activities. If we projected these values out of sample to someone who did not have a dishwasher and was forced to wash dishes, the utility we would get from washing dishes would be dramatically overstated (the unpleasantness would be understated).

In practice, how could such selection bias the results? The way that activity level affect is measured is through probabilistic sampling of a person's day. The more they like an activity, the more they will engage in an activity. The more they engage in an activity, the more likely that activity is going to be sampled. As a result, the affect measures will tend to be biased toward sampling activities that people like. Applying the affect measure for such activities to all others will likely overstate the utility (understate the unpleasantness) of the activity.

Second, given that changes in technology change the costs and benefits of engaging in certain activities, the selection I previously alluded to can be more or less pronounced when comparing activities across time (as the authors do). For example, as technological advances have occurred for food preparation (microwaves, take-out food, dishwashers, etc.) during the last forty years, the cost of reducing time inputs into food preparation has fallen. If food preparation is relatively unpleasant, we should see less people engaging in food preparation today. Those that do engage in food preparation should be those that relatively enjoy food preparation (because they chose not to purchase cheap market substitutes). Even if individuals' tastes have not changed over the last forty years with respect to the unpleasantness of preparing meals, the measured U-index would likely decline for food prep.

There is some evidence that the degree of selection has changed substantially over time. The fraction of households who engaged in some sort of food preparation in 1965 was 65 percent. In 2003, only 55 percent of households engaged in some sort of food preparation. Similar patterns are found among all home production time-use categories (and for market work for men). During the last forty years, people have seemed to substitute away from unpleasant activities. Conversely, the fraction of households who watch television on a given day has increased by 10 percentage points over this time period. Households should be substituting toward relatively more enjoyable activities and away from less pleasant activities.

Overall, the choice to spend time on an activity is related to how much one enjoys that activity relative to other activities. The U-index is based on enjoyment measures only for people who allocate time to a given activity. The more time that they allocate to an activity, the more likely it is that their enjoyment will be a component of the U-index. Given this, the U-index will be biased downward (enjoyment will be biased upward) relative to people's underlying preferences. This creates a problem with trying to project the U-index out of sample.

One solution to this problem is to ask people about their expected enjoyment if they were doing alternate activities. However, this method would be subject to the filtering issues associated with recalling distant memories that the authors are trying to avoid. A second solution is to just sample everyone's entire day with respect to measuring their affect (and do no projection out of sample).

In summary, I would like the authors to discuss this selection issue in their work and think about ways to address this issue when predicting out of sample. Otherwise, if the selection issue cannot be overcome (perhaps because there are no instruments to deal with the selection), it severely limits the usefulness of the U-index relative to other existing measures of subjective well-being.

8.4.2   Selection Issue Two: Individual Fixed Effects

The authors already recognize the potential selection issue arising from individual fixed effects. However, when doing different analyses (like measuring trends in happiness over time), they do not account for such selection. The relevant issue for this type of selection is that different types of people do different types of activities. Also, different types of people have differing underlying levels of happiness. If the choice of activities is correlated with the underlying level of happiness, the U-index will be confounding individual fixed effects with the activity's latent enjoyment level.

The best way to deal with this issue is to remove individual fixed effects when computing the U-index. The authors do this in their chapter. They are able to do this, given that they have multiple observations of affect for a given individual. While they did not emphasize this directly, the level of affect changes dramatically once conditioning on individual fixed effects. For example, the data suggest that low educated individuals watch much more television than high educated individuals. Additionally, low educated individuals do much less exercising than high educated individuals. The happiness literature (as well as the U-index) suggests that low educated individuals are much less happy than high educated individuals. If this is the case, we would speculate that television watching has too high a U-index (because it is more intensively consumed by low happiness individuals) and exercise has too low a U-index (because it is more intensively consumed by high happiness individuals).

Comparing tables 1.8 and 1.9 confirms my predictions. Without controlling for individual fixed effects, exercise and television watching look very much different with respect to their unpleasantness (7.4 and 18.1, respectively—a gap of 10.7 on the U-scale). However, after controlling for individual fixed effects, the two activities look much more similar to each other. Specifically, the respective U-index for exercise and television watching are now 11.9 and 15.7 (a gap of only 3.8 on the U-scale). In fact, the gap in the U-index between television watching and almost all other leisure activities is relatively small once controlling for individual fixed effects. However, the U-index for housework and food prep did not change much after controlling for individual fixed effects. This is not surprising, given that there is a much smaller education and income gradient with respect to time spent in nonmarket work within the population.

So in summary, in all future work, I recommend that the authors only work with the fixed effect version of their U-index. Also, I would encourage them to highlight this issue in future iterations of their work. If this research was implemented in different settings, those implementing their methodology should be encouraged to take multiple observations of affect for the same individual so individual fixed effects can be removed from their analysis.

8.4.3   Selection Issue Three: Time-of-Day Effects

One thing I would have liked to see is a control for time-of-day effects when comprising the U-index. If one's U-index changes throughout the day (regardless of activities) and some activities are more intensively consumed at certain times of the day (like television watching), the U-index for certain activities could be contaminated by time-of-day effects.

For example, the authors show that individuals are more likely to report being tired at the end of the day (figure 1.3). The end of the day is when people are most likely to watch television. So, if we classify television watching as a less enjoyable activity, is it because people find television more unpleasant than other activities, or is it because people watch television at the end of the day—when all activities are more unpleasant? To make policy prescriptions about moving individuals across different activities, we would want to know the true unpleasantness of the activity.

In summary, I would like to see the authors pull out time-of-day effects when computing their U-index measure for different activities. Again, I would also like them to caution other researchers who are trying to implement their research design that such time-of-day effects can be important.

8.5   Conclusions

Overall, this is a very ambitious and worthwhile project. The main short-term goal is to assess the value added by measuring changes in the U-index to assess changing well-being relative to changes in other existing measures of well-being (wages, GDP, happiness indices, etc.). If a large-scale data collection effort is to be created to measure the U-index, we need to understand the value added so as to start to think about the appropriate cost-benefit analysis. Only time will tell if the U-index adds substantive value to our understanding of the evolution of societal (or individual) well-being. The work of Krueger et al. provides a necessary first step in this evaluation process.

References

Aguiar, M., and E. Hurst. 2007. Measuring trends in leisure: The allocation of time over five decades. *Quarterly Journal of Economics* 122 (3): 969–1006.
U.S. Department of Labor, Bureau of Labor Statistics. 2003–2005. *2003–2005 American Time Use surveys.* Washington, D.C.: Government Printing Office.

9

Rejoinder

Alan B. Krueger, Daniel Kahneman, David Schkade,
Norbert Schwarz, and Arthur A. Stone

The contributors to this volume raise several valid points about the strengths and weaknesses of our proposed method for National Time Accounting (NTA), particularly regarding the idea of measuring subjective well-being by the fraction of time people spend in an unpleasant emotional state (the U-index; see chapter 1 of this volume). To be clear, we should emphasize that in our contribution, we did not attempt to provide a comprehensive measure of all aspects of well-being. We offer a new measure of an aspect of well-being that is: (a) relevant to people's daily lives, (b) distinct and measured separately from other aspects of well-being in the existing literature, and (c) related to possible policy actions (e.g., overtime restrictions) and technological developments in society because of the link to time use.

In this brief rejoinder we concentrate on responding to the main criticisms raised. But we should not lose sight of the generally positive and encouraging reactions to the approach that we proposed, especially by J. Steven Landefeld, whose agency is charged with measuring the National Income and Product Accounts (see chapter 4 of this volume). Our goal here is to highlight what can be done to improve the measurement of evaluated time use and to clarify what our approach adds and does not add, rather than to defend our approach as the only way to proceed.

In chapter 2 of this volume, George Loewenstein states, "I believe that much if not most of what makes life worthwhile is *not* captured by moment to moment happiness, but corresponds more closely, if not perfectly, to what Krueger et al. acknowledge to be absent from NTA, namely 'people's general sense of satisfaction or fulfillment with their lives as a whole, apart from moment to moment feelings.'" This theme also emerges to a lesser extent in David Cutler's chapter (see chapter 3 of this volume). We already have acknowledged that our approach to NTA excludes one's sense of meaning and fulfillment, although we suspect that a high sense of fulfillment will not be without positive emotional consequences. Still, we think that NTA, and the U-index in particular, capture a good deal of what makes life miserable, if not what makes it worthwhile. First, people who are in pain or depressed much of the time are probably miserable; they certainly spend their time in more restricted ways than others who are not in pain or depressed, and they express low levels of life satisfaction. Second, the approach can be extended to measure additional features of experience related to whether time use is worthwhile, such as whether people consider their specific uses of time to be a waste of time or meaningful. Third, one could perform a horse race to examine whether cumulative affective experience or self-reported life satisfaction does a better job predicting objective outcomes, such as health and mortality. We hope this test will be conducted in the future. Fourth, we think the U-index has measurement properties that are superior to standard measures of life satisfaction, such as being an ordinal measure at the level of feelings experienced in situ. Moreover, standard measures of global life satisfaction are subject to numerous contextual influences (Schwarz and Strack 1999), which are attenuated under episodic reporting conditions (Schwarz, Kahneman, and Xu 2009). Lastly, we note that even if global evaluations of life satisfaction and fulfillment are considered to provide a more accurate reflection of the extent to which life is worthwhile, experienced well-being measures still provide additional information about the emotional experience of daily life.

David G. Blanchflower raises the question of whether experienced well-being and the U-index yield many new insights beyond what has been learned from studies of life satisfaction and overall happiness (see chapter 7 of this volume). He emphasizes that results using data on either self-reported happiness or the U-index find that subjective well-being is higher for those who are older, white, married, and employed, and for those who are more highly educated and have higher income. We view findings such as these as partly validating our measure of experienced well-being. At the same time, the correlation between experienced well-being and a circumstance like household income is substantially weaker than the correlation between life satisfaction and income, suggesting that a different process relates circumstances to people's experienced happiness than to their global judgments of well-being. Indeed, the Easterlin paradox of a weak correlation between income (or changes in income) and subjective well-being (or changes in subjective well-being) seems to apply more strongly when subjective well-being is measured by experienced affect than by a judgment of life as a whole (see Stevenson and Wolfers 2008; Kahneman et al. 2006; Krueger 2008).

If the only goal of NTA was to describe people or demographic groups, then we would agree with Blanchflower that it is possible to collect subjective well-being data more efficiently than with evaluated time use. However, characterizing people is not the only goal, or even the main goal, of NTA.

An important application is to understand from where differences in well-being arise. National Time Accounting provides insight into this issue by illuminating how different sociodemographic positions are associated with different time use and different emotional experiences, providing information that is policy relevant. Moreover, cross-national comparisons on the basis of NTA data provide insight into how different organizations of daily life relate to the well-being of citizens by permitting a decomposition of differences in subjective well-being between countries into differences due to time allocation and differences due to the emotional experience of a given set of activities. For international comparisons, Blanchflower acknowledges that one obtains meaningfully different results using affect reported for episodes of the previous day—or even the previous week—and reports of overall happiness and life satisfaction. The reversal of the ranking of the French and American comparison in our chapter is a vivid example of this phenomenon, and Blanchflower provides additional data to this effect. Likewise, changes for a nation over time can be traced to changes in time use and changes in emotional experiences for a given time allocation. These decompositions are not possible with standard satisfaction data. Part of what makes life more enjoyable is spending more time in enjoyable activities; this is highlighted in NTA. We also note that none of the previous studies in the time-use literature that touched on NTA actually applied the technique to compare differences between countries or changes within countries over time.

Another goal of NTA is to characterize the emotional experience of time use during certain activities and situations. Our and others' (e.g., Csikszentmihalyi 1990; Robinson and Godbey 1997) measures of experienced well-being have added new insights in this regard. For example, we find that child care and adult care appear to be particularly unpleasant activities while they are being conducted. We also find that commuting ranks as one of the most unpleasant activities of the day, while watching television is an affectively average activity. And we find that interacting with others generally raises the emotional experience of an activity. Findings like these extend the boundaries of what has been learned from global judgments of life as a whole.

William Nordhaus maintains that there is a fundamental flaw in attempts to use subjective well-being as a social indicator (see chapter 5 of this volume). He argues that emotions, and subjective well-being more generally, are not—and cannot be—interpersonally cardinal variables. Nordhaus argues that an interpersonally cardinal variable "must have a uniquely defined zero and a well-defined unit of increment, and there must be a method to compare the values across individuals." He further argues that the zero point (and presumably the increment) must be stable across time and people. He claims that there simply is no interpersonal scale for reporting subjective data such as happiness and pain. "Neither blue rivers nor blue moods," he argues, "constitute a meaningful index of emotions because they are not based on interpersonally cardinal variables."

Before responding, it is useful to be clear about terms. Subjective data are reports of variables that only the person doing the reporting can observe. Objective data can, in principle, be observed by an external party (or parties) in addition to the person doing the reporting. Feelings are clearly subjective. No one else can experience your emotions to verify how you feel, although others can see likely correlates of your emotions (e.g., whether you smile or grimace). Life satisfaction is also an inherently subjective variable. Height, consumption, and income are objective variables. What makes objective data, like height or consumptions, interpersonally cardinal variables is not that they can be observed by a third party, however, but that a common convention is used to measure and report them. For example, height can be measured in inches or centimeters for someone in shoes or bare feet. Without the convention of a ruler, height does not meet Nordhaus's interpersonally cardinal criteria. Even for objective variables, there are situations in which there is not an accepted convention of measurement. For example, prior to the advent of railroads and time zones in the nineteenth century, every local town set its own time; zero hour was different in different locales. Greenwich Mean Time enabled time to be measurable.

At one level, we have some sympathy for Nordhaus' critique—indeed, the U-index was developed largely to relax some of the restrictive measurement requirements of social indicators. The U-index *does not* require a unique and universally defined zero point and increment to be a useful social indicator. It was developed precisely to avoid the need for interpersonal comparisons of interval scaled data, which is the thrust of Nordhaus' critique. Yet at another level we disagree with his critique, even as it applies to more standard measures of subjective well-being that preceded the U-index.

Nordhaus asserts that subjective variables such as pleasure or pain and likes or dislikes are not interpersonally comparable. He asserts this on principle and provides no theoretical or empirical justification for his contention. Yet the extensive material reviewed in sections 1.3.1 to 1.3.3 of our chapter provides substantial evidence that measures of subjective experience are meaningfully related to physiological indicators and are predictive of important real-world outcomes, from marriage to immune system function to mortality. This evidence is difficult to reconcile if differences in subjective reports of well-being across subjects are meaningless because they are not interpersonally comparable. There are numerous examples where conventions of measurement have been successfully used to report and compare ratings of emotions and subjective evaluations across individuals. Consider the following scenarios. College students are routinely asked to rate the quality of their professors on a numerical scale, and the average rating across students is used for tenure and salary decisions. Netflix asks subscribers to rate how much they liked movies on a scale of one to five and then uses this information, along with other subscribers' subjective ratings, to provide recommendations for new movies. Companies routinely survey their employees' and customers' satisfaction. Doctors in every hospital in the United States ask patients how much pain they feel on a scale of zero to ten, sometimes associating faces with the different ratings, and the responses are used to guide a course of action. Even the *Journal of Political Economy* asks referees to give a subjective rating of the quality of the paper they reviewed, from one to one hundred. Unless one believes that all of these efforts are pure folly, providing no useful information, it would seem that subjective variables pass a market test of being interpersonally cardinal. In sum, making interpersonal comparisons of individuals' subjective ratings has proved a valuable and enduring practice in numerous fields, and the mere fact that the cardinality criteria that Nordhaus lays out are hard to substantiate does not imply that the measures fail to capture meaningful information.

At a conceptual level, thousands of years of evolution have probably abetted the development of conventions to enable people to communicate and convey the intensity of their emotions. It is in one's survival interest to be able to detect and express how much something hurts, for example. The socialization process also guides people to express the strength of their emotions in an understandable way. Verbal descriptions of feelings come to have somewhat common meanings, although there can be a lot of noise in the way people express themselves. Nonetheless, this process enables interpersonal measurement conventions to be established for subjective variables. It is also worth noting that in surveys, it is common to give respondents verbal anchors to guide them (e.g., a zero means the feeling was not present, and a six means it was very much part of the experience) so they have a common zero point and a sense of what the interval between scales is in reporting subjective responses.[1] Although we would not push this argument too far, there are reasons to believe that social conventions can make it possible to report and contrast emotions.

We recognize, however, that language and custom can affect the convention that is used to report subjective variables. Different societies develop different conventions. Indeed, we argue in chapter 1 that this is an issue for comparisons of life satisfaction between France and the United States. This is one reason why we proposed the U-index. The U-index is robust to the interpersonal measurement convention, as long as a given person uses the same convention for positive and negative emotions.

As Nordhaus acknowledges, the U-index "would appear to avoid the difficulties of some happiness indices by its creation of an ordinal index."

---

1. It seems to us that the absence of feeling an emotion like pain *does* provide a natural zero point, even if the width of the interval of increments may be vague. Thus, we think it should be noncontroversial to develop an index that measures the percentage of time that people spend in some pain.

A measurement parable

One of the anonymous reviewers of this volume suggested the following response to William Nordhaus's claim that "hedonic measures do not meet the standards for an interpersonally cardinal variable that are required to construct a meaningful quantitative social indicator."

> Imagine a world where lots of people smoke. However, this world has not progressed enough scientifically to have anything like twenty-first century measures of health. All that this world has achieved, sad to say, is some rough subjective measures of health. There are in this world some surveys that look at just those. In them, human beings fill out forms where they report how they feel in response to questions such as "My health is excellent . . . fairly good . . . poor . . . very poor?" and they give other social and economic data. But there are no blood test readings or heartbeat count or scans or anything like that. . . . But they can, in this world, run regression equations. Their dictator must have been a theoretical econometrician.
>
> A commentator of the day, called BN, makes a big speech and says there is no point in trying to use these subjective health measures for anything. You should all pack up and go home, he says.
>
> But, to show he is wrong, a group of researchers tries to estimate Subjective Health equations and they find that smoking comes in with a big negative coefficient, whether controlling for everything else or not controlling (it does, incidentally, if you estimate Subjective Health equations on twenty-first century data). They then prescribe anti-smoking restrictions. BN writes complaining letters, lamenting the end of the scientific measurable method, to the *New York Times,* but the researchers press ahead. Millions of lives are saved. They become heroes. Yet according to BN not a single interpersonally cardinal health indicator exists in this world.

The referee's parable, which is not so far removed from reality, highlights the point that progress has been made by comparing individuals' subjective evaluations of their health and other domains of life.

*In his original draft, Nordhaus used the phrase "measurable variable" instead of "interpersonally cardinal variable." We have edited the referee's passage to accord with the revised version of Nordhaus's paper.

However, he argues that our procedure "simply pushes the difficulty into the background." To us, the appeal of the U-index is that different people do not have to use the same convention to measure their emotions, as long as the emotion that they rate highest is the one that they feel most intensively at the time. Stated simply, the requirement for the U-index is for someone to be able to decide at a given moment if they are feeling more happy than sad or more pain than pleasure. Nordhaus argues that the intensity of emotions cannot be compared because there is no conceivable zero point or increment for emotions, even for a given person at a given moment in time.

Nordhaus accepts that emotions can satisfy an ordinal ranking, presumably meaning that someone can determine that he or she feels more or less pain in a given situation. He does not believe that it is possible for someone to decide whether he or she feels more pain than pleasure during that situation, however. Thus, the runner who reports in our surveys that while jogging, his pain is high but his happiness is even higher is not providing meaningful information, according to Nordhaus; nor is the runner who says he felt more pain than pleasure when he sprained his ankle. It is not clear, however, why ordinality would apply within emotions but not between them. Emotions have some properties in common. If the human brain is capable of deciding that something hurts more or less in a given situation, why can it not decide that a given situation is more painful than pleasurable?

No evidence is presented to substantiate Nordhaus' claim that the strength of emotions at a point in time cannot be compared, or that in principle, there is unlikely to be a natural zero point for pain and other emotions. Indeed, Nordhaus implies that no evidence (such as the correlation between self-reported emotions and brain imaging) could persuade him that emotions can be compared, because they are not measurable variables. His argument rests on the presumption that the (conceptual) zero point and increment for measuring emotions "will vary with mood, circumstances, genetics, context, history, and culture." This is a more difficult argument to defend when it comes to the U-index, however, as the U-index tries to measure mood as an outcome, and the zero point and increment can be person specific for the U-index—so genetics, history, and culture are not stumbling blocks. While the factors that Nordhaus raises may well add noise to the measurement of the U-index, they do not seem to make it meaningless for individuals to rate the intensity of how they feel at a point in time along various affective dimensions.

To the extent that one considers evidence relevant, the evidence does suggest to us that there is much useful signal in the U-index, and evaluated time use more generally. As detailed in our chapter, reports of the intensity of emotions across individuals do correlate with physiological measures. If self-rated emotions were not comparable across people, at least to some extent, we would expect a correlation of zero. In addition, the pattern of the U-index across demographic groups and activities is, for the most part, intuitive. Finally, cognitive interviews indicated that subjects selected the affective dimension that they assigned the highest numerical rating to as the most intense feeling they had during the episode.

Nordhaus misrepresents the U-index when he writes, "This approach is equivalent to assuming that there are interpersonally cardinal subindices in an underlying preference function, $U(P, H)$." The underlying preference function does not need to be interpersonally cardinal—it can vary across individuals. Moreover, $U(P, H)$ can vary for a given individual over time, and it is unnecessary for the researcher to specify the $U(P, H)$ function for the U-index to be a meaningful social indicator. The experience of a given person feeling more pain than pleasure is of relevance even if the underlying preference function changes.

Nordhaus goes beyond the requirements for interpersonal cardinality in criticizing the U-index, because the U-index is an ordinal measure at the level of emotions. He argues that "blue moods" or unpleasant experiences cannot conceivably be defined or measured because there is no natural zero point or standard increment for a given person's emotions.[2] In this view, no latent variable can conceivably indicate a person's likes and dislikes or pleasure and pain. However, this standard would seem inconsistent with the underpinnings of the "standard ordinal preference function" as well. If a person can decide that one bundle is preferred to another, then Nordhaus would presumably accept that there is an underlying latent variable with a common zero point and well-defined increment that enables the two bundles to be compared. Thus, the extent to which someone liked something would have to be a conceivable latent variable for that person to decide that he or she preferred one bundle over another and therefore chose it (presuming that people choose the bundle they like most). The only difference in measurement requirements between the U-index and the standard ordinal preference function is that in the former, a person is assumed capable of comparing whether he or she is more happy than sad at a given time, and in the latter, the person is assumed capable of comparing how much he or she would like alternative consumption bundles that he or she may or may not consume.

All social indicators require assumptions and entail some noise and uncertainty. The assumptions underlying our proposal for National Time Accounting seem to us to strike a reasonable balance between measurement requirements and practicality. We did not develop the U-index from first principles as a comprehensive indicator of the well-being of society. Instead, we offer it as a plausible indicator of the relative frequency of misery experienced in certain settings and by various groups. We hope that the U-index and related indicators can provide a useful indicator of situations that are associated with unpleasant emotional experiences and of groups that are more likely to endure emotionally unpleasant experiences. We would not expect a goal of public policy to be to minimize the U-index, but instead for the U-index to highlight areas that are worth further investigation. We also hope that NTA can provide a means for tracking

---

2. Presumably, to define a blue mood, all one would need is a zero point—the absence of feeling blue—because the width of the increment is irrelevant if the goal is to derive an indicator of the presence or absence of any nonzero level of the emotion.

whether societies are spending their time in more or less enjoyable ways, which can be an input along with others to derive a picture of the progress of society.

In conclusion, it is useful to recall Jan Tinbergen's (1976) advice: "Progress in our understanding can only be based on the push for measurement of phenomena previously thought to be non-measurable" (51).

References

Csikszentmihalyi, M. 1990. *Flow: The psychology of optimal experience.* New York: Harper Collins.

Kahneman, D., A. Krueger, D. Schkade, N. Schwarz, and A. Stone. 2006. Would you be happier if you were richer? A focusing illusion. *Science* 312 (5782): 1908–10.

Krueger, A. 2008. Comment on Stevenson and Wolfers, "Economic growth and subjective well-being: Reassessing the Easterlin paradox. *Brookings Papers on Economic Activity* (Spring): 95–100. Washington, D.C.: Brookings Institution.

Robinson, J., and G. Godbey. 1997. *Time for life: The surprising ways Americans use their time.* University Park Pennsylvania State University Press.

Schwarz, N., D. Kahneman, and J. Xu. 2009. Global and episodic reports of hedonic experience. In *Using calendar and diary methods in life events research,* ed. R. Belli, D. Alwin, and F. Stafford, 157–74. Newbury Park, CA: SAGE.

Schwarz, N., and F. Strack. 1999. Reports of subjective well-being: Judgmental processes and their methodological implications. In *Well-being: The foundations of hedonic psychology,* ed. D. Kahneman, E. Diener, and N. Schwarz, 61–84. New York: Russell-Sage.

Stevenson, B., and J. Wolfers. 2008. Economic growth and subjective well-being: Reassessing the Easterlin paradox. *Brookings Papers on Economic Activity* (Spring): 1–87. Washington, D.C.: Brookings Institution.

Tinbergen, J. 1976. More empirical research. In *Economics in the future,* ed. K. Dopfer, 39–52. London: Macmillan Press.

Contributors

David G. Blanchflower
Department of Economics
Dartmouth College
6106 Rockefeller Hall
Hanover, NH 03755

David M. Cutler
Department of Economics
Harvard University
1875 Cambridge Street
Cambridge, MA 02138

Erik Hurst
Graduate School of Business
University of Chicago
Hyde Park Center
Chicago, IL 60637

Daniel Kahneman
Woodrow Wilson School
Princeton University
322 Wallace Hall
Princeton, NJ 08544

Alan B. Krueger
Industrial Relations Section
Princeton University
Firestone Library
Princeton, NJ 08544

J. Steven Landefeld
Bureau of Economic Analysis
1441 L Street NW
Washington, D.C. 20230

Richard Layard
Centre for Economic Performance
London School of Economics
Houghton Street
London, WC2A 2AE, England

George Loewenstein
Department of Social and Decision
  Sciences
Carnegie Mellon University
208 Porter Hall
Pittsburgh, PA 15213

William Nordhaus
Department of Economics
Yale University
28 Hillhouse Avenue
Box 208264
New Haven, CT 06520

David Schkade
Rady School of Management
University of California, San Diego
Otterson Hall, Room 4S144
9500 Gilman Drive #0553
La Jolla, CA 92093

Norbert Schwarz
Institute for Social Research
University of Michigan
426 Thompson Street
Ann Arbor, MI 48106

Arthur A. Stone
Department of Psychiatry and
    Behavioral Sciences
Stony Brook University
Putnam Hall
Stony Brook, NY 11794

Author Index

Subject Index